Social Movements in Br

Over the last thirty years across Europe and America, more and more people have been turning their backs on mainstream politics and parties, and pursuing more unconventional ways of making themselves heard. Recent research suggests that as many people in Britain are active in protest or similar movements as in the conventional political parties. Social scientists have revived the idea of 'Social Movements' to explain this.

Paul Byrne's accessible and engaging study explores the theories surrounding these new movements of the 1980s and 90s. He begins by summarising these theories and describing how such movements as Greenpeace, Friends of the Earth, the Women's movement and the Green Party have all developed in Britain. Importantly he asks: 'who gets involved?'; 'why do they get involved?'; and 'why do they act as they do?'. Combining theory and practice to compare the British experience with the continental European and American theories, the study argues that in Britain there are important differences between 'social' and 'protest' movements which have hitherto been overlooked.

Designed to help students understand complex theoretical arguements, this book will be essential reading for those studying politics, sociology and those involved in the increasingly prominent movements.

Paul Byrne is a Senior Lecturer in Politics, Loughborough University.

Theory and practice in British politics
Series editors: Desmond King and Alan Ware

This series bridges the gap between political institutions and political theory as taught in introductory British politics courses. While teachers and students agree that there are important connections between theory and practice in British politics, few textbooks systematically explore these connections. Each book in this series takes a major area or institution and looks at the theoretical issues which it raises. No other textbook series offers both a lively and clear introduction to key institutions and an understanding of how theoretical issues arise in the concrete and practical context of politics in Britain. These innovative texts will be essential reading for teachers and beginning students alike.

Other titles in the series

The Law
Jeremy Waldron

Electoral Systems
Andrew Reeve and Alan Ware

The Civil Service
Keith Dowding

Political Parties and Party Systems
Moshe Maor

Social Movements in Britain

Paul Byrne

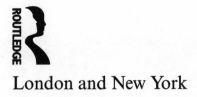

London and New York

First published 1997
by Routledge
11 New Fetter Lane, London EC4P 4EE

Simultaneously published in the USA and Canada
by Routledge
29 West 35th Street, New York, NY 10001

© 1997 Paul Byrne

Typeset in Times by Routledge
Printed and bound in Great Britain by T.J. International, Padstow,
Cornwall

British Library Cataloguing in Publication Data
A catalogue record for this book is available from the British Library

Library of Congress Cataloguing in Publication Data
A catalogue record for this book has been requested

ISBN 0 415–07122–4 (hbk)
ISBN 0 415–07123–2 (pbk)

Contents

Acknowledgements

I should like to thank Mike Gane, Des King, Joni Lovenduski and Alan Ware for their comments and criticisms on earlier drafts of some of these chapters; they are not responsible for any errors that may remain. I am grateful to all those activists in the various British movements who have found the time and patience to talk to me about their experiences, and to my students who have provided much useful feedback as the project has developed. I am obliged to *Parliamentary Affairs* for permission to reproduce in part material on the Women's movement which first appeared in the January 1996 issue of that journal. I should also like to thank Val Byrne for her forbearance and support while this book has been in preparation.

1　Introduction

Over the last thirty years, hundreds of thousands of people in Britain have been inspired to take part in a 'new' kind of politics. Not content to choose just from the programmes offered by mainstream parties, they have advanced ideas previously ignored by established politicians. They have often by-passed conventional political processes, taking part in campaigns and protests, and sometimes even putting their personal liberty at risk. They have championed radical causes like environmentalism, feminism and disarmament which not only challenge the postwar orthodoxy, with its espousal of industrialisation, economic growth and nationalism, but also often seem to benefit others as much as themselves. They have blurred the line between the 'personal' and the 'political', arguing that the causes they advocate are too important and wide-ranging to be dealt with by change only in the public sphere – people's attitudes and lifestyles also have to change.

The national political scene may remain dominated by conventional Parliamentary politics, but there has been a distinct trend of people showing less enthusiasm for the main parties and more interest in 'single-issue' politics. When people have felt strongly about an issue, they have not just made their views known to politicians or within parties, but gone out and organised their own campaigns, groups and self-help organisations. The mainstream political parties have responded by trying to incorporate some of these concerns into their programmes, but the 'new' politics continues.

It is not just the style of politics which seems to have changed, but also its subject matter. Largely as a result of such activism, ideas and causes previously missing from 'normal' political debate have become common currency. Some, like unilateral nuclear disarmament or the rights of women, have been around before, but have been revived with a new impetus. Others are new – like the 'dark green' environmentalism which questions the whole ethic of economic growth. Perhaps most significantly, new political identities have emerged. People no longer classify themselves just as Conservatives, Socialists and so on, but as 'feminists' and 'greens'. While most of these people have left-wing rather than right-wing sympathies, they tend to see themselves as apart from (often, indeed, above) the conventional left/right dichotomy. This has not been something unique to Britain, but has occurred throughout the world, and especially in the Western liberal democracies.

They have also redefined the scope of politics. By stressing the importance of personal change, as well as looking to the state for action, they have argued that 'politics' is not something that just takes place in Westminster, Whitehall or the Town Hall, but in people's everyday lives in their homes and workplaces. Who does the housework and takes care of the children; how often you use your car; what kind of food you eat – in the 'new' politics, such questions have as much relevance as what laws are passed and how they are put into practice by the authorities.

Recognising the different nature of this kind of politics, social scientists have differentiated it from 'conventional' politics by reviving the term *Social Movements*. This book is about such movements in Britain, and looks at what we know about who these people are, what they have done and why they have done it. We cannot promise definitive answers; in some instances the information simply is not available. As we shall see, one of the distinctive features of social movements is their nebulous nature. This has not prevented commentators from speculating in theoretical terms about why some people (and not others) have gone down this road, how they have gone about it, and what has been achieved. This in turn raises interesting questions about motivation and strategies of political action which are relevant across the whole political spectrum, not just social movements. In what follows, we shall scrutinise these theoretical ideas, looking at how theories have been derived from new kinds of political activity, and trying to assess how useful they are.

POLITICAL PARTICIPATION

Before beginning our assessment, we need to establish the general context within which these developments have occurred. After all, we are examining the motives and behaviour of a minority of the population. If we are to assess the importance of a new kind of political activism, it would be as well to have an idea of the nature of political participation in Britain generally.

Although we shall be looking at what appear to be some new features of political behaviour, many of the old, established ways of conducting politics remain intact, and the majority of people appear content to restrict their political involvement to the 'normal' channels. Having said that, we must remember that political activism of all kinds is a minority sport in Britain. Most British people do participate in their political system; roughly speaking, three out of four vote in General Elections and about half as many take the opportunity to vote in local elections. For the vast majority of people, however, participation is sporadic and limited to voting or perhaps contacting an MP or Councillor over a specific issue. Relatively few people are sufficiently interested to become active in the main political parties. Although many belong to interest groups of various kinds, their participation rarely extends beyond paying their subscription. Any meaningful assessment of unconventional activism, therefore, should measure it against not just the total population but also the numbers really involved in conventional politics.

If we do this, then it is clear that significant change has taken place. For example, the mainstream parties have ruled in Parliamentary terms throughout the post-war period, but the loyalty they have been able to inspire among their supporters has declined since at least the early seventies.[1] Electoral volatility has increased, as more people change their political allegiances between elections. Membership of the mainstream political parties has fallen significantly. Whereas millions were members of the main parties in the fifties, today the Conservative Party's membership is estimated to be below half a million, and Labour can only boast of some 400,000 individual members – and before the strenuous efforts made by the Blair leadership in the nineties to boost such membership, the total was around 250,000. In contrast, campaigning groups and movements have boomed over the last twenty-five years. The Campaign for Nuclear Disarmament (CND) and the associated Peace Movement, for example, saw its support rise from around 4,000 in the seventies to a height of some 250,000 in the mid-eighties; it has fallen back considerably in the nineties, but still claims the support of some 60,000 people. Friends of the Earth saw its membership rise from around 1,000 in 1971 to almost 20,000 at the beginning of the eighties, and 140,000 by the end of that decade. Greenpeace in the early nineties had some 400,000 supporters in Britain out of a global total of 5 million.

It is dangerous to cite specific examples out of context. Internecine strife in the Labour Party in the seventies and early eighties may have done little to stimulate new membership of the party. It may be that specific issues were the main stimulus for growth in some campaigning groups – the decision to site American Cruise missiles was an important factor in the revitalisation of CND, for example. Before moving on to place these developments within their specific contexts, therefore, we should examine what we know of societal trends in political participation and activism during the last thirty years.

The authoritative account of the differences in political culture across the developed world at the beginning of the sixties[2] portrayed Britain as a deferential culture which produced a high level of regime support – in other words, most of the British people were, for most of the time, content to limit their participation in politics to the 'normal' channels of elections and mainstream political parties, and to leave the details of politics in the hands of established politicians. This appraisal was comparative rather than absolute; the point being made was that British citizens were less likely than citizens of other liberal democracies to resort to protest and even violence to resolve political arguments, not that such activities were totally absent.

Subsequent research in the seventies threw up findings which suggested that, even if the picture of a consensual society content to confine itself to conventional politics was true in the sixties, changes had taken place by the seventies. In an influential work published in 1977, Alan Marsh used survey evidence to argue that people had become significantly less deferential towards established institutions and practices, and wanted more opportunities to participate in and influence decision-making than those conventional avenues offered.[3] Marsh's study was concerned more with attitudes than actual behaviour. He used his survey questions to try to ascertain what he termed 'protest potential'; that is, rather than concentrating upon who had actually performed some kind of 'unconventional' political participation, he was trying to identify who might, and what those who would not contemplate such action thought of those who did. He found that over half of his respondents approved of the use of unconventional protest activities. Not only did some 55 per cent approve in general terms of such actions as (legal) demonstrations, but as many agreed with the proposition put to them that there were times when 'it is justified to break the law to protest about something you feel may be very unjust or harmful'. Further comparative research confirmed a similar trend in other Western liberal democracies;[4] many more people were ready at least to consider the possibility of unconventional participation and protest than had been the case a decade earlier. Some commentators were sufficiently moved to argue that Britain's political culture had been transformed, and that the stability which had been the hallmark of British politics was consequently under threat.[5]

Any survey-based evidence, no matter how carefully constructed, must always be questionable to some degree. One can never be sure that the sample chosen is completely representative, nor that survey questions have not simply prompted respondents to come up with opinions which did not exist prior to the questioning. Moreover, critics have pointed out that these surveys conducted in the seventies do not have much to tell us about actual participation in unconventional politics as distinct from feelings about such activities.[6] The trend of such evidence was clear, however; people were continuing to participate in conventional politics, even if with rather less enthusiasm than had been the case, but they were more ready to see as justifiable the kind of unconventional activities that all but a small minority had spurned in the twenty years after the war.

What is more, the evidence we have suggests that this trend continued unabated into the eighties. A highly comprehensive account of contemporary participation provided by Parry *et al.* concluded 'protest has become firmly established as part of the array of actions citizens and groups might consider using to make themselves heard. It cannot be ignored as part of any present-day study of political participation.'[7] Whereas previous investigations had been directed towards attitudes towards protest and other unconventional participation, this study provided data on actual participation. Among its findings were that almost as many people had signed a petition (63.3 per cent) as had voted in local elections (68.8 per cent); almost twice as many had attended a protest meeting (14.6 per cent) as had attended a rally organised by a mainstream political party (8.6 per cent); and as many people had been on a protest march (5.2 per cent) as had participated in fund-raising (5.2 per cent), canvassing (3.5 per cent) or clerical work (3.5 per cent) on behalf of political parties.[8]

We have to be careful not to over-state the case; one must distinguish between the attitudes people have towards others undertaking protest activity, and their readiness to engage in it themselves. While Marsh may have found a majority willing to see illegal protest as sometimes legitimate, later surveys have found far fewer people who have actually engaged in such protest or who are willing to contemplate doing so. Parry *et al.* found that 72.4 per cent of their respondents 'would never consider' going on a protest march, and 36.4 per cent had similarly negative feelings about attending a protest meeting.[9] On the other hand, conventional participation is not exactly wildly popular. Parry *et al.* group their respondents into a small number of categories, ranging from 'just voters' to 'complete activists'. Over 75 per cent of their sample either voted regularly but undertook little other participation, or did not even vote with any regularity. As they put it, 'less than a quarter of British citizens (23.2 per cent) actively sustain the citizenry's role in political life'.[10] Within this active quarter of the population, direct action of various kinds attracts just as many people as does the opportunity to work on behalf of the conventional mainstream parties.

In short, there has not been a revolution in the conduct and practice of British politics. Most people, for most of the time, continue to participate only sporadically, and politics remains a relatively low priority in their everyday lives. What has changed, however, is that there are many among those who are actively interested for whom politics no longer means just participating in national parties, local politics and conventional interest groups like trade unions.

THE CULTURAL CONTEXT

People's involvement in politics is, of course, affected by the rules of their society. In the UK, for example, all adults have the right to vote, with some exceptions (prisoners, lunatics, peers of the realm). People may write to their MPs, but they cannot gather to register a protest within the immediate vicinity of Parliament. They may organise a petition among their neighbours or fellow workers, but there are now strict limits upon mounting public demonstrations. Such rules are the 'codified' part of the political system, so called because the opportunities for and limitations upon political activity are formally expressed and given the force of law.

Having said this, there are comparatively few formal laws governing political behaviour in the UK. There is no comprehensive written Constitution and/or Bill of Rights, laying down in law how people should participate and interact on a political level. Instead, the UK has a 'residual' system – that is, certain aspects of behaviour are protected or forbidden by law, but outside of those the assumption is that people may do as they wish.

It is not just the formal or legal rules which govern participation, however; there are also informal expectations about what are considered to be 'legitimate' forms of political participation. These expectations on the part of people (usually termed 'norms', meaning customary behaviour) can be hard to identify precisely, not least because they are not formally expressed or written down, and we cannot always be sure of their origins. Nevertheless, they form as important a part of the opportunities open for political participation as the legal rules. If you feel strongly about a particular issue, you may express your feelings in a way which is within the law – for example, having your body covered in tattoos saying 'End the Bloody Whaling Now' – but contrary to the prevailing norms of political behaviour. Ignoring or rejecting conventional means of political activism entails the very real danger of your message being treated with ridicule, or opposed simply because of how you have chosen to express your views – regardless of the merits or otherwise of those views. In other words, conventional wisdom suggests that, if you want your participation to be effective, you are best advised to pay heed to what political scientists term political culture – that is to say, those values and beliefs on the part of both politicians and public about not only what should be done but also how it should be done. In short, political culture mediates the form and effectiveness of demands for change.

Society is dynamic, however, and it is both the changes in society and the forces or actions which bring about those changes which interest us. A country's political culture is not immutable; on the contrary, it is constantly changing, not only because of changes in the law but also because attitudes and values change over time. Occasionally, changes in the law can precede attitudinal change; that is to say, the Government (or, more accurately, Parliament) can pass laws which are in advance of public opinion. The wave of 'moral' legislation in the late fifties and sixties, which saw legal restrictions relating to homosexuality, divorce and abortion relaxed or abolished, are commonly cited examples of Parliament enacting changes for which there was little evidence of widespread public support at the time.[11] Although all remain contentious issues, many more people are now much more relaxed about the changes than they were at the time. Such instances tend to be the exceptions that prove the rule, however; it is far more common for attitudinal changes to take place first, followed by changes in the law, as political parties seek to identify popular trends in the electoral marketplace.

Just what it is that causes people to change their attitudes is a highly problematic question. Personal experiences, the experiences, arguments and examples of others, domestic and international developments – and the crucial role of the media in reporting and interpreting all of these – are all important factors. Whatever the reasons, at any one time there are always some people who are questioning both the contemporary laws and the attitudes which are prevalent in society. Some remain strictly a minority interest; paedophilia and pagan worship, to take two unrelated examples at random, have their advocates, but very few in society have been convinced of their virtue. Others, however, do strike a chord, and result in far-reaching changes in both attitudes and law. The role and status of women in British society is a good example. While there are powerful arguments that British society has a long way to go before real equality between the sexes is achieved, it is clear that many significant changes have occurred over the last fifty years. Some of these developments have been in the 'public' sphere – that is to say, laws now exist governing the way in which women must be treated in terms of employment or their right to obtain an abortion. Others have been attitudinal changes, taking place in the 'private' sphere – for example, expectations about the division of responsibilities within families have changed (even if the dice are still loaded in favour of men), although governments have not passed laws to cause this to happen.

It is, of course, one thing to identify change, and quite another to prove causality, to demonstrate beyond all reasonable doubt that such changes have been caused by certain factors or actions. Nevertheless, it is worth noting that, in at least some of these areas of significant change, we also find new forms of political action. Issues like feminism or ecological awareness have been put on the political agenda at least partly because of people engaging in an almost bewildering variety of collective action, much of which has been outside the normal channels of conventional politics, and contradicting the prevailing norms of political behaviour. Although in the nineties all the main parties now have policies in such areas, they did not give people a lead on them. That lead came from people who, for various reasons, supplemented the 'respectable' ways of making political demands with more direct strategies of action. When faced with something they did not like or approve of, these people did not just express their discontent by making their views known to elected representatives, they also took direct action – making changes in their personal lives, organising their own self-help activities and sometimes protesting in public.

It would be as well to stress here that some of these 'new' features are not, in fact, that new – it is more a case of them lying dormant for some time and re-emerging over the last few decades. The suffragettes fighting for basic political rights for women in the nineteenth and early twentieth centuries displayed many of the same characteristics and employed the same kind of tactics as feminists have over the last twenty-five years, and, as we shall see, protest has been an endemic feature of British politics throughout this century. Nevertheless, although we are therefore talking about cycles or waves of protest, between the wars such activity was largely conspicuous by its absence.

In conclusion, we have clear evidence that the 'rules of the game' have changed to some extent in post-war British politics. New issues have been put on the political agenda, and new ways of mobilising people around those issues have been employed. This is not a zero-sum situation; traditional conventional politics have continued. It does, however, represent a new dimension in recent and contemporary British politics. Alongside the 'normal' avenues of political participation – parties, protectional interest groups and even promotional pressure groups – we have a new form of political action, social movements. These movements have radical aims which question some of the core ideas associated with advanced industrialised societies. The motives of their supporters, and the ways in which they pursue these aims, seem to be significantly different from those found in 'mainstream' politics. Social scientists have been challenged to explain these developments, and have done so by proposing new theoretical insights. Our purpose is to examine these insights, and relate them to the actual practice of this new politics in the UK. To do so, we must first define our terms; as the next chapter shows, this is far from straightforward where social movements are concerned.

2 Defining social movements

The first problem any student of social movements faces is defining just what we mean by a 'social movement'. The term has been used rather indiscriminately during the last thirty years, applied to anything from localised protests over single issues within a particular country to ideological standpoints which have had a global impact. A moment's thought about the term itself gives us some indication of the difficulties we face in pinning it down; a 'movement' does not have the clear boundaries of a party or a group, and 'social' covers all aspects of behaviour from the public and collective to the private and personal.

The ambiguities have arisen not least because the causes advanced by social movements, and the ways in which they have sought to advance those causes, confounded the conventional view of political behaviour which held sway in Europe and America during the fifties and sixties. Prior to the emergence of social movements, the generally held assumption had been that people got involved in politics because of self-interest, and, having perceived a grievance or opportunity for advancement, then pursued that through the established channels of political access. By this sort of criterion, social movements seem to be unpredictable, irrational, unreasonable and disorganised. They are:

- unpredictable, in that they do not always arise where there seems to be the greatest 'need'; environmental movements have not always developed in societies with the greatest environmental problems, or women's movements in societies where women are most disadvantaged, and so on;
- irrational, in that their adherents do not seem to be motivated by self-interest or material advantage;
- unreasonable, in that their adherents appear to think they are justified in flouting the law or disregarding 'normal' ways of doing things;

- disorganised, in that they deliberately refrain from formalising their own organisations, even when it would seem advantageous to do so.

Social movements, then, are amorphous entities which resist neat classification. It is hard to delineate them in organisational, tactical or ideological terms. Let us take some examples to illustrate this. The women's movement has never had an organisation, in the sense of a single, over-arching or 'peak' organisation which brought together all those who supported feminism. It may have come close to one in the early seventies, in the form of the Women's Liberation Movement (WLM); even at the time, however, many women who subscribed to the ideas of feminism remained outside the WLM, and from the late seventies on the movement has been a 'complex coalition'[1] which incorporates many different groups, from women's committees in local authorities, to those involved in Peace Camps such as Greenham Common, and to the Working Mothers' Association. The tactics employed by feminists have ranged from the conventional lobbying of decision-makers, to 30,000 women linking hands around American nuclear bases, and to the setting up of refuges for victims of domestic violence. Ideologically, the movement encompasses those who conceptualise their fight as being all about equal rights, particularly in the workplace, to those who believe that lesbianism is an essential prerequisite for 'true' feminism. The Peace Movement, despite having an organisation kernel in the form of CND, has cast its net much wider; at its height in the mid-eighties there were estimated to be some 150,000 supporters in local peace groups in addition to the 100,000 who had joined national CND. Its supporters have employed tactics which extend from serious academic work on the probable effects of nuclear warfare, to mass demonstrations, and to a wide variety of non-violent direct action. Ideologically, the movement includes both 'nuclear pacifists', who object to nuclear weapons but not conventional armed forces, and 'outright pacifists', who reject all kinds of warfare and the political system which they see as underpinning it. The Environmental Movement is perhaps the most extreme example of blurred boundaries. Organisationally, it stretches from long-established (and eminently 'respectable') groups like the Council for the Preservation of Rural England, through to more activist groups like Friends of the Earth and Greenpeace, and out as far as the Sea Shepherd Conservation Society which has recently acquired its own submarine for use against whaling ships. Moreover, it is, of course, the movement which has spawned its own political parties – in 1994, no less than thirteen legislatures in Europe had Green members. Tactically, the movement can be argued to encompass everyone from those who take their newspapers down to the local supermarket once a week for recycling to those who have organised their own systems of local bartering; from the intellectual arguments of Transport 2000 to the sabotaging of bulldozers by Earth First!. If one subsumes animal welfare under the heading of environmentalism, then it even encompasses the public campaigning of the RSPCA and the car-bombings attributed to extremists associated with animal rights groups. Ideologically, the movement attracts support from those who equate environmentalism with recycling and energy conservation to those who see it as *the* ideological paradigm replacing both capitalism and socialism.

This is a superficial account of such movements, and raises many questions which we will be addressing in more detail subsequently. Hopefully, however, it serves to illustrate the myriad problems of defining the term. It gives rise to one question immediately – if it is so difficult to say what is and what is not a social movement, then how are we justified in referring to feminism, pacifism and environmentalism as if they are self-evidently examples of such movements? The easy answer to that is to say, well, everyone else does. People may disagree on whether particular groups or networks are actually part of these wider movements, but a common theme since the late sixties has been that these three areas constitute the irreducible core of social movement activity. We can take things a little further than this, however, as empirical observation of these movements has in turn produced new theoretical ideas which aim to clarify what distinguishes social movement activity from more conventional political participation.

There have been many attempts to identify the features which distinguish social movements from other forms of political action. Indeed, in America and continental Europe, such theorising has outweighed empirical studies[2] – possibly because the nebulous nature of movements make them harder targets than parties or conventional interest groups for behavioural research, and sometimes because the people involved are engaged in illegal direct action which they are understandably reluctant to discuss with anyone outside their movement. As we shall see in the next chapter, there are many disagreements between theorists. We shall come back to those; for now, we shall restrict ourselves to noting some of the main characteristics of social movements on which most of the theorists agree.

VALUES AND IDENTITY

Social movements are like political parties, in that their adherents share a common outlook on what should and should not be happening in society. They differ from political parties, however, in that their adherents are motivated by *expressive* as well *instrumental* considerations; indeed, some theorists argue that expressive politics lies at the heart of social movements.

Parties have beliefs and principles which they seek to translate into action by competing for control over the governmental or state apparatus. Their motivation is instrumental, in that their *raison d'être* is political power. Their fundamental beliefs may set limits upon their room for manoeuvre, but if they wish to change their ideological priorities they can at least attempt to persuade their members and supporters to follow them on the grounds that such change is necessary in order to win or retain power.

Social movements are expressive, in that they have beliefs and moral principles, and they seek to persuade everyone – governments, parties, the general public, anyone who will listen – that these values are the right ones, but do not compete for political office. They argue their viewpoint in all sorts of ways – in the political arena, but also often in 'non-political' contexts such as personal relationships and lifestyles (though they would argue that such areas do, in fact, have a political dimension). The one constant that does not and cannot change is the basic value they espouse. What matters to social movement adherents is keeping their beliefs unadulterated; this takes priority over short-term tactical gains, like getting one particular policy adopted, because the belief is the cement that keeps the movement together. A peace movement cannot trade-off the abolition of one specific form of weapons system in return for abandoning its campaigning against others, or an environmental movement agree to stop arguing against river pollution if a government agrees to do something about air pollution; if they did so, then their adherents would rightly argue that they had ceased to be a peace or environmental movement. The purity of the cause is all.

For social movements, values are non-negotiable, and in this sense social movements have characteristics in common with religious groups as well as political parties. Indeed, in some societies, religion is the basis for social movements. America is the best example, where Christian fundamentalism and the 'Moral Majority' have become powerful political forces, and are rightly analysed in terms of being social movements. It is interesting to note that there is little evidence of such developments in Britain, yet religious belief does impact upon social movement activity. As we shall see, religious convictions play an important part in the peace movement, and the churches have become involved in the debate over abortion which has formed an important part of the women's movement agenda. Islamic fundamentalism has become politically contentious, not just because of specific events like the Salman Rushdie affair, but also in the whole debate over the role and place of religion in education. To date, however, such concerns have been subsumed, either within conventional institutions like parties or social movements like the peace and women's movements.

It is values, then, rather than a formal structure, that hold social movements together; supporters of social movements identify themselves with the overall message of the movement, and experience a sense of belonging and solidarity with those who agree with them. Melucci argues that the formation of a collective identity is one of the main objectives of a `social movement; once formed, adherents incorporate this new perspective of themselves in their self-awareness.[3] As importantly, adherents are perceived by others, who are apathetic about or disagree with the movement's aims, as being part of an identifiable group.

This does not mean that there is no room for disagreement within movements; as we shall see, it is common for tactical disagreements to occur, and the loosely structured nature of movements tends to accentuate this. People are attracted by, and become active in, only some aspects of a movement – one particular campaign but not others. Nevertheless, for a movement to exist, there must be a collection of individuals who not only have shared values or moral principles, but also give these values and principles a high priority. For such people, the *symbolic* aspect of social movements is important; by becoming involved in a movement, they are making a statement about themselves. One might become a member of a mainstream political party because of a fervent belief in the virtues of free enterprise or public ownership, but equally one's motivation may be much narrower – one wants to see specific changes in taxation, for example, or in education. Becoming involved in a movement, however, entails a commitment to values as well as specific issues; saying 'I am a Feminist' or 'I am a Green' means adopting broad values and beliefs which are applicable across one's entire lifestyle as well as stances on particular issues of public policy. In· this sense, movements are engaged with the *cultural* dimension of society as much as the political.

STRUCTURE

Although social movements may have groups within them that are formally structured in the way that conventional parties are (with formal membership, written constitutions, decision-making conferences, etc. – CND within the broader peace movement is a good example), movements as a whole are not formally organised. As Diani has argued from a European perspective, social movements 'are networks of interaction between different actors which may either include formal organisations or not, depending on shifting circumstances';[4] for those who prefer transatlantic terminology, Gerlach and Hine offer the acronym SPIN – segmented, polycephalous (many-headed), interaction networks.[5] The key term is 'networks of interaction'; movements come about when people get together and, through interaction that may be on a one-to-one basis, within a group or between groups, come to share the same values and outlooks. Networks are the basis on which movements are built, and they perform different kinds of functions – as means of teaching people about the values of the movement and of reinforcing solidarity, as well as the more obvious functions of exchanging information and organising activities.

As networks rather than formal organisations, movements attract supporters or adherents, rather than members. Although those supporters are often more committed than those who have formal membership of political parties (being prepared, for example, to risk hardship and/or punishment by undertaking direct action), decisions on what to do are taken locally or individually. It is rare for any significant effort to be made to coordinate supporters' efforts nationally, and even rarer for such efforts to succeed. *Autonomy*, then, is an important defining feature of social movements, and one which, as we shall see, reflects the strong beliefs about democracy and participation which are held by most social movement supporters.

One other aspect of the fluidity of movements should be mentioned here; they fluctuate over time. This has been noted by commentators who talk in terms of 'waves' of movements or, in the case of Tarrow, 'cycles of protest'.[6] Why movements should ebb and flow, sometimes having a high profile and other times lying apparently dormant, is open to question. Some, like Tarrow, argue that there are particular historical periods which are more conducive to collective protest than others; others, like Kitschelt,[7] stress the 'political opportunity structure' of different political systems (meaning both institutional factors like electoral and party systems and prevailing cultural attitudes), and make the point that movements will adapt to changes in that structure over time. For some movements, of course, external events provide the stimulus for action – it was the decision to deploy Cruise missiles in Europe which revived the peace movement at the end of the seventies, for example. We will discuss these ideas further when looking at particular movements. The point to note in this context is that movements do not have the permanence associated with more institutionalised groups.

Some would go further, and argue that movements do not have the visibility of more organised groups. This argument, found among European commentators rather than their American colleagues, stems from the stress they lay on movements as agents of *cultural* change – that is, the values people hold and the way in which they interpret what is happening in society. Melucci, in particular, argues that, even when movements seem to be dormant, we cannot assume they have disappeared; he contends that movements operate just as much at the level of interpersonal relationships. Movements, then, can be elusive animals – sometimes active and visible, sometimes not; some theorists argue that movements rarely die, but only lie dormant, ready to be revived when the circumstances are right.

Having said that, we should not lose sight of the fact that social movements do have a political dimension; they may be much looser organisations than parties and interest groups, and they may be more concerned with values than specific policies, but they nevertheless are committed to seeing those values reflected in public policy. If this political dimension is missing, then we may talk of social networks or groups, but not social movements. Take, for example, the issue of the legalisation of cannabis, something which has been sporadically on the political agenda over the last thirty years. It is an issue which is of apparent concern to a considerable number of people – estimates of intermittent or regular users of cannabis in the UK are usually between one and two million, with four or five times that many having tried it at some time. There is clearly a network in operation here, at least in terms of supply and distribution (the market is totally unregulated, and yet price levels show remarkably little variation across the country). There is little or no evidence, however, to suggest that cannabis users have shared attitudes or beliefs, what we might term a common culture. There may have been some grounds for arguing for such commonality in the late sixties, when cannabis use was strongly associated with the 'alternative' culture which fused radical politics, the student movement and the explosion of pop and rock music. Since then, although cannabis use is still found predominantly among the young, it has spread across social groups, and is now as likely to be found among young people on the right of the political spectrum as among those on the left. Moreover, there has been little attempt to mobilise around the issue of legalisation, apart from very occasional 'open letters' or advertisements in the national press in which some public figures have indicated their support. There is nothing particularly surprising in this; cannabis use, after all, is illegal, and public mobilisation would bring with it the unwelcome possibility of attention from the authorities.

The point we are seeking to make, however, is that networks must have both a cultural and political dimension if they are to be dubbed social movements. Gay people are a case in point. Like cannabis users, their activities have been subject to legal restraints, but (largely, one suspects, because of the lead given by the gay community in America) gay people in the UK have constructed a strong sense of identity, and have mobilised in both the cultural and political sphere. It is interesting to speculate whether this would have happened so quickly and to such an extent without the catalytic effect of AIDS, but the fact remains that gay people now have a sufficiently strong sense of group identity that it has overt manifestations in the economic, political and social spheres. They differ from the peace and environmental movements, in that they are not suggesting that their attitudes and values be adopted right across society; but they are akin to the women's movement, in that they also are arguing for their 'space' in society, for recognition that their outlooks are as legitimate as any other.

'OUTSIDERS'?

A persistent theme in analyses of social movements is that, in various ways, they *challenge* the existing order and way of doing things. Melucci, for example, argues that one of the defining features of social movements is that their ideas are so radical that they 'break the limits of compatibility of a system'[8] – in other words, their aims cannot be achieved by reform, but require a thoroughgoing revision of some of the basic ideas which underpin the whole functioning of that system. Thus, for example, one could argue that feminist aims cannot be wholly realised just by passing laws relating to equal opportunities, but also require an end to patriarchy itself; dark green environmentalism does not just call for pollution controls, but an end to the ethic of economic growth itself.

Even those authors who concentrate upon the 'political' rather than 'cultural' dimension of movements acknowledge that one of the main aims of movements is to change the agenda of politics, to put on to that agenda new concerns and issues and, more generally, to create new political and social 'spaces' – put simplistically, getting society to recognise the validity of new ideas like feminism or environmentalism. As such, movements develop when people realise they have a common interest or concern which cannot be pursued through the existing parties, interest groups and institutions in a society. There are two important caveats to be made here.

First, this does not mean that social movements will always develop among people who feel excluded from existing political institutions and power. This was one of the first things to be discovered about social movements. When the early post-war movements first became active (the civil rights movement in America was particularly important), the assumption was that they arose from people feeling disadvantaged, developing a sense of grievance as a result, and consequently mobilising into movements. It quickly became clear, however, that this analysis did not hold water. It was pointed out that there were all sorts of disadvantaged people in society, but only some were coalescing into movements. In other words, a sense of grievance or exclusion (whether defined objectively or subjectively) might well be a *necessary* condition for the creation of social movements, but it was not *sufficient*. There had to be other factors at work to explain why movements emerged in some areas, but not others. It was this kind of reasoning which led to the development of the influential *resource mobilisation* approach, of which more later.

Second, just because we are talking of social movements developing among those whose interests and concerns lie outside the established political elites and institutions does not mean that their adherents are found only among the 'underclass' in society. On the contrary, in fact. As we shall see, there are many gaps in our knowledge of who gets involved in social movements, and why they do. We do have some information on this, however, and the striking feature of such studies on the composition of movements is that their support is found predominantly among the relatively advantaged in society. All social movements number among their adherents people who are unemployed and/or have little in the way of educational qualification, and so on; but all the evidence we have to date – over the last thirty years, and in Europe and America – suggests that the 'typical' supporter of a social movement is someone who is both educated to an above-average standard and employed. They are predominantly, to take a short-cut for the sake of brevity, middle-class. There are many qualifications to be made to this, which we shall examine when looking in more detail at who gets involved in social movements. Suffice it to note here that those who are attracted to social movements do seem to come from a particular part of the middle class – they are more often than not employed in the public rather than private sector, for example, in the 'caring' and educational professions, and thus are not among the economically better-off. As we shall see, this has led some commentators to talk in terms of there being a discrete segment of society which they label the 'New Middle Class'.

Education and occupation are not the only distinguishing features of social movements. The gender balance is equally striking, with a much higher proportion of women being involved in movements than is typical in mainstream politics. Adherents also display a strong tendency to have left, rather than right-wing views. They tend to be found among the young in society, although the evidence here is less clear-cut. All these are features of social movements we shall examine in much more detail in subsequent chapters; the point we seek to make here is that 'outsider' status must not be equated with disadvantage. If anything, social movements attract the more articulate in society; as we shall see, those who are active in movements also tend to be active in 'conventional' politics. Movements supplement rather than replace conventional participation.

TACTICS

If there is one characteristic which sets movements apart from other forms of political action, it lies in *what* they do. All movements engage in at least some action outside of the institutional or legal channels of political access. We need to draw a distinction here between 'institutional' and 'legal'. Direct action can often be adjudged illegal, either because a specific law is breached (for example, trespass) or because the manner in which a legal action, such as a public demonstration or march, is undertaken is seen by the police (if not always the courts) as constituting a breach of the peace. Such direct action is a relatively common occurrence in some movements (the peace movement, parts of the environmental movement) but much more infrequent in others (the women's movement). To a large extent, this is dependent upon the nature of the 'target'. Where a movement is mobilising against something which is predominantly a matter of governmental policy – nuclear weapons or road-building are classic examples – protest and direct action leading to overt confrontation with the authorities tends to occur. If a movement is primarily trying to influence attitudes across society rather than just within government, instances of such action are more rare. Law-breaking, then, can be a feature of social movement participation, but it is not an essential defining characteristic; even in movements where it does occur with some regularity, the few who engage in it are heavily outweighed by the majority who refrain from actions which could lead to arrest.

What is widespread within movements, however, is action outside of the institutional channels. Indeed, this is one of the main factors distinguishing movements from both mainstream political parties and interest groups. We cannot talk of completely clear-cut boundaries here; parties and conventional interest groups will occasionally engage in campaigns or even (at least in the case of interest groups) protest actions. On the whole, however, their energies are concentrated upon the established channels of access and influence – Parliament, local government, the Civil Service. Social movements cast their nets much more widely. They also will seek to influence the political elites through lobbying and persuasion, but this only ever represents a part of their efforts, often quite a minor part. Their prime target is the population as whole, and their actions are often unfocused, in that they are more akin to 'bearing witness' in public about their particular values or beliefs than they are aimed at influencing certain decision-makers over particular policies – although, of course, the media is often the focus for movements, with some organisations within movements (Greenpeace being a good example) making this attention on the media quite explicit.

Tactics and beliefs come together; one important aspect of movements' beliefs is a rejection of the existing order – not just its conventional values, but the way of conducting politics itself. One of the main attractions of movements, especially to young people, is precisely that they do not seek to achieve their objectives through the conventional political system. Pakulski encapsulates this neatly when he observes that movements' tactics can be expressed as a paraphrase of McLuhan's famous slogan; for movements, the message is in the medium they use – they 'use examples rather than discursive arguments; they aim at moralising politics through action, reforming social life and changing individual orientations, all in the name of values and principles seen as neglected, distorted or corrupted.'[9]

Some examples may help clarify our discussion at this stage. The 'New Right', evident in British politics from the early seventies, dominant through the eighties, and still a very powerful force, displays many characteristics in common with social movements. It is a loose grouping of like-minded individuals; although it contains some clear-cut organisations, in the form of 'think-tanks' such as the Centre for

Policy Studies founded by Sir Keith Joseph, the Adam Smith Institute and the Institute of Economic Affairs, it has operated very much as a network rather than a single, formally organised pressure group. It has certainly had very definite and wide-ranging beliefs and aims, arguing that government should relinquish many of its responsibilities to market forces and the private sector, and applying this line of analysis to virtually every aspect of contemporary government. During the seventies, it was an 'oppositional' force, in that it was fighting against the consensus on the appropriate role for government that it saw existing among all the mainstream parties, including the Conservative Party. Its motivation has been instrumental rather than expressive, however, in that the target of its arguments have been the political elite rather than the population at large. While it may have been an 'outsider' within the Conservative Party before Margaret Thatcher became leader in 1975, it was fighting from a position of strength from within the party thereafter, and became the dominant force between 1983 and 1990. The New Right can still be considered as a 'movement' within the Conservative Party. Its adherents identify themselves as supporters of its values and beliefs, and are identified by others as such; it has its own heroes (Thatcher, Portillo, and Redwood following his stand against Major), and a clear agenda for action. It cannot be conceptualised as a social movement, however, because, although its prime concern is with questioning the way *government* is conducted, it does not question the existing conduct of *politics*. It is and has been a movement pressing for change from within the existing political system, not from outside it. Another example might be the Welsh nationalist party, Plaid Cymru. While its Scottish counterpart, the SNP, does include cultural concerns on its agenda, its prime concern is with economic and political issues. Plaid Cymru, however, places as much, if not more, stress upon cultural issues as it does upon the economic sphere. One of its main priorities is the preservation of the Welsh language and what it conceives to be a distinctive Welsh culture under threat of cultural domination from England. In this sense, Plaid Cymru is as much a movement of cultural change (or rather defence) as it is one pressing for specifically political change. As it restricts itself to fighting for seats in Parliament and local government, however, and goes to some lengths to distance itself from the direct action engaged in by more militant individuals, it also lies outside our definition of a social movement.

Action outside of existing channels and institutions, then, is a defining characteristic of social movements, although this does not preclude movements also employing more conventional tactics as well.

The wide variety of tactics employed by movements can lead to dissent within the movement, usually when a single organisation becomes dominant, either through sheer weight of numbers or through the image inculcated by the media. As we shall see, CND has had its share of internal tensions. The most striking instances of internal divisions, however, have occurred within the environmental movement. Greenpeace, for example, was founded by activists who had become frustrated by the tactics of the American conservation group the Sierra Club; in their turn, radical groups dedicated to direct action, such as Earth First!, the Sea Shepherd Conservation Society and several groups in the UK, have all been formed by activists who disagreed with the tactics employed by Greenpeace. One can observe a process of incremental militancy taking place. Virtually all the political parties formed out of environmental movements have experienced serious internal rifts over the tactics and direction they should pursue.

Green parties aside, such internal disagreements are not life-threatening for a movement in the way they are for more formal organisations. Social movements are sufficiently loose in an organisational sense to allow for a large variety of tactics to take place within a movement without it causing the movement to break up. By and large, movement adherents are sufficiently tolerant of each other's views on preferred tactics to live and let live, the justification being that each has to pursue the movement's aims and beliefs in the way they see fit. Disagreement over appropriate tactics – for example, lobbying, demonstrating or direct action – rarely leads to terminal splits. Moreover, a considerable part of a movement's energies may be taken up with persuasion and self-help within the movement, rather than directed at those outside the movement. Consciousness-raising, support groups and workshops are all found much more commonly in movements than in more conventional groups, and perform the dual function of educating movement supporters and reinforcing their commitment and belief.

PROTEST CAMPAIGNS AND SOCIAL MOVEMENTS

A social movement is something more than just a handful of events or actions, more than just a protest against a single act or policy. A local protest against a construction project or a particular instance of sexual discrimination may give rise to demonstrations or even direct action, as well as more conventional lobbying; but it cannot be said to represent a movement if it does not seek to engender support at least across the whole of a society, if not internationally. Movements aim for societal, not just localised, change. Similarly, even a national protest cannot be said to constitute a movement if it concentrates upon a particular act or policy. The introduction of the Community Charge (Poll Tax) in 1990 sparked off a wave of protest demonstrations, involving tens of thousands of people and some outbreaks of serious violence.[10] An Anti-Poll Tax Federation was created, largely inspired by members of the left-wing Militant Tendency, which claimed to have up to 1,500 local branches. This was a campaign which was national in scope, was organised on a network basis, and used public demonstrations as an important part of its tactical repertoire. It was not a social movement, however, because its target was one specific policy; once the policy was changed, the *raison d'être* of the campaign disappeared, as did the protest. A social movement, because of its emphasis upon widespread beliefs and values, has a *scope* and potential *durability* that a protest campaign does not. For collective action to be dubbed a social movement, then, it has to persist over time, and have aims and beliefs which are applicable to many public policies, not just one.

This does not mean that social movements cannot *contain* protest campaigns within them. If anything, this is the norm, and in most cases does not pose us with too many definitional problems. Campaigns are normally focused upon one particular area or issue – for example, favouring public transport over the construction of more roads or the extension of child-care facilities. Such aims can usually be identified as synonymous with the broader aims of social movements, and as such the campaigns can be conceptualised as part of that overall movement. This does not mean that the movement controls the campaign in any way, merely that the campaign is one component of many which go to make up the constellation that is the movement. Some campaigns transcend movements; the Greenham women were clearly part of both the peace movement and the women's movement, and, as we shall see, there were many single-issue campaigns during the eighties which reflected the broader aims of both the peace and environmental movements. The definitional point is that, while a campaign reflects and may be inspired by the broader aims of a movement, it is the social movement itself which articulates those aims. It is really only in the peace movement that the distinction between a single-issue protest campaign and a social movement is problematic, because the peace movement is so dominated by just one campaign, CND. There are particular reasons for this, largely to do with the nature of the issue and the political opportunity structure, to which we shall return when examining the peace movement in more detail.

THEORY AND PRACTICE: SOCIAL MOVEMENTS IN BRITAIN

As this discussion doubtless illustrates, there are many grey areas when it comes to defining just what is and what is not a social movement. It may help to focus our thinking if we consider, in general terms, where social movements might 'fit' in a continuum of political action which stretches from mainstream political parties at one extreme, through protectional and promotional interest groups, to social movements and politically-inspired riots and civil disobedience at the other. We can do this by constructing a matrix which correlates these different forms of political action with such factors as ideology, organisation and tactics. It is a clumsy exercise, in that we are imposing simple categories. In the matrix shown in Table 2.1, ideology is summarised as either 'reformist' (working for change within the existing system) or 'radical' (seeking changes which would necessitate a complete overhaul of the economic/social/political system); organisation as 'formal' (relatively centralised, elected officials, a national decision-making structure) or 'informal' (decentralised, either no elected officials or some elected decision-makers who have little effective authority over local groups/supporters); and tactics as 'conventional' (working through the existing channels, like elections, or lobbying), 'unconventional' (using direct action, usually non-violent) or 'personal' (encouraging and facilitating personal change). Nevertheless, it does bring out the important differences between social movements and other forms of political mobilisation.

When we think of social movements in this context – as one form of collective political action among others – I think we can appreciate that there is not really just one decisive break-point between 'conventional' and 'unconventional' politics. This is why we talk in terms of a

Table 2.1   Varieties of collective political action

	Ideology	*Organisation*	*Tactics*
Political Parties	reformist	formal	conventional
Protectional Interest Groups	reformist	formal	conventional (excluding strikes)
Promotional Interest Groups	reformist	formal/informal	usually conventional
Social Movements	reformist and radical	some formal; mostly informal	conventional and unconventional; often some emphasis upon the personal
Riots	usually radical	informal/none	unconventional

continuum of political action. Having said that, I think the matrix above does bring home to us the qualitatively different nature of social movements when compared with more mainstream forms of collective political action. Movements represent the point on the continuum where ideology, tactics and organisation *may* become rather different. As we shall see, one of our contentions is that, at least in the British context, we actually have to distinguish both between movements commonly labelled as 'social movements', and indeed between different parts of those movements. More of that later; the defining characteristics above are intended only as a starting point. As we look at different theories in more detail, and then how they relate to the specifics of how movements have developed and behaved in Britain over the last thirty years, we can investigate in more detail how theory and practice do not always 'fit'. Before we move on to this, let us establish the recent historical context out of which this new form of politics has arisen.

3 The resurgence of social movements

It is generally agreed that there have been four major new social movements in advanced industrial societies over the last thirty years – centred on students, women, environmentalists and peace activists. As we have seen, one reason why there is general agreement that these movements constitute the core of social movement activity is because they have ideological, tactical and organisational similarities which set them apart from more conventional political participation. Another reason why these four are singled out is their quite remarkable degree of parallel development cross-nationally. Some countries have been more receptive than others; America, Britain, Germany, Italy and the Netherlands have all seen considerable social movement activity, whereas it has been a less notable feature of political protest and participation in France, Belgium and the Iberian countries. As we shall see when looking at the idea of 'political opportunity structures', one can attempt to explain this variance by reference to the particular political circumstances of each nation-state. The fact remains, however, that the trend across most of the Western democracies has been broadly similar – each has developed its own versions of the core movements and, what is more, they have grown in each country almost simultaneously. One of the notable features of new social movements is this way in which they transcend national boundaries, and the relative speed with which they do so. Hardly surprising, then, that many theorists (particularly in Europe) have seen social movements as evidence of new kinds of power and value relationships common to capitalist societies in the late twentieth century.

Another striking feature of any overview of social movements over the last thirty years is the degree of overlap between them. It is common for groups within movements, and sometimes whole movements, to grow out of existing groups and movements. Often this is because of disagreement over priorities and tactics; Greenpeace was formed by activists disillusioned with more conventional conservation groups, Earth First by ex-Greenpeace activists who thought that Greenpeace had gone soft, and so on. Even where this is the case, there is not a complete break with the past, and new groups and movements often, consciously or not, carry over with them basic ideological and tactical orientations from those they have left. Neither of these phenomena are particularly surprising. Disagreement over aims, priorities and tactics is to be expected, given that movements place so much stress upon idealistic and wide-ranging goals and expect a higher degree of commitment than more conventional political groupings. We shall return to this when considering the ideology of movements. Nor is it exceptional that movements adopt and adapt tactics employed by their predecessors. As theorists have noted, one of the prime objectives of social movements is to open up new 'spaces' in politics – to get issues and ideas, previously ignored, on to the political agenda, and to win cultural and political acceptance of the methods used to propagate their message. Movements learn from one another, not least because there is a relatively high degree of overlapping support. Tactics do not have to be successful, in the sense of having achieved the movement's aims, for them to be taken up by others. The fact that they have been used at all, and have thus entered the public domain of forms of political activism, encourages others to follow.

This can be illustrated by considering the question of what one takes as the starting point for the rise of social movements in the second half of the twentieth century. It is generally agreed that the student movement of the late sixties was the genesis of the women's and environmental movements, and, perhaps to a lesser extent, the peace movement. Yet, in both America and the UK, the student movement had influential predecessors. In the American case, it was the civil rights movement of the early sixties. This was an important precursor of the student movement. While itself adopting tactics developed by others (the Ghandian principle of non-violent resistance, for example), it also introduced new forms of action – sit-ins, teach-ins, occupations, and so on[1] – which were subsequently taken up by the student movement. Opinions differ on whether or not the American civil rights movement was a 'social' movement; some argue that it was more in the nature of a single-issue protest group, others that it qualifies for social movement status by virtue of its stress upon collective identity. This does not concern us in this context, although it raises questions about the distinction between social movements and protest campaigns, to which we shall return. The point to note here is that, when the student movement began to mobilise, it had a new and radical style of participation upon which to draw. Its 'action repertoire' now included new forms of direct action inherited from the civil rights movement; it then went on to develop its own new forms of action, as the social movements which followed it developed their own by building on the example of the student movement. The parameters of protest had changed.

One can see a similar process taking place in the UK. The first signs of a willingness to break with conventional mainstream politics came between 1957 and 1963, with the creation of one of the best known protest campaigns in recent British politics, the Campaign for Nuclear Disarmament (CND).[2] Following the debacle of the Suez crisis, many of those on the left of British politics were questioning Britain's role in the world and both the moral and pragmatic justifications for possession of an 'independent' nuclear deterrent. Such arguments were initially conducted within the confines of conventional politics, primarily in the Labour Party. The hopes of the left-wing activists within the party of converting Labour to the cause of unilateral nuclear disarmament received a crushing blow in 1957, however, when one of their own great heroes, Aneurin Bevan (then shadow Foreign Secretary) argued against unilateralism. With the Conservative Government firmly wedded to the concept of British nuclear weapons, and a Labour leadership now set against unilateral nuclear disarmament, anti-nuclear protest began to develop outside conventional politics, culminating in the formation of CND at the beginning of 1958. We shall be looking at the experiences of CND in more detail subsequently; suffice it to note here that, between 1958 and 1963, protest over the nuclear issue set the pattern for subsequent movements – direct action (motivated by moral reasons rather than narrow self-interest), differing degrees of militancy and consequent internal splits.

The first leaders of CND were highly regarded members of the intelligentsia who, although without doubt on the left of the political spectrum, expected the new group to function primarily as a kind of intellectual pressure group, using the sheer weight of argument to persuade decision-makers. They were taken by surprise not only by the amount of public interest the new group inspired, but also by the insistence of many of their supporters that intellectual argument should be supplemented by public protest and non-violent direct action.[3] Protest initially took the form of demonstrations (the Aldermaston marches), the first of which attracted some 10,000 participants, with subsequent marches numbering up to 150,000 people. Having tried at first to distance themselves from such activity, CND's leadership realised they could not ignore such levels of interest and took on the role of organising the marches from 1959 onwards. They could not bring themselves to endorse other forms of direct action, however, such as the 'sit-down' protests which led to many arrests. Nor could they accept that CND should widen its ideological stance from a single-issue organisation (unilateral nuclear disarmament) to one which advocated a completely pacifist stance. Internal tensions became overt in 1960, with the breakaway of the more militant supporters to form the Committee of 100, which was both pacifist and explicitly committed to the practice of non-violent direct action. While CND saw nuclear weapons as a particular issue of concern within an otherwise broadly legitimate political system, the Committee of 100 conceptualised the nuclear issue as just one feature of a political and social system which legitimised violence; for them, non-violent direct action was not just a tactic, but an inherent part of their broader ideological vision in which society had to be reconstructed on a non-violent basis.

The fortunes of both CND and the Committee of 100 became embroiled with the on-going struggle within the Labour Party, support for unilateralism becoming an important symbol of left-wing credentials among party activists. We shall be looking at this in more detail later, when discussing the motivation for protest and the ways in which protest is expressed. Partly because of this and the election of a Labour Government in 1964, and partly because of developments in the international sphere (notably the Cuban missile crisis of 1962 and the agreement of a Partial Test Ban Treaty in 1963), anti-nuclear protest dwindled into virtual insignificance after 1964. The importance of this first phase of anti-nuclear protest should not be underestimated, however. It established a precedent for 'respectable' protest. The protesters were ridiculed by much of the media for being duffel-coated, sandal-wearing do-gooders. Even their most vehement critics, however, could not overlook the fact that the campaign attracted well-educated people, many of whom were in relatively high-status occupations such as teaching and the Churches.[4] Moreover, it was clear that morality played a central part in both their motivation and their action; their arguments were couched in terms of what was good for Britain and the world, not just for themselves, and non-violence even at the expense of personal risk was a defining characteristic of their behaviour.

The arrival of the Labour Government in 1964 brought about the temporary demise of unconventional protest; after thirteen years of uninterrupted Conservative rule, it seemed as if people were willing to see what could be achieved through conventional Parliamentary politics. By 1967, however, many such hopes had been dashed. While the Wilson Governments had introduced some radical reforms (comprehensive education, for example), there was little to suggest that they contemplated radical change in the economic sphere or in international relations. Nuclear disarmament was not on their agenda, and the Labour Government remained firmly committed to membership of NATO and the post-war 'special relationship' with America. It was this latter aspect of the Government's policy which provided a stimulus for the next wave of unconventional protest, the student movement of the late sixties.

The rise of the student movement, which grew almost simultaneously in America and Europe from the mid-sixties to the early seventies, has to be appreciated in the overall context of industrialised society at the time. Once in a while, a decade catches the popular imagination. It comes to be seen as a turning point, as a time in which fundamental changes in people's attitudes and behaviour occur and have a lasting effect for years to come. Such perceptions are rarely accurate. They are often based upon what was happening in just one section of society, and conveniently ignore the fact that most people, for most of the time, remained untouched by whatever the exciting new developments were. Nor do shifts in culture take place in neat ten-yearly intervals, starting as if by magic on the stroke of midnight at the beginning of each decade. Nevertheless, some decades acquire a resonance which overrides such details, and in post-war Britain the sixties is a classic example. The sixties is seen as a time in which people broke free; if the thirties was characterised by economic depression, the forties by war and the fifties by gradual recovery, it was in the sixties that people found the economic and political confidence to experiment with new forms of self-expression. This was especially the case with young people. Born after the war, their childhood may have been marked by some deprivation, but, as they grew into adulthood, the world seemed to be becoming a much easier place in which to live. Unlike their parents, they were coming of age in an era when living standards were rising, the threat of conventional war was remote and even the potential horror of a nuclear holocaust appeared to recede after the Superpowers drew back from the brink of the Cuban missile crisis in 1962.

We must not forget that many, if not most, of this post-war generation of young people carried on their lives in ways not dissimilar to those of their parents; they had more in the way of material possessions, but they continued to live in conventional marital relationships, to pursue careers in the established professions and occupations and be content to express any political feelings through the 'normal' channels of mainstream Parliamentary parties. A significant minority did not, however; their reaction to greater affluence and relative economic security was not to embrace it with a mixture of enthusiasm and relief, but rather to question it. They were no longer prepared to show deference to established political leaders and institutions, but wanted a more active say in how their world was run. They developed a preoccupation with what has become known as 'lifestyle'; that is, they saw economic growth as involving at least as many problems as it did benefits, posing a threat to individual autonomy and opportunity for self-expression. They may only have been a minority, but innovations such as a distinctive culture based upon pop and rock music and the rapid growth of the electronic media acted as catalysts to the development of an international consciousness, a conviction that, while they might be outnumbered in their particular societies, at least there were many others around the world who shared their views and concerns.

Originating in the civil rights campaigns of the fifties and sixties, and subsequently focusing on involvement in Vietnam, the student movement first came to prominence in America. The Vietnam War sparked off widespread protest, especially among the young, which coalesced around the universities. It quickly spread to Western Europe, particularly France, Germany and Italy, and had a significant impact in Australia. Unlike the protest over nuclear disarmament, it was a genuinely international phenomenon.

It was inspired by a combination of factors. One rallying call was a rejection of the colonialism that Vietnam (and American foreign policy towards Central and South America) was seen to represent. There were also more localised factors stemming from the rapid expansion of student numbers since the early sixties; higher education underwent a dramatic expansion throughout most of the Western democracies, with the number of students doubling or even trebling in some countries. This shift away from an elitist system of higher education led in some countries (notably France and Italy) to over-stretched facilities, and disgruntled students perceived their university authorities to be unresponsive and unduly authoritarian in response to such problems. While student radicalism was to lay the foundations for terrorism in Germany and Italy during the seventies, it was in France that it had its most immediate and dramatic impact. For a brief period around May 1968, French students and radical socialists formed a common front[5] which appeared to threaten a genuinely revolutionary situation, resulting in overt confrontation with the government.

The student movement in Britain was a much more low-key affair, with little or no interest being shown by the Labour Party or the trade union movement. Direct action took the form of protest marches and 'occupations' of university property. Even the most famous of these, the demonstration (or 'riot', as the media termed it) outside the American Embassy in London's Grosvenor Square organised by the Vietnam Solidarity Campaign in 1968, resulted in only about 40 arrests and the same number of people injured. While tear gas and cobble-stones flew on the streets of Paris, demonstrators and police in Grosvenor Square sang a chorus of 'Auld Lang Syne' together before dispersing.[6]

If the student movement took a less extreme form in Britain than elsewhere (and, indeed, rarely spread beyond a handful of universities), it should not be discounted. Its importance lay not so much in the numbers involved, but in the kind of thinking and tactics it inspired. Initially motivated by specific issues like Vietnam, the student movement quickly developed wider interests, rejecting the dominant political institutions and practices of both capitalism and state communism. They were motivated by a belief in the development of a new lifestyle – one that centred upon the explosion of pop and rock music (fuelled by relative affluence), sexual freedom (fuelled by new developments in contraception such as the 'birth control' pill), an espousal of revolutionary and feminist thinking, and the beginnings of a concern with environmental issues. Activists were clearly dissatisfied with the moderation of the mainstream left at home, as represented by both the Labour Government and a trade union movement preoccu-pied with seeking material advantages for its membership. They were equally disenchanted, however, with the direction taken by Communist states in Eastern Europe, turning instead to Trotsky, Mao-Tse Tung, Che Guevara and the revolutionary movements in the Third World for their inspiration. Even here, however, they were far from slavishly following any particular dogma, adopting only the libertarian core of revolutionary socialism espoused by such thinkers, and adapting it to their own concerns. It led to the first real interest in ecological issues and feminism – even if the latter was, somewhat ironically, stimulated by the leading role played by men in the movement.[7]

This emphasis upon libertarianism was also important, in that it conditioned the student movement's views upon its own organisation. The movement was held together by shared ideas and ideals rather than by any formal structure. Hierarchy was firmly rejected, and participation by all who wished to express a view was seen as not just desirable but essential. Communication between activists was achieved through informal networks rather than formalised meetings or structures. In this way, the student movement did not just introduce many young people to radical ideas, it also taught them new ways of mobilising around those ideas. The rapid expansion of television, new youth-oriented and pirate radio stations, and the growth of an 'underground' press made possible by technological innovation – all contributed to a climate in which both national and international communication between like-minded individuals became much easier.

This mixture of a radical ideology and new action repertoire was what gave the emerging women's, environmental and peace movements their distinctive character. All had their antecedents. The CND of the eighties was a revival of fortunes after some fifteen years of near-dormancy, rather than a 'new' movement; the environmental movement grew out of existing, more conventional groups; and the women's movement is often termed 'second-wave' feminism, referring to the 'first-wave' of the suffragettes' campaign which peaked between 1900 and 1914. Yet each was qualitatively different in its new guise. CND attempted to spawn a wider peace movement, and, while its prime aim remained the same, expanded its action repertoire from demonstrations to many different forms of direct action, as well as placing its conventional lobbying and use of the media on a much more professional footing. The women's movement added to its representational aims a new dimension which stressed the acceptance of difference as much as it stressed equality, and developed a whole new strain of intramovement 'self-help' tactics. The environmental movement changed even more dramatically. As we shall see, its ideology moved from a conservationist to a 'dark green' ecological perspective; its action repertoire expanded to include direct action (even, in a minority of cases, violent direct action), and it even founded its own distinctive political party. Yet there was a unity underlying all these changes, both across the different movements and in different countries. All emphasised their distaste for formal organisation and hierarchy; all drew the bulk of their support from the same sector in society; all, in different ways, questioned the prevailing paradigm of economic growth and modernisation.

Of course, there have been differences between countries. The peace movement has been strong in the UK and Germany, for example, yet much weaker in France and Italy. The women's movement quickly became semi-institutionalised in America (in the sense of having quasi-formal organisations which entered into coalitions with more conventional parties and groups), whereas its counterparts in the UK and Germany have remained much more autonomous and loosely organised. The Netherlands has been a fertile territory for all kinds of social movements, while neighbouring Belgium has not. Sometimes the reasons for such different development seem clear. As far as the peace movement is concerned, for example, the UK did have its own nuclear weapons, whereas Italy did not; most Germans were uncomfortably aware that if nuclear war did break out in Europe, their country was first in the firing line. Neither factor applied to France, however, which is why we have to look at the particular political contexts in which the movements operated. We shall be doing this via the concept of 'political opportunity structures' – the cultural and institutional arrangements which hold sway in different countries. For now, though, our point holds true in broad terms. There has been a wave of new forms of political action, espousing new kinds of aims, occurring virtually simultaneously throughout Western societies. Before we move on to examine this in detail in the British context, let us take an overview of how social scientists have reacted to this, because it is the validity of their ideas to the specific experiences of social movements in the UK which we will seek to test.

4 Theoretical ideas

Social scientists reacted to this new style of politics in different ways. They had a number of things to explain, depending upon their view of society, but the common feature to all was the challenge of explaining the revival of such discontent and alienation, and its apparent concentration among the better-off and better-educated in society. Social scientists have risen to this challenge with a plethora of theoretical ideas – theorising has proved much more popular than empirical research. We shall be examining these theories in more detail when looking at what movements in Britain have actually done over the last thirty years, but it might be useful to take a broad overview of each one now. What follows does not lay claim to being an exhaustive summary of every theoretical insight which has been put forward, but I think some five broad categories can be discerned, some of which have important sub-categories. These are:

- theories which conceptualise social movements as instances of more or less spontaneous outbursts of anger and frustration on the part of individuals who, as a consequence of rapid social change, feel disadvantaged (the *classical* approach);
- theories which concentrate upon organisations within social movements, seeing those organisations as mobilising people and resources, competing with one another and adapting their aims and tactics in order to survive (the *Resource Mobilisation* approach);
- theories which argue social movements result from, and contribute to, over-arching changes in the structure and nature of advanced industrialised societies (the *New Social Movements* approach). Within this school of thought are those who see the protest associated with social movements as a recurring feature of social development over the last few hundred years, with movements activity since the sixties being the most recent 'wave' (the *cyclical* approach),

and also those who argue there is something qualitatively different about the post-war period (the *post-industrial* approach);

- theories which overlap to some extent with the post-industrial approach and which concentrate upon a 'new middle class'; while some argue this new class becomes active in movements for the instrumental motive of improving their own interests, most argue that it differs from others in society because it has different values which give it an expressive rather than instrumental motivation (the *post-materialism* approach);

- and finally a school of thought which accepts many of the insights offered by the above, but argues that social movements have to be assessed within the particular confines of the political system and culture within which they operate (the *Political Opportunity Structure* approach), and that movements arise because conventional politics offers too little in the way of opportunities (the *exclusion* argument).

Before looking at each of these, one general point needs to be made. Much of the research to date on social movements has been undertaken in America and continental Europe. One of the striking things about this theoretical work is the different focus of European and American social scientists. It may well be that this is changing; a number of deliberate efforts have been made in recent years to bring the two 'sides' together.[1] The bulk of the work published on social movements over the last thirty years, however, bears the hallmark of one or other of these distinctive approaches. To a large extent this is because they are influenced by their own intellectual and political cultures, which have led them to look at different things and from different perspectives. What follows is very much an overview, with all the over-simplification this implies; not all Americans subscribe to the 'American' perspective, nor Europeans to the 'European' view. Nevertheless, it is important that we have an idea of the intellectual traditions of each, which colour our five different schools of thought.

American commentators over the last few decades have been accustomed to a political culture and system in which groups play as important a part in politics as parties. Their starting point tends to be pluralism, a political system in which power is, at least in theory, relatively dispersed – through the separation of powers between legislative, executive and judicial branches of government, through a federal system, and through the legitimacy accorded to organised groups and the lobbying they undertake. Given this, unconventional or extra-systemic protest is particularly problematic – at bottom, what has to be explained is why people turn to such protest when, in theory, they have a perfectly open political system within which they can make their views heard. This has led to two perspectives which differ from the European approach.

First, American analysts tend to focus upon the 'political' or 'overt' side of social movements. By this, I mean that American social scientists tend to look for protest activities, rather than the emergence of contentious ideas in society, as evidence of social movement activity. Much of the empirical work in America has been based upon particular protest groups or actions, rather than discussion of major ideological and structural changes in advanced capitalist societies. Those from the European perspective can be quite scathing in their criticism of this eclectic approach, arguing that American commentators are prone to labelling almost any collective action not apparently based upon 'rational' self-interest as evidence of a social movement at work.

Second, American social scientists have an enduring interest in the 'rationality' of protest, and indeed of all political behaviour. Their initial response to unconventional protest was to label it 'irrational', evidence of an inability for various reasons to play a full part in 'normal' politics. Since the seventies, this viewpoint has been largely replaced by one which argues that it is rational, talks of 'entrepreneurs' who are capitalising upon opportunities to create social movements, and explains social movements in terms of interactions between groups and institutions rather than focusing upon individuals. They are interested in why some causes or sets of beliefs produce social movements, while others do not, and how the social movements which do arise interact, not just with the political authorities, but also with each other. As such, their concern lies primarily with the *organisational* aspects of social movements.

Continental European observers, on the other hand, who have a long tradition of emphasising the theoretical rather than the empirical aspects of social science, take phenomena like feminism or environmentalism as evidence of a new and fundamental cleavage in society. As the struggle between classes has largely failed to evolve in the direction envisaged by Marx, social movements are seen as taking the place of the proletariat as the oppositional force in the on-going fight between haves and have-nots. While American scholars are preoccupied with the visible aspects of movements (what they do, how they do it), their European colleagues are more interested in social movements as *ideological forces* in society. They are not so much interested in how a social movement goes about its activities as what the existence of a movement tells us about the culture and values of a society. From the European perspective, a social movement does not have to be particularly active (in the sense of mounting public campaigns, demonstrations, direct action, etc.) to be important; even when apparently dormant, movements can have an impact on what is termed 'cultural production', that is they can be influencing the way their own adherents and those opposed to them *think* about how society should be organised.

Different intellectual traditions, then, have caused different questions to be asked; our concern is not to pronounce which is the 'best', but to accept that each may have something to offer us. We begin our account with theories associated with the American perspective, largely because they were the first to be developed. American social scientists had to cope with the rise of the civil rights and anti-Vietnam War movements some five to ten years before their European counterparts were spurred into action by the student movement of the late sixties. Research on social movements in America is usually summarised as belonging to two schools of thought: the 'classical', and a subsequent rejection of the classical by 'Resource Mobilisation'. There are no hard and fast boundaries between these, each of which accuses the other of having only a partial explanation to offer. In the early days of the Resource Mobilisation approach, its devotees were concerned to distinguish clearly their new approach from that which had gone before, and perhaps over-stated the differences between them. As Resource Mobilisation became more accepted, the proselytising fervour of its advocates has lessened, and there is more willingness to accept that there are overlaps between them. Nevertheless, for our purposes, we will concentrate for now upon the essentials of each, which are indeed rather different.

THE CLASSICAL APPROACH

The fifties and sixties saw the development of the classical approach, one that was preoccupied with explaining why individuals participated, not why movements arose at certain times and not others, and explained such behaviour in terms of 'irrationality' on the part of those individuals. Its focus, then, was on the individual on the one hand, and society on the other. If we can explain why some people behave in this fashion, the argument was, then we do not need to account for why a particular society at a particular time has certain social movements and not others – they have them because individuals have been motivated to protest. The classical approach had different component parts, the principal ones being 'collective behaviour',[2] 'mass society'[3] and 'relative deprivation'.[4] There were important differences between them, but that lies outside our scope in this context; what they had in common was that they saw protest behaviour stemming from a mixture of societal and individual stresses. Rapid social and economic change disturbed the smooth functioning of society; individuals developed grievances because their expectations were not being met, which led to frustration and outbursts of anger. Such people were likely to be 'atomised' – a sociological concept meaning essentially a detachment from established social and other networks – and their protest was likely to be transitory. As Mayer notes, 'the actors for this non institutional politics are the backward, marginal alienated elements of society'.[5] In the classical model, then, social movements were outside of 'normal' politics. Given that, in the eyes of the classical theorists, such movements and individuals were living in a pluralist political system which provided access for all, their motivation could only be that they did not have the cognitive skills necessary to work within the pluralist system. Hence their proclivity for 'irrational' outbursts.

RESOURCE MOBILISATION

This approach was stimulated by what were perceived to be a number of flaws and omissions in the classical approach: that it did not explain the participation in movements of socially integrated and well educated people; that it did not explain why some movements developed while others did not; that it did not recognise that grievances were more widespread in society than the classical model assumed; and that it did not recognise that movements developed as a rational response to inadequacies in the representational approach rather than being merely an instance of 'irrational' behaviour.

The participation of the educated middle classes in social movements was first highlighted by the civil rights movement of the fifties and sixties and the anti-war/student movement which grew up from the mid-sixties. The 'riot dimension' of the early sixties civil rights movement could possibly be explained by classical model assumptions, but what was one to make of the involvement of middle-class whites (who by no stretch of the imagination were 'atomised'), and what of the important role played by already-existing organisations such as the Churches? If the civil rights movement appeared to show up inadequacies in the classical approach, it was the subsequent anti-war/student movement which persuaded most social scientists that a new approach was needed. Despite the increase in numbers of students, graduate employment prospects remained good. These were among the most advantaged in society in material terms, not only raised during a period of increasing material prosperity but also with good expectations of continuing to benefit in the new 'affluent society' – not least because, as capitalism developed, more and more of a premium was being placed upon 'knowledge' as distinct from ownership of the industrialised means of production. Nor were they under any special threat from specific developments such as the Vietnam conflict; conscription was a worry for many in America, but much more so for those outside higher education. Yet not only were they ignoring the conventional avenues for political participation, they were also advocating causes and ideas like civil rights, freedom and peace, which were altruistic rather than self-centred. Both the object of their concerns and the means which they adopted to pursue them appeared to defy explanations of individual motivation which rested upon social alienation. An additional factor may well have been that many American academics, like their European counterparts, were themselves active in these movements, and may have been uncomfortable with a theory which labelled them as among the political and social 'underclass' of society.

Resource Mobilisation theorists thought that the answer lay, not in concentrating upon the social psychology of the individuals concerned, but instead in looking at how movements develop. In other words, while the classical model concentrated upon the 'macro' level (societal stresses) and the 'micro' level (the psychology of the individual), Resource Mobilisation suggested we turn our attention to the intermediate or 'meso' level of the organisations around which movements cluster. Crucial to the Resource Mobilisation analysis is the argument that grievances in society are important, but not nearly so important as the classical approach suggested. The argument here is that 'grievances' and dissatisfactions are inherent and widespread in society. At any one time, there are *always* going to be some people in society who feel they are not getting their due or their fair share. It follows from this, according to the Resource Mobilisation school, that we should not spend our time trying to establish what particular grievance gives rise to what particular movement. Instead, we should be asking why only some grievances and dissatisfactions produce movements and others do not. The answer lies in the availability and use of *resources* – hence the term, Resource Mobilisation.

There is no commonly accepted definition of what exactly does and does not constitute a 'resource', even among Resource Mobilisation theorists. The term is taken to mean both tangible resources such as money, facilities, photocopiers and computers, but also more intangible assets such as any professional skills supporters may have, or even the amount of time they can make available to the movement. It can also be taken to mean the ability to attract the support of more established groups and organisations in the political and social system.

It was not just the emergence of middle-class protest which inspired such thinking, but also related developments in other parts of social science, particularly among those who were studying more 'conventional' interest groups. Without doubt, the single most important influence here came from the work of Olson[6] in the mid-sixties. Conducting research upon economic producer groups, Olson developed a theory of collective action which suggested that the whole process of mobilisation was much more fraught with difficulty than the classical approach assumed. Olson's starting point was the assumption that individuals act 'rationally', by which he meant they will seek to maximise their own interests and any benefits they can obtain, while simultaneously seeking to minimise any costs to themselves. Olson's point was that groups often pursue a 'collective benefit'. For example, a motorists' organisation might press for more spending on roads and lower taxation on vehicles and fuel, which would benefit all motorists, not just those belonging to the organisation; or an environmental group might press for pollution controls which, if accepted, would benefit all, not just those who fought for the change. Olson argued that any such group faced the problem of what he termed 'free-riders'. It would not be 'rational' for an individual to incur the 'costs' of involvement if the group was going to obtain the benefits anyway; and, if the group was already of a certain size, then it would not be 'rational' for any one individual to suppose that their contribution would make any significant difference to the outcome. Following on from this, Olson argued that the only way groups could motivate people to make the effort to become involved and incur the costs of such commitment was to offer 'selective incentives' – that is, rewards or services which were only available to members of the group. Thus, for example, motorists' groups do not just press for changes which they perceive as beneficial to all motorists, but also (indeed, primarily) offer various services like breakdown recovery and legal assistance which are only available to members. It was only in this way, Olson argued, that the cost–benefit equation could be made to work; if people were to incur the costs of involvement, then their rewards had to be available on this selective basis.

The particular strengths and weaknesses of Olson's argument need not concern us here; what is important is that Olson provided a theoretical underpinning to the disquiet felt by Resource Mobilisation theorists about the assumptions of the classical approach. They took Olson's insights and applied them to social movements, arguing that they refuted the idea that grievances were somehow automatically translated into movements. If Olson could show that mobilisation was problematic even for mainstream producer interest groups, then it must be much more so for social movements – because, at least on the face of it, they were all about 'collective benefits' and had no 'selective incentives' to offer. The anti-war/student movement was not offering those who supported it the chance to avoid conscription and having their tax revenues contribute to the defence budget while those who did not support the movement would have to pay for and fight in the war; nor was the civil rights movement able to argue that only those who actively participated would benefit from any resulting political and social change.

American commentators upon social movements have not taken Olson's thesis as the last word on the subject. In particular, they have questioned his definitions of both the 'costs' and 'rewards' of collective mobilisation. Hirschman, for example, has argued that Olson views costs and rewards in a purely instrumental sense – if I get involved in this, what material benefits will I receive?[7] Hirschman maintains that, particularly when applied to social movements, this misses the point that motivation may be more expressive than instrumental in nature. In other words, what may seem to an outsider to be 'costs' – involvement and commitment – are seen by participants as 'rewards', as they actually enjoy devoting their time and money to a particular struggle. Such activism is its own reward, even if the movement fails to achieve its objectives.

Chong takes this line of argument a stage further.[8] He agrees with Hirschman that one has to take into account more than just material incentives, and that some activists do see participation as its own reward. He parts company with Hirschman, however, by arguing that one can also discern some *selective* incentives which underlie such apparently expressive behaviour. He distinguishes between two sorts of selective incentive, in addition to Olson's material incentives – psychological and social. By psychological, he means the 'feelings of efficacy, self-esteem, righteousness, and competence that are part and parcel of playing an active role in the affairs of society'.[9] The motivation does not always have to be quite so high-minded as this list might suggest; Chong acknowledges that sometimes the motivation to participate is 'like a desire to gain revenge',[10] although we should bear in mind he is writing in the context of a study of the civil rights movement in America. The point remains that this psychological motivation is a selective incentive because you cannot experience it without participating, and it can also be seen as rational because you are fulfilling a personal need to fulfil such feelings. It is Chong's idea of social incentives which has attracted more attention, however. Here, he is making the point that people are social beings, with on-going social interactions with family, friends, colleagues and so on. If those around you are all convinced feminists, or believe in unilateral nuclear disarmament, then there will be some pressure upon you also to adopt such attitudes – 'the desire to gain or sustain friendships, to maintain one's social standing, and to avoid ridicule and ostracism are all social goals that constitute selective incentives for individuals to participate in collective action'.[11] Chong's argument is that 'fitting in with others' can be seen as a selective incentive because it can be seen as developing a 'reputational concern' – by which he means developing, through one's participation in activities where there seems to be no material self-benefit, a general reputation which can, as it were, be 'cashed in' at some future date. 'The selective incentives to participate are the accumulated future benefits that we will reap as a reward for co-operation in the current collective endeavour.'[12] Such insights give rise to further questions: why, for example, some people seem more concerned than others about their reputation – a point which Chong does not really address. He does acknowledge that even those motivated by the attitudes of, and their standing with, other people are more likely to become involved if there is already some kind of movement or organisation in existence, with at least an outside chance of being successful, and here he sides with the Resource Mobilisation theorists by pointing to the importance of pre-existing social networks, on which emerging movements can 'piggy-back' their way to public attention. Even so, it means that those who *start* a movement have to be motivated by something rather stronger and deeper than reputational concerns. Overall, however, the central point remains: people are social beings who can be motivated by incentives which are not material, but may well be selective – you have to take part if you want the credibility or reputation. So, for example, in the British context, this could translate into something like: 'I was a member of CND in the eighties because I was active in the Labour Party, wanted to be accepted as part of the left in the party, and support for CND was perceived by others in the party as an essential element of one's left-wing credentials'; or 'I am going on an anti-nuclear march and making a donation to Greenpeace because this reaffirms my own self-image, gives me a chance to mix with like-minded people and (perhaps above all) demonstrates to others what kind of person I am'. This instrumental/expressive dichotomy is one to which we shall return when discussing European responses.

Oberschall takes a different tack, questioning the validity of Olson's definition of rewards.[13] He argues that it is the status and access to political elites which are important. If an aggrieved group in society feels it has little chance of achieving social mobility or inclusion in the political decision-making process, then the potential rewards of unconventional protest are that much greater. Peace movement activists may feel the potential costs of involvement are outweighed by the potential reward (unilateral nuclear disarmament), which are almost certainly never going to result from conventional dialogue with the political authorities; black people or women might feel they will never be accepted as equals by those with power, so the potential rewards (acceptance and inclusion) justify the potential costs of becoming active. Fireman and Gamson argue that people participate because they realise that the collective good would never be achieved if everyone reasoned like Olson's rational individual.[14] They maintain it is not selective incentives but group solidarity, group interests and personal interests in the collective goods, along with the perceived urgency of collective action, that motivates people to participate.

Such arguments raise wider points about the nature of motivation, to which we shall return. In this context, the point to note is that American social scientists differed with parts of Olson's argument; his rational choice theory could explain why people would not support social movements, but was much less useful when it came to explaining why some did. His central thrust, however – that there was nothing automatic about interests and grievances producing groups and movements, and that costs and rewards were an on-going concern for groups if they wished to maintain their support – was seized on with alacrity. Drawing on the implications of Olson's thesis, the Resource Mobilisation school developed theories relating to both the growth and the subsequent development of social movements.

Resource Mobilisation is perhaps at its most convincing when it discusses the origins and early development of movements. The classical model had implied that movements grew more or less spontaneously, as outbursts of anger and frustration led to imitative behaviour. Resource Mobilisation operates more at the collective level, seeing movements emerge out of networks, groups and movements which already exist. One important factor lies in informal social networks which already exist within the aggrieved group. For example, they argue that the emergence of the civil rights movement was facilitated by the involvement of many black people in various Churches – these informal networks already in existence laid the foundations for the creation of a wider movement. The more networks which exist within an aggrieved group, the easier it will be to mobilise. Another important factor is the relationship with groups outside the aggrieved group. McCarthy and Zald argue that what they term 'conscience constituents' are important resources for movements.[15] These are groups of people who do not stand to benefit directly from a movement's aims, but can be persuaded to offer support – an example would be a peace movement seeking to gain the support of Churches.

Having said that, one cannot assume that striking alliances with established organisations or institutions is necessarily always beneficial for a movement. The new allies may well agree with the central thrust of a movement's aims, but have their own, more general, values and attitudes which, if adopted by the movement, may well impede that movement's chances of success. For example, we have mentioned the importance of the role of Churches with respect to peace movements. Outside Britain, the Church has also been important for the women's movement, particularly in Catholic societies. In countries such as Belgium, Italy, Spain and Switzerland, the good news for women's movements has been support both from the Church and from established Socialist parties for such basic rights as suffrage. However, as both Lovenduski[16] and Banaszak[17] have noted, the Catholic Church has also endorsed women's 'traditional roles as caregiver, mother and religious keystone'[18] and encouraged non-confrontational strategies, while the support of Socialist parties 'strong enough to engender a negative reaction, but not powerful enough to institute woman suffrage on their own'[19] can actually be counter-productive. In more general terms, then, the point is that support from established players in the system may come at a price; their way of doing things may well rub off on a movement, leading it to become less adventurous in its aims and/or tactics, and so reducing its chances of making a successful impact upon society.

Returning to the more material aspects of 'resources', McCarthy and Zald also point to what they see as the importance of movements obtaining resources (usually financial) from charitable foundations, private-sector companies and even the government (normally on a regional or local level). It is from this that we get the idea of movements competing for resources. McCarthy and Zald, for example, use the terminology of Social Movement Organisations (SMOs), meaning organisations within movements which mobilise resources for the wider movement – examples would be Friends of the Earth and Greenpeace within the environmental movement. While accepting that SMOs may well enjoy good relations and, more likely then not, a degree of cross-cutting membership and support, the Resource Mobilisation perspective nevertheless sees them as being in competition for scarce resources – the time, energy, knowledge and commitment of individuals and the money and physical resources of sympathetic organisations in the wider society.

It is quite widely accepted by now that at least some of this kind of thinking reflects the distinctive features of the American system. For example, the relatively decentralised structure of the American federal system means more opportunities exist to seek funding at state and local level than is usually the case in unitary systems like that of the UK. Moreover, there is a strong tradition in America of private-sector organisations and wealthy individuals funding charitable foundations, and so on. The basics remain valid, however; Resource Mobilisation draws our attention to the possibility of competition (implicit or explicit) between apparently allied social movement organisations, and it also reminds us that we have to account for both initial recruitment into social movements, and the subsequent retention of those recruits' support.

Much more contentious has been the elaboration of what might be termed an 'organisational and tactical imperative' by some of the Resource Mobilisation school. Building on the arguments from Olson about costs and benefits, and drawing on the earlier works of such theorists as Max Weber and Michels about how organisations develop and try to prolong their own lives, some[20] have argued that this will inevitably mean that SMOs will both develop certain forms of organisation and 'tone down' their tactics and aims. Over time, it is argued, SMOs will not only become formally organised, with professional staff and a bureaucratic structure, but also lean more and more towards conventional participation rather than outright protest – because this enables the SMO to encourage recruitment and, crucially, mount long-lasting campaigns. There are two facets to the argument. One is that the more formally organised the SMO is, the better it is able to vary its tactics to suit particular circumstances – 'organisational planning means that the tactics of the SMOs are not based on emotional outbursts of frustrated citizens but on conscious calculations of how best to advance the organisation's goals – whether through dramatic protests or quiet political lobbying.'[21] The other is that a combination of having professionals working for the SMO and moving towards more conventional means of making their views heard reduces the 'cost' of support for sympathisers. This operates at both an individual and organisational level. The argument is that charitable foundations, localised political institutions (for example, local authorities in the UK) and so on are more likely to offer financial and other support if the SMO does not concentrate exclusively on unconventional, possibly illegal protest. Similarly, individuals do not have to incur the 'costs' of unconventional protest (up to and including imprisonment), as the SMO restricts itself to 'legitimate', legal means of expressing their viewpoint. Nor do they have to confront the time-consuming problems of the day-to-day running of the organisation, as that is undertaken by paid staff.

Such ideas have proved contentious in both theoretical and empirical terms. Gerlach and Hine, for example, have advanced a counter-argument that informal, decentralised organisational structures are actually more effective.[22] Precisely because a movement is little more than a collection of loosely coordinated localised groups, it can be hard to suppress (there is no 'head' which can be lopped off by the opposition) and different local groups can try different sorts of tactics. Others have argued that if one studies the development of movement organisations, the thesis simply does not hold true empirically. Against this, first impressions of an SMO such as Greenpeace, for example – which, as we shall see, runs itself in a fashion not dissimilar to a private-sector company – lead one to think it is at least worth exploring.

NEW SOCIAL MOVEMENTS

While American commentators were preoccupied with such organisational questions, continental Europeans were much more interested in what social movements symbolised in terms of macro-societal change. The central question they identified was not the rationality or otherwise of social movements, but how such movements related to what had previously been seen as the real forces for change in society. The problem for those who conceptualised society in collective rather than individualistic terms was that, until the sixties, it had been assumed that the 'real' challenge to the existing order would come from the working class, particularly the industrialised working class. The fact that such a challenge had been conspicuous more by its absence than anything else was explained away by 'false consciousness' – the working class being misled by ideological manipulation on the part of the ruling class into thinking that reformism, rather than revolution, was the way forward.

Yet here was a challenge which not only emanated from the more privileged in society rather than the worse-off, but in which the challengers were also apparently uninterested in seizing control of the state apparatus. The new protesters did not want to storm Parliament or replace senior civil servants and judges with their own kind; they were not revolutionary socialists. Nor were they demanding the right or opportunity to be included in the 'normal' political system and process, in the way that trade unions and social democratic/Labour parties had during the preceding decades. They wanted freedom, but not freedom from economic exploitation so much as freedom to live their lives as they wanted, without interference from the state. They did not want power over society, but rather autonomy. They were seen as being *anti-modernistic*, in that they rejected the capitalist ethic of growth, and had aspirations which overturned the conventional ideas of bettering oneself in material terms. For the New Social Movement theorists, such motivations and behaviour were the result of structural changes in advanced capitalist societies, as automation and other technical advances made *production* less important and *knowledge* much more important.

'Knowledge' has a particular resonance for some commentators. Eyerman and Jamison, whose work concentrates upon environmental movements, distinguish different dimensions of 'knowledge' which they argue are central to the study of social movements.[23] On one level, social movements are seen as the bearers of new ideas in society; established intellectuals develop new ideas and perspectives around which social movements then form. An example would be the way in which established scientists developed a critique of the consequences of 'conventional' science and technology in the sixties, leading to the creation of an environmental perspective. Movements then mobilise and agitate to create new 'public spaces' for such new ideas – not just getting such issues on to the political agenda, but also introducing them into everyday life and the way in which people see the world they live in. On another level, however, social movements do not just seize on a new idea and start championing it. New ideas stimulate people to come together and discuss them; it is through this interaction – at first between individuals and later, as the idea spreads, between different groups and organisations, and between them and those that oppose them – that the identity of a movement is hammered out in a process termed 'cognitive praxis' by Eyerman and Jamison. 'Knowledge is . . . the product of a series of social encounters, within movements, between movements and even more importantly perhaps, between movements and their established opponents.'[24]

Sociologists may be more comfortable with such ideas than political scientists, falling as they do within the broad area of the sociology of knowledge. They raise ideas which are definitely within the remit of political science, however, as they draw our attention to a number of points relating to the distinction between 'public' and 'private', and the relationship between 'means' and 'goals'. This is well illustrated by the work of Melucci.[25] He argues that the *raison d'être* of a social movement is challenging the dominant values and cultural codes in society. Consequently, it may be necessary to analyse the 'visible' aspects of movements (such as protests and demonstrations), but it is not sufficient on its own. Analysis which examines only collective public activity such as protest overlooks 'the network of relationships which constitutes the submerged reality of the movements before, during and after events'. In other words, he is arguing that movements do not just exist in the dimension of public actions, but also in the dimension of everyday life: 'conflicts do not chiefly express themselves through action designed to achieve outcomes in the political system. Rather, they raise a challenge which recasts the language and cultural codes which organise information'.[26] In short, movements aim to change attitudes as well as public policy, and interpersonal and small-group interaction is a vital component of this. It follows from this that the way in which movements organise themselves, and the things that they choose to do, should be assessed not just as means to an end but as ends or goals in themselves. A movement may choose to remain loosely organised and decentralised, and to stress internal participation, even if it means it takes a long time to reach decisions, not because this makes it less vulnerable to attack from opponents, but because such a way of going about things is in itself an important part of the movement's appeal. It is part of the movement's *identity*.

THE CYCLICAL APPROACH

As one might expect, authors of the cyclical school tend to adopt a much longer time-span than others, dealing in centuries rather than decades. Tilly, for example, looks at the forms protest has taken (the 'action repertoires' of movements), and draws a distinction between patterns of protest in the eighteenth century and those of the nineteenth and twentieth centuries.[27] He argues that earlier protest was characterised by its reactive nature, in that people were protesting against decisions by authorities, often on a local level, and the protests took the form of violent uprisings or riots or the refusal to pay taxes. By the nineteenth century, he maintains, the focus of protest moved to the national level, and the forms of protest became those with which we are familiar today – mass demonstrations, rallies and so on. The essence of his argument is that the people, and the issues involved, change over time, but one can discern patterns of activity which give such protest a unity over time. Tilly focuses, however, upon *political* protest. He is discussing the process whereby those who were previously disenfranchised mobilise in order to be included in political decision-making. This is obviously relevant to earlier struggles, such as that of the trade union movement, to gain recognition and become part of the conventional political process. Although useful in reminding us that what appears new may just be a revival of the past in a different guise, however, his approach is less relevant when it comes to understanding movements from the sixties onwards, precisely because political inclusion was not their sole, or even their prime, motive.

Tarrow has provided analyses which are both contemporary in focus (protest in post-war Italian politics[28]) and more wide-ranging historically and geographically.[29] Unlike Olson, Hirschman, Chong *et al.*, Tarrow is not preoccupied with why individuals become involved with movements, but rather with why movements seem to ebb and flow over time. He argues that one can discern a cyclical process in which movements grow out of small-scale spontaneous protest into fully-fledged movements. These movements then peak as they are partially accommodated by the authorities (both in terms of meeting some programmatic demands and including some of their 'leaders' into existing political elites); subsequently they decline, partly because at least some victories have been won and partly because of disappoint-ment felt by movement activists that compromises have been agreed and more has not been achieved. Tarrow also has much to say on the way in which movements can learn from each other, developing what he terms a 'modular' repertoire of different forms of action and mobilisation, the point being that as one movement builds on the success of another, so the cumulative effect is to increase the opportu-nities for all – although it is arguable that this overlooks the fact that movements, and organisations within them, are often effectively in competition with each other. It is a point to which we shall return when discussing political opportunity structures, but one cannot dispute that, more than most, Tarrow manages to convey the way in which particular movements, and indeed movements as a whole, will inevitably fluctuate over time and both act upon and react to a constantly changing political and societal environment.

Like Tilly, Tarrow's primary concern is with protest rather than movements as such, and with how previously excluded groups gain access to political power. Brand, our final example of the cyclical school, has a wider focus, in that he discusses cultural rather than specifically political protest.[30] His thesis is that social movements appear in waves, triggered off by periods of 'cultural crisis' in which people question the whole idea of modernity and progress, becoming critical of such trends as bureaucratisation, political centralisation and industrialisation, and shattering the 'technocratic consensus of the post-war decades'. He substantiates this thesis with empirical evidence by examining the growth and decline of pacifism, environmentalism and what we now know as feminism. He makes the point that, at least for pacifism and environmentalism, one can identify three distinct phases of interest and mobilisation – 1830–1850, 1890–1914 and the period since the 1960s; although women's rights appeared later on the scene, he argues that this also fits the model in its latter two stages. He backs up his point that they all spring from a common feeling in society – a 'pervasive mood of cultural criticism' – by pointing out the largely parallel nature of the mobilisation phases of the individual movements; that is, they tend to occur at the same time. As we shall see, while others agree that social movements tend to feed off each other, one movement providing the impetus, resources and even supporters to create another movement, they interpret this more in terms of organisational resources than any underlying cultural mood.

POST-INDUSTRIAL SOCIETY

A second school of thought is one which conceptualises the apparently new style of politics in terms of a move from an industrial society to one which is 'post-industrial'. The argument is that the structure of capitalist society has changed. In the nineteenth and the early part of the twentieth century, capitalist society had been conceptualised in essentially bipartite terms; those who owned or controlled the means of production, and the industrial working class – what Giddens has termed 'the main dichotomous class system of capital and wage-labour'.[31] In the latter half of the twentieth century, technological and political change combined to introduce new elements; a growing role for those with professional and technical knowledge, whose power was based upon their expertise rather than their property or physical labour, the creation of a welfare state, and the rapid growth of the service sector in the economy. Some, such as Habermas,[32] draw attention to the expanding role of the state (not just in terms of its welfare function but also its attempts to intervene in and direct the economy), and argue that the new politics represented by the student movement and subsequent social movements can be seen as a defensive reaction against 'inner colonisation' of civil society by an increasingly technological state. Touraine also sees the technocracy as a key element, in that he argues that opposition to the 'programmed society' is the core conflict in contemporary society.[33] Touraine's approach is highly distinctive and wide-ranging, re-casting many assumptions found in mainstream sociology, and a comprehensive account of his thinking is not possible in this context. Suffice it to say that he rejects any idea of structural causes for conflict in society (that is, the argument which says that if a class is exploited, then sooner or later – depending upon false consciousness – it will mobilise against its exploiters). In Touraine's analysis, sociocultural conflict has come to replace the kind of socioeconomic conflict found in industrial capitalism. Touraine conceptualises society as an on-going struggle between those who define the dominant rules (including cultural norms) in society, and those who are fighting to impose their own social identities and new social order – what he terms 'historicity', the 'overall system of meaning which sets dominant rules in a given society'.[34]

These are meta-theories, which help us to put our evidence in context, but are otherwise beyond our area of concern. More specific ideas which are closer to our interest centre upon the idea of a new class which has been thrown up by the move from industrial to post-industrial society.

THE 'NEW' MIDDLE CLASS

The argument here is that the post-war period has seen the rise of a 'new' middle class alongside the 'old' middle class. While the power and influence of the 'old' middle class was, and still is, based upon ownership or control of the means of (primarily industrial) production, this 'new' middle class derives its occupation, status and power from its *knowledge*. This is partly a function of the rise of welfarism: as the state assumes the responsibility for health, education and social integration generally, so a new middle class of teachers, lecturers, social and health workers arises. It is also a function of an increasingly technocratic society, which needs engineers and scientists in order to function efficiently. Consequently, most accounts of the 'new' middle class differentiate between a technocratic element (incorporating both technical specialists like engineers and scientists, and managers and administrators) and a 'humanistic' element (incorporating areas like education, the caring professions, the Church, journalism and the arts).

Some identify this new class, and agree that it is prone to new forms of political action, but argue that its motivations are not dissimilar to those of its predecessors. Burklin[35] and Frankel,[36] for example, both argue that a strong motivation for involvement of the new middle class with social movements is that such movements are perceived as pursuing aims which, if secured, would have the effect of boosting career opportunities and job security for the new middle class. We shall examine these arguments in more detail when looking at the reasons for people's involvement with movements. In this context, the point to note is that some commentators see this new class in post-industrial society *behaving* differently but with *instrumental* motives – seeking material gains.

Others are prepared to assign more altruistic motives to the new middle class. Offe, for example, argues that social movements are a response to the failure of conventional political and economic institutions to resolve problems in society.[37] He points out that, despite the growth of bureaucracy, state intervention and the regulation of both social and economic life, industrialised societies seem unable to tackle such problems as pollution or gender inequality. Social movements arise to protest at both the direction public policy is taking (growth-orientated) and the manner in which it is implemented (the restriction of personal autonomy by an invasive bureaucratic state). Offe argues that the new middle class become involved because they have the knowledge and intellectual ability to see what is going on. It is in their own interest to resolve these dilemmas of post-industrial society, but they are proposing courses of action which would benefit all, not just themselves – as Offe puts it, politics of a class, but not on behalf of a class.

A more common approach has the same starting point – a recognition that many of those active in social movements are drawn from the new middle class – but interprets this as expressive rather than instrumental behaviour. That is to say, people may well be pursuing certain policy changes via social movement activity (banning the bomb, reducing pollution, and so on), but their motivation for involvement is as much a desire to make some kind of statement about their values generally as it is an attempt to achieve any specific material changes. Britain has produced some good examples of this approach, notably through Parkin's work on the peace movement and Cotgrove and Duff's analysis of the environmental movement. Cotgrove and Duff argue that the new middle class is concentrated in what they term the 'non-productive' sector of the economy (education, welfare, and so on), that these professions lack the economic clout of their 'productive' counterparts, which in turn means that they enjoy less political power, and that they support social movements as a way of throwing what weight they have behind forces which question the existing balance of economic and political institutions. They are not seeking special accommodation for themselves in the political and economic system, but expressing their general disagreement.[38]

Parkin was among the first in the field, with his argument that support for CND in the late fifties and early sixties represented a 'capsule statement' of values.[39] The 'education, welfare and creative' sectors of the middle class who were so prominent in CND's early days were, according to Parkin, the new radicals in society, but their radicalism was based upon altruistic values and a high regard for morality rather than any desire to seize political power. Parkin acknowledged that this radicalism and oppositional stance was linked to the 'status inconsistency' of the new middle class, particularly those drawn from the humanistic side. Such people were highly educated and qualified, and yet of relatively low economic status. What was important in Parkin's thesis, however, was that he did not think there was a simple deterministic relationship between this disparity and involvement in social movements. Rather, he argued, it was a case of people with such radical values being attracted to such professions in the first place. This was a crucial insight, directing our attention away from the idea that economic and political disadvantages stemming from a particular structural location in society *caused* involvement in social movements, and suggesting instead that perhaps there were certain values at work here which both led people into certain occupations and motivated them to become involved in movements.

POST-MATERIALISM

It was this kind of thinking which led to the development of an approach known as post-materialism. The best known proponent of such an argument is Inglehart.[40] His proposition, based upon a survey made across nine European countries in the early seventies, is that the post-war generation has different values to those of the preceding generation. He argues that the relative prosperity of Europe after 1950 has meant that people are less concerned than before with material goals (employment, housing, consumer goods, and so on) because such needs are already met, and more or less taken for granted. Drawing on the work of Maslow – who developed the idea of hierarchies of motivation,[41] the thesis of which was that as one set of needs is met, people 'move up' to another level of needs and desires – Inglehart argues that the post-war generation is concerned with 'higher order needs'. These are defined as a desire for opportunities for personal growth and development, and a rejection of formal hierarchies in favour of participation at all levels of decision-making – expressing oneself rather than acquiring more and more material goods. Having enjoyed both relative affluence and freedom from warfare during their childhood, Inglehart argues that the post-war generation have been socialised into such higher order or 'post-material' values, and it is this which motivates their support for social movements. Socialisation is an important element in Inglehart's argument. He argues that values formed when people are relatively young tend to persist over time; this, he argues, is why post-material values have persisted in the face of economic recession over the last twenty years. We shall examine the validity of this, and some of the apparent flaws in Inglehart's thesis (for example, why so many of the post-war generation still resolutely espouse materialistic values), in more detail when looking at the question of why people support social movements. For now, we shall simply note the central thrust of Inglehart's argument, which has much in common with European commentators' perspective; both see changes in the nature and structure of post-war society providing a breeding ground for the emergence of social movements.

There is a clear parallel between Inglehart's thesis and Parkin's argument that values precede and to some extent determine social and economic location and political activism. There are differences of emphasis, however. Inglehart offers us a comparative work covering many societies; as such, he concentrates upon the relationship between an individual's psychology of motivation and the overall nature of Western industrialised societies. Parkin's study was of one movement in one society (CND in the UK). Although, as should be clear from the previous section, out of this he developed generally applicable insights which remain among the most useful even today, he was led to explore something of the particular circumstances obtaining in Britain in the sixties. He identifies a set of 'dominant values' – support for the monarchy, established Churches and private property ownership – and then proceeds to demonstrate that most CND supporters were 'deviant', in the sense of that they disagreed with such values. What is more, he sees the adoption and development of such deviant values as preceding recruitment into CND – 'if the reasonable assumption is made that the supporters subscribed to this particular constellation of deviant values before the emergence of the unilateralist movement, then it makes sense to claim that they were, so to speak, "prepared" for it before the question of nuclear weapons became a major political issue.'[42] The point is not so much that values can precede action (a view shared by Inglehart), as that our attention is drawn to why certain movements arise at certain times, and the form and tactics they adopt – why did Parkin's 'deviants' turn to CND and not to some other movement? It is one thing to suggest that there develops in society a group of people who are 'deviant' or 'post-materialistic'; it is another to explain why such values get expression in the form of a peace movement in one country and a green movement in another, or why a movement such as the women's movement can develop into a relatively institutionalised organisation in one society, yet remain a very informal, loosely structured network in another.

POLITICAL OPPORTUNITY STRUCTURES

It is this kind of question which is addressed by our final category of approaches, one which offers the concept of a 'political opportunity structure'. This is not really a competitor to any of our other approaches, but more of a reminder to us that we can only fully understand particular movements by viewing them in their societal and political contexts. The type of political system, the timing of particular technological or international developments, the cultural attitudes towards various types of behaviour which exist within different societies – none of these may *determine* whether and how a movement develops, but they may well have a substantial *influence* upon this. Moreover, as Jenkins and Klandermans remind us, this is a two-way process; movements can be instrumental in bringing about changes in the political system and its principal agents, which creates new opportunities for further action.[43]

Kitschelt, for example, conceptualises political opportunities in terms of 'open/closed' and 'strong/weak' dichotomies.[44] He argues that some political systems are relatively open to inputs from society (they have proportional representation, multi-party systems, strong legislatures and an accepted role for pressure groups) and weak in output terms (national governments compelled to share power with regional and/or local governments, a strong and independent judiciary). This, he argues, will lead movements to integrate to some extent with mainstream institutions, through lobbying and perhaps even participation in elections. Other societies are relatively closed to inputs and strong in outputs (first-past-the-post electoral systems, one or two dominant parties, strong executives reluctant to consult with pressure groups); he argues that movements in these societies will tend to adopt a much more confrontational approach, in which public demonstrations and varieties of direct action play a much greater role.

There are some potential flaws in this argument – for example, political systems may be open in some policy areas (environmental initiatives) but closed in others (nuclear disarmament). We shall investigate this in more detail when looking at the tactics employed by movements. Nor can we assume that similar movements, operating in what appear to be similar political opportunity structures, will necessarily develop along similar lines. This is a point developed in some detail in Banaszak's study of campaigns for women's suffrage in Switzerland and the USA.[45] Although separated by some fifty years (women winning the vote in America in 1920, and in Switzerland in 1971), Banaszak notes that there are and were many similarities between the two political systems – both, for example, having federal systems with their consequent decentralisation of power, and both having relatively weak and decentralised political parties. The suffrage movements developed quite differently, however, particularly in terms of tactics and impact, which Banaszak attributes to the way in which the American movement developed a national community (thus enabling geographically and socially diverse groups to learn from each other's experiences), while the Swiss movement remained isolated in local campaigns which often simply did not know what their counterparts were doing. In short, the political opportunity system may be a factor in how and why movements develop, but it does not appear to be a determining factor.

However, it is the central thrust of the argument which is of interest to us here, and a number of commentators have drawn attention to various aspects of the political opportunities approach. Summarising their work, Tarrow categorises these as not only openness or closure of the political system, but also the stability or otherwise of political alignments (this would include both parties and electoral behaviour), the presence or not of allies and support groups, the extent of any divisions within elites, and the policy-making capacity of the particular government.[46] As might be inferred from this, precise measurement of many of these variables could well be problematic. It is one thing to establish some basics on party systems and electoral behaviour, but quite another to pronounce upon policy-making 'capacity' or degrees of 'openness'. One might also wish to see more emphasis upon the role of the media in different societies, which for some movements, and particularly for specific campaigning groups within those movements, can be of major importance – Greenpeace being an obvious example.

Nevertheless, the political opportunities perspective provides a welcome note of caution to some of the more macro-societal views. Consider, for example, the environmental movements in the UK and Germany. Macro theories have a valid point in arguing that the very existence of such movements in both countries may well be a consequence of common structural factors like the nature of the class and capitalist system. When studying the different ways in which each movement has developed, however, it is surely important to bear in mind that the German movement is operating within a system which does make it relatively easy for smaller political parties to operate effectively (because of both the electoral system and the importance of regional government), just as it is to remember that the UK has a long history of popular conservationist pressure groups (well-established in conventional politics) which pre-dated the rise of green politics. Similarly, the recent history of CND might well have been significantly different had the Labour Party been in power during the eighties, rather than in opposition.

These are specifically *political* factors, and it is no accident that much of the macro-theoretical thinking has come from sociologists, while the political opportunities perspective is largely the preserve of political scientists. In this sense, the political opportunities perspective sits more easily with the Resource Mobilisation approach than the New Social Movements school of thought. The political opportunities perspective can be seen as an extension of Resource Mobilisation concepts or, perhaps more accurately, as a focus upon particular aspects of those concepts, the relationship between movements and political institutions. The stress found in New Social Movement theorising upon the *cultural* aspects of social movements (new 'identities' in society, new lifestyles) tends to play down the importance of looking at how movements 'negotiate' with the state to secure the freedom of manoeuvre needed to let new cultural ideas flourish.

EXCLUSION

Some authors take this idea of accounting for the development of movements by reference to the nature of the political system those movements work within a stage further by arguing that the disposition of political institutions, parties, conventional interest groups, and so on, is an important *causal* factor in the origins of movements. They are arguing that the nature of a particular political system and culture not only has a significant effect upon how social movements go about their business, but also when and if movements arise at all. Kitschelt, for example, maintains that movements only arise when aggrieved groups cannot work through existing channels; the closure of existing channels of participation, such as those provided by parties or established interest groups, is a necessary though not sufficient condition for the emergence of unconventional, disruptive and sometimes violent collective mobilisation.[47]

Scott offers a similar analysis.[48] He argues that movements are of two types. On the one hand there are movements which articulate the grievances and demands of people who are excluded from the benefits typically available to average citizens. They are concerned essentially with rights, and have to interact with political institutions to obtain them. On the other hand are movements which articulate the grievances of those 'who are excluded from established elite groupings and from processes of elite negotiation';[49] their demands are typically more to do with arguments about participation rather than with citizenship rights. In both cases, however, Scott maintains that exclusion is a precondition for movements to arise. This can be exclusion resulting from corporatist styles of government, in which a trinity of government, employers and labour organisations effectively 'freezes out' other interests, or simply a failure on the part of established parties and groups to adjust to social change. An important point to note is that Scott is talking in terms of the exclusion of both people and ideas – movements are trying to bring about change 'by thematizing issues excluded from normal societal and political decision-making, and by articulating the grievances of groups who are themselves excluded. These two aspects – exclusion of issues and exclusion of groups – are not separate spheres of social movement activity.'[50] As Scott rightly notes, the implication of his argument is that movements are striving for integration; the apparent disappearance of a movement could well be evidence of its success.

CONCLUSIONS

As we can see, social movements have attracted interest from quite a wide spectrum of different intellectual disciplines and traditions. It is impossible to pull this together into one coherent thesis, not least because different scholars have sought to explain different aspects of the phenomenon. What we can do, however, is extract some 'core' propositions, not necessarily found in every approach, which relate to key aspects of movements. I take these aspects to be: who gets involved in movements; what are the aims of movements; how are they organised; what tactics do they use; and why do movements behave as they do. We have seen from our overview in this chapter that different explanations are offered for each of these. People become involved either because:

- they have grievances and, being politically disadvantaged, they pursue those grievances through social movements; or
- they have different values from their parents and grandparents; those values find expression in both the aims and methods of social movements.

The aims of movements are either:

- a fundamental challenge to the dominant norms of advanced industrialised societies, having a clear cultural as well as political dimension; or
- more piecemeal in nature, political rather than cultural, and subject to adaptation if that would help to preserve the social movement organisation.

Movements are organised on a network basis rather than a formalised, hierarchical basis; such informality will either:

- become more formalised over time, as the movement engages with mainstream political institutions; or
- remain informal, because this is more effective.

Tactics employed by movements mix the conventional and unconventional; over time, either:

- tactics will become progressively more conventional and less risky for participants; or
- unconventional tactics and direct action will always be a part of a movement's repertoire.

Movements behave as they do either because:

- they are outsiders seeking integration into the mainstream of politics, and movements are seen as the best vehicle for this; or
- in their aims, tactics and organisation, they are expressing something which cannot be expressed within the confines of conventional politics.

These are the differing propositions which we will use to structure our examination of what are held to be the clearest instances of movements in recent British politics, the environmental, women's and peace movements. We shall be taking each in turn, describing its development and assessing it in the light of the propositions above, with one exception. The question of who becomes involved in movements is difficult to answer because the available data is somewhat patchy – we shall deal with this aspect first in general terms.

5   Who are they?

Much of the extensive literature on social movements has two things in common which frustrate those who like their academic research to be neat and with no loose ends. There is the difficulty of defining exactly what is and what is not a social movement, which we have already discussed; and there is the lack of empirical information on just who these people are who get so involved with movements. Largely thanks to survey-based research, we now know plenty about the social and economic backgrounds and priorities both of voters and of members of conventional parties and groups. When it comes to social movements, however, there is a dearth of such information. This is understandable; after all, it can be difficult to 'find' social movement supporters. There are few formal organisations with handy computerised membership lists in the social movement sphere; people's involvement can be intermittent (perhaps supporting some particular campaigns and not others within the movement), and some of the actions undertaken by movements, such as marches and demonstrations, are deliberately mounted in order to maximise 'casual' as distinct from long-term support. In short, social movements are very 'open'. They seek support from right across the social and economic spectrum. They expect that support to be expressed in action rather than formal membership, and that action can often occur in the 'private' sphere (e.g., consisting of attitudes which impinge upon interpersonal relationships) rather than the 'public' arena. Consequently, given the difficulties this gives rise to in delineating supporters of a movement, empirical investigations tend either to look at specific organisations within a movement, and extrapolate characteristics for the whole movement from this, or to attempt to extract relevant data from surveys of the population as a whole. Each method has its dangers; supporters of a particular organisation within a movement may not be representative of the movement as a whole, and working with general attitudinal surveys can lead to undue emphasis being put upon responses to just a few questions in the effort to identify a movement sub-group within the total population.

Despite these difficulties, we do have some material to work with and – fortunately for us – the investigations into the composition of movements have produced broadly similar findings. Fortunate, in that the investigations undertaken to date have been of different movements, in different countries and at different times. Had they produced dissimilar findings, we would not be able to make any generalisations at all; as it is, we still have to be wary of drawing conclusions – we must remember, for example, that the particular political events and circumstances at the time at which an investigation is undertaken could well affect the results – but there is enough of a common thread running throughout to justify talking of distinct trends.

The picture that emerges is one of social movements apparently holding a particular appeal for one segment in society, those who are well educated (and thus usually middle-class) and who are not employed in the private sector. If there were such a thing as a 'typical' supporter of a social movement, he or she would be a graduate working in the public sector with an income which was above average but below that of similarly qualified people in the private sector. As we shall see, although there is evidence to suggest that sympathy for social movement beliefs and tactics among the population as a whole tends to be more widespread, the more active a supporter someone is, the closer he or she conforms to this stereotype.

Students of social movements did not discover this segment of the population. Before much attention was devoted to social movements, scholars of social structure were noting the changing nature of capitalism and the effect this was having upon our view of classes in society. At the beginning of the sixties, commentators such as Galbraith[1] and Bell[2] were noting that the powerful were no longer just those with capital in the form of wealth and/or property, but also those whose influence was based on *knowledge*. The 'middle class' was thus reconceptualised as having two distinct elements – the 'old' middle class (or bourgeoisie) whose power rested on ownership (if not always control) of the means of production, and a 'new' middle class – who did not own the means of production, but whose expertise, skills and experience gave them a measure of control over those means of production. As research progressed, it became clear that this 'new' middle class contained at least two elements which were sufficiently disparate that they should be distinguished from each other. Galbraith, Bell and Gouldner[3] were all drawing a distinction between different types of intelligentsia within the new middle class – the 'technocratic' and 'humanistic' elements we noted in Chapter Four.

The technocratic/humanist distinction within the new middle class continues to be employed as a conceptual tool today, although, as one might expect, there have been numerous modifications suggested along the way – indeed, by 1979, Bell was describing the 'new class' as a 'muddled concept'.[4] The gist of the argument – that one can distinguish a grouping in society with above-average status and influence derived from knowledge rather than ownership, and that there are valid sub-divisions within this 'new' middle class – remains intact, however, even if there are disagreements about the nature of these sub-divisions. Although the labels might differ, there is still a general acceptance that the technocrat/humanist split is a useful perspective, not least because it is a distinction which is emphasised by the occupational location of these two elements. The 'technocrats' are concentrated in the private sector, are well educated and enjoy significantly above-average incomes; the 'humanists' are concentrated in the public sector, and, while being at least as well educated, do not enjoy the same degree of material advantage as their technocratic counterparts.

This debate has been of particular interest to students of social movements because movements of all persuasions and beliefs draw a surprisingly large amount of their support from just one element of this new middle class, the 'humanists'. In other words, supporters of movements seem to have a lot in common, which has led some commentators to talk in terms of a *structural location* for social movements – meaning that there are some features of these people's social, economic and political 'place' in society which predisposes them to become involved in movements. Before discussing why such people become involved, let us examine what data we have concerning the composition of movements in order to assess the validity of this apparent relationship between movements and the 'new middle class'. The popular image of feminists, environmentalists and so on is one of a teacher or social worker (who is just as likely to be female as male), educated but not rich, and almost certainly something of a 'lefty'. Let us see if the evidence bears this out, by looking at such areas as education and occupation, political orientation, age and gender.

EDUCATION AND OCCUPATION

In the British context, an obvious starting point lies with the peace movement – or, more specifically, with CND. This is where we can find the most data, with important investigations having been undertaken covering both periods of CND's popularity in the sixties and the eighties. That we know more about CND than other campaigns and movements is not surprising. Post-war, CND has been around longer than other social movements in Britain, and is a quasi-formal organisation which forms the core of 'its' movement in a way that is not found in other movements. We may not be able completely to equate CND with the broader peace movement, but partly because of its size and partly because the aims of the peace movement are rather more tightly focused than those of the women's or environmental movements, we can be reasonably confident that CND supporters are unlikely to differ significantly from their non-CND compatriots in associated or localised elements of the whole peace movement.

Parkin's study from the sixties[5] advanced arguments, particularly about the motivations of supporters, which are still influential today. We will examine his thesis subsequently, but we are concerned here with the empirical data he produced. In a dual study of 445 youth and 358 adult CND supporters in 1965/6, Parkin found clear evidence that CND was a 'predominantly middle class movement'. No less than 83 per cent of the adult sample and 62 per cent of the youth sample were professional, managerial or white-collar workers – indeed, there were more clergymen and university lecturers than unskilled manual workers. Both adult and young supporters were well educated. Sixty-one per cent of the youth sample had been educated in grammar or public schools (twice the national average) and 55 per cent were receiving further or higher education post-18. Among the adults, 68 per cent had attended grammar or public schools and 54 per cent had benefited from further or higher education. Parkin's samples were also distinctive in occupational terms. Although he only investigated the occupational backgrounds of adult male supporters, Parkin found a clear clustering around what he termed 'welfare and creative' professions (social work, education, journalism, etc.) as distinct from 'business and commerce' – some 64 per cent of the middle-class males working in this area. Moreover, they were employed primarily in the public sector or in non-profit-making organisations. Some two-thirds of the middle-class males fell into this category, compared with a third of the working-class male supporters.

Twenty years on, the demographic profile of CND was largely unchanged. A survey of its current membership commissioned by CND itself in 1982 found that their members were still overwhelmingly middle-class.[6] Three years later, when I undertook a sample survey of CND's national membership,[7] the membership had grown by almost 200 per cent, and yet the social composition remained almost identical.

Eighty-five per cent of the 620 respondents in 1985 provided information on their occupational background, and 74 per cent of these (63 per
cent of the whole sample) had middle-class jobs. As with Parkin's
sample, they were well educated; 57 per cent held a degree or diploma,
and only 15 per cent had finished their education at 16. Gender, an area
not really investigated in the sixties, did not produce significant
differences; half the respondents in my survey were women, and their
educational profile almost exactly matched that of their male counterparts – 56 per cent of women holding degrees or diplomas, and 14 per
cent finishing their education by 16. As with Parkin's survey, employment in the public sector was common (over 60 per cent of those
responding to this question), with only those lower down the occupational scale being more likely than not to work in the private sector.

The type of job that supporters had in the eighties was also very
similar to twenty years earlier; in the 1985 survey, some 63 per cent
were employed in occupations corresponding to Parkin's 'creative and
welfare' sectors, with almost 40 per cent being employed in just two
areas, education and the 'caring' professions. Harrison's survey of 198
supporters in two local CND groups in 1991 again found little change
in the demographic composition of peace movement supporters.[8]
Sixty-three per cent of his respondents were classified as having
middle-class occupations, with some 40 per cent being employed in the
non-commercial sector (including 22 per cent in education and 15 per
cent in the caring professions). The only striking difference between the
1985 and 1991 results in demographic terms was the proportion of
unemployed respondents – 4 per cent in 1985 and 21 per cent in 1991;
even among these, the middle class predominated, over 60 per cent of
the unemployed in the 1991 survey having a degree or other professional qualification.

The educated middle class are not only disproportionately represented in numerical terms, they also tend to be among the most active
in CND. Forty-five per cent of the 1985 survey respondents were
'active' (attending meetings or actions on a regular basis), and over
two-thirds of those were well educated with middle-class occupations;
of the 11 per cent of the sample who were 'highly active', no less than
70 per cent were from this background. This was a trend also noted by
Kriesi, who investigated attitudes towards social movements in the
Netherlands in 1986; he found that, while sympathy for such movements as those centred on peace, the environment, women and
squatters was surprisingly widespread in Dutch society, those from a
'social and cultural' background (teaching, social work, health, etc.)
formed the 'avant-garde of the New Social Movements'.[9]

These are only surveys, covering hundreds out of the tens, if not hundreds, of thousands of people who were involved with the peace movement. The consistency over time, however, is remarkable; although CND has attracted support from across the social and economic spectrum, it has always attracted more support from among the well educated middle class, employed in public-sector or non-profit-making organisations than from any other sector in society. What is more, such data as we have on other movements, in Britain and abroad, produces a similar picture.

Cotgrove undertook a study incorporating members of environmental groups in the late seventies.[10] Of the 441 responses he received, 38 per cent were employed in 'service, welfare and creative' occupations, compared with 14 per cent employed in commerce and industry. Sixty-four per cent were classified as having 'non-market' occupations; 63 per cent had been educated for at least 14 years (compared with a national average of 28 per cent). Their average income, however, was lower than their non-environmental middle-class counterparts. A smaller-scale survey of Green Party members in the Midlands in 1991 revealed similar results.[11] Of 340 respondents, 38 per cent were employed in the public sector, compared with 24 per cent in the private sector; no less than 23 per cent were teachers or students. Again, the majority was highly educated – 60 per cent held a degree or a diploma.

This was a finding mirrored in a survey of the existing literature on environmental concern among the American public in the late seventies (covering over 20 separate studies), which noted that 'environmentalists' were disproportionately well educated, but were not always among the economically better-off.[12] In another review of investigations into American environmental activists in the mid-eighties, Morrison and Dunlap confirm a similar picture; activists were typically well educated, in a professional occupation. Their income was above average, although not to the same extent as their educational and occupational characteristics.[13] Offe, in his influential overview of social movements in advanced Western societies up to the mid-eighties, reiterates the theme; he notes the preponderance of people with high educational status and relative economic security among the core supporters and activists in social movements.[14]

We do not have more recent data on the environmental movement, nor is there much at all on the women's movement. In both cases, therefore, we have to extrapolate data from other sources. One of the most authoritative recent sources is the British Political Participation Study, based upon a sample survey of some 1,600 people across Britain in the mid-eighties.[15] This seeks to investigate the extent and type of participation in contemporary Britain – who participates, and how and why they do so. Although social movements as such are not addressed by this study, it does offer us a wealth of empirical data and at least two perspectives which are particularly relevant to our interests.

First, the study looks at the whole range of participation, some 23 types of activity extending from voting via collective action to protest and direct action. These are then divided into five broad forms of participation – voting, party campaigning, contacting (MPs, local councillors, etc.), collective action and direct action. The latter two are the ones of most interest to us, as they centre on the kind of activities associated with social movements. Collective action includes working through organised or informal groups and 'mild' protest – signing or circulating a petition and attending a protest meeting. Direct action includes blocking traffic and taking part in a protest march, political strike or political boycott. Clearly, the net cast by these two measures is sufficiently broad that it encapsulates many who would not be considered active in a social movement. Participation in a trade union, for example, would qualify for inclusion under the 'collective action' and possibly the 'direct action' headings, and there are many conventional groups who inspire participation. Nevertheless, it is interesting to note that education again seems to have a clear bearing upon differential rates of participation. The study notes that education not only significantly increases participation across the board – 'degree holders are not only an educational elite, they are also a participatory elite'[16] – but is also clearly related to a propensity to engage in direct action. As Parry *et al.* put it, 'protest is not located where some might expect to find it, at the bottom of the educational hierarchy, but among those at the top – those who have, to this extent at least, been successes in life.'[17] Although the study investigates the relationship between participation and occupation, it does not find evidence of any strong correlations except the propensity for those employed in the public sector to participate more than their private-sector counterparts.

Having identified the more active in each of its categories, the survey offers a profile of the people in each. The 'collective activists' are educated (26.4 per cent graduates) and relatively well-off if not rich – over 40 per cent are in the richest 25 per cent, but most of these are in the second richest 20 per cent rather than the top 5 per cent. The occupational distribution matches this, with almost 36 per cent of the group coming from the salariat, compared with 25 per cent of the total sample. The middle class is 'over-represented' among the collective activists, then, but it is not their exclusive preserve. Over a third of the group (35.5 per cent) come from the working class, and 34.2 per cent have no educational qualifications. When one remembers that this category includes formal organisations like trade unions, however, the fact that the well educated middle class form almost twice as great a proportion of this group as they do of the whole sample is worth noting. The 'direct activists' are a more mixed bunch (although it should be borne in mind that only 50 respondents fell into this category). The educated and middle class are certainly present, and once more 'over-represented': 28.6 per cent are graduates (16.5 per cent in the whole sample) and 30.6 per cent are from the salariat (25 per cent of the total). There are fewer wealthy people, although 23.3 per cent come from the wealthiest 25 per cent (25.2 per cent of the whole sample) and the poor are under-represented (14.1 per cent, compared with 24 per cent of the total sample).

Summarising this, the authors draw our attention to the clear relationship between wealth and direct action, especially when applied to the educational elite of graduates. The graduates most prone to collective and direct action are found in the intermediate wealth bands rather than among the richest 5 per cent of the sample – as the authors put it, 'it is the combination of graduate educational status and neither very high nor very low material position that seems to define, in individual resource terms, the principal locus of direct action in our sample . . . [such graduates] are not restrained to anything like the same extent as those fellow graduates from the materially richest 5 per cent from adopting political tactics that might put such possessions and life-styles in danger.'[18] Little there to contradict the 'new middle class' thesis.

Second, the study devises four sets of 'value orientations' in order to investigate the linkage between values and the extent and type of participation, and prompted at least in part by the idea of a 'new politics' in which issues like environmentalism and feminism become important influences on participation. The first set of values to be measured are the 'traditional' ones of left and right. The main conclusions are that, unsurprisingly, those with strongly held views participate more than average; perhaps less predictable are the findings that those on the left are significantly more keen to participate, especially when it comes to direct action, but that there is much less difference in the realm of collective action. As this latter category spans a broad range, from participating in organised groups through to attending a protest meeting, it is hard to draw conclusions from this, although it raises the interesting possibility that at least some of the right's showing may be due to participation in localised protest over environmental issues.

The other three categories are more directly relevant to our concern, as they seek to measure participation among those who are committed to the causes of 'green/peace', 'feminism' and 'participation' itself. A warning note should be sounded here. The study only identifies those who agree with the various causes, which does not mean such respondents are necessarily active in a social movement in that area; and (as is common with such surveys) it identifies them on the basis of their answers to a few 'key' questions – which does involve making certain assumptions that those questions do indeed reveal the 'true believers'. With those caveats in mind, however, the study does suggest certain trends in behaviour which accord with the evidence we have already examined.

The 'green/peace' supporters are identified as those who strongly believed that the government should not build any more nuclear power stations (25.3 per cent), and that the government should remove nuclear weapons from Britain (26.3 per cent) – those who agreed strongly with both propositions comprise 16.6 per cent of the total sample, and are taken to form the 'green/peace' sub-set. The authors are surprised to find that this sub-set in fact mirrors the total sample rather closely. It is not just the young – the age profile is similar to that of the whole sample, and indeed the proportion of 18–29-year-olds subscribing to the 'green/peace' value set is actually slightly lower than their proportion in the total sample. The proportion of women is higher (59.9 per cent as against 56.6 per cent of the whole sample), but the difference is slight. Given our preceding evidence, perhaps the real surprise is in the educational and social class backgrounds of the 'green/peace' supporters. They are not better educated than the whole sample; only 7.3 per cent are graduates (6.6 per cent of the total sample) and the proportion with no educational qualifications is actually higher (55.6 per cent) than in the whole sample (45.7 per cent). The class background produces the same picture; half the 'green/peace' supporters are from the working class (compared with 38.3 per cent of the whole sample) and only a fifth are salaried (24 per cent in the whole sample). Suddenly we do appear to have some evidence that casts doubt upon the 'new middle class' thesis.

However, the authors offer a possible explanation for this, though they stop short of claiming to have the definitive answer. They remind us that the survey was carried out at the end of 1984, when both nuclear weapons and (perhaps to a lesser extent) nuclear power were high-profile issues in the electoral battle between the main parties. Labour had included cancellation of Trident, opposition to the deployment of Cruise and the removal of all nuclear bases (British and

American) from British soil within five years in its 1983 election manifesto; the Conservatives, riding on a wave of post-Falklands euphoria, had made defence a key issue in the election, and leading figures on the right of the Labour Party had openly questioned the Party's policy. At the time the survey was conducted, Neil Kinnock had become Labour leader and was still a member of CND; the 1984 Labour conference had re-affirmed its commitment to non-nuclear defence. It was, in short, a time when nuclear disarmament was at the centre of the political agenda, and was arguably a symbol of left-wing credentials within the Labour Party and trade union movement, as it had been at the beginning of the sixties.

Given this, the authors suggest that there could be a strong party effect at work, with a wider-than-expected measure of support for 'green/peace' values emanating from the lead given by the Labour Party and leading trade unions. They point out that a clear majority of the 'green/peace' group were also Labour supporters (62.9 per cent), while more than a fifth were very strong identifiers with the party. On a left–right scale, three-quarters of the 'green/peace' supporters were to the left, and over half were among the 25 per cent at the furthest end of the scale. Viewed from another angle, they point to the finding that young graduates showed below average support for 'green/peace' issues, and say the explanation would appear to be that over half of them were Conservatives who would be opposed to nuclear disarmament. In short, they are suggesting that the lower-than-expected incidence of the highly educated middle class and the higher-than-expected incidence of the poorly educated working class can both be explained by the impact of party politics. The polarisation between the parties and the high profile of the defence issue mobilised opinion on both sides of the debate, and this leads the authors to suggest that the 'green/peace' supporters comprise two strands – 'there are those whose educational resources are high but whose material resources are at average to lower levels – the less well off graduates. But there is also a strong phalanx of the generally low resourced – with few educational qualifications, poor and working class, as well also as the unemployed.'[19]

There is an intuitive appeal to this argument, given the particular salience of the 'peace' issue at the time, although it would have been useful to see more analysis which distinguished between the 'green' and 'peace' supporters. The argument is certainly helped by the findings of the survey in relation to feminist values, because here is an issue which was not at the top of the political agenda at the time, and which attracts supporters who fit the 'new middle class' thesis rather better than the 'green/peace' group. Feminists were again defined by attitudes rather than activism. The survey did identify some respondents who were members of a feminist group; as they comprised only 1.3 per cent of the total female sample, they are not investigated in depth. Consequently, the feminist sub-set was derived by way of answers to two questions: whether working women should enjoy equality of opportunities with men; and whether abortions should be made easier to obtain for women who want them. As it turned out, almost everyone in the total sample agreed that women should enjoy equal opportunities (92.2 per cent agreeing), with over 40 per cent agreeing strongly with the idea. Relaxing restrictions on abortion also found favour with over 48 per cent of the whole sample, but only 13.4 per cent thought it very important. Altogether, some 46 per cent of the sample agreed with both propositions, and could be regarded as having pro-feminist values, but the survey isolates only those who agreed strongly, which reduced the size of the feminist sub-set to 8.3 per cent of the total sample – half the size of the 'green/peace' supporters.

As one might expect, the majority of the feminist sub-set were women (69.2 per cent); the sizeable minority of men in this sub-set were not investigated in detail, although the study does point out that, when responses from the total sample on the abortion/equal opportunities questions were analysed, men were just as supportive of 'feminist' values as were women. As with the 'green/peace' supporters, the expectation that young people would predominate among the feminists was confounded; they also were to be found right across the age range. The difference between the two sub-sets is found elsewhere, as the feminists fit the 'new middle class' mould more closely than their 'green/peace' counterparts. Of the feminists, 11.3 per cent were graduates, compared with 6.5 per cent of the total sample. Of these, 11.7 per cent came from the wealthiest 5 per cent in the whole sample; the proportion with salaried jobs matched that of the total sample (24 per cent), but only 29.6 per cent of the feminists were from the working class, compared with 38.3 per cent in the survey. Moreover, when the whole sample is scrutinised in terms of agreeing or disagreeing with feminist values, young graduates emerged as being among the stronger backers of the feminist cause, particularly those who were relatively less well-off.

All in all, the survey concludes, the feminist movement 'fits somewhat more closely with the expected pattern that radical causes will be associated with a certain level of affluence.'[20] This is true, but the striking thing about the differences between the 'green/peace' and 'feminist' supporters is not so much the unexpected showing of the poor and working class among the former as the sheer spread of support among the feminists. More were from the working class than from the salariat; almost a third were men; almost 90 per cent were not graduates; their age profile matched that of the total sample. It suggests that support for feminist values is relatively dispersed among the population. This is borne out when the partisan affiliations of the sub-sets are examined. As we have seen, 'green/peace' supporters are clearly located on the left of the political spectrum; the feminists are much more evenly spread. They do include people with a left-wing outlook – over 14 per cent were on the 'far left', and 36.7 per cent identified with the Labour Party (30.8 per cent of the whole sample); but there is also a strong contingent from the centre and the right of the political spectrum, with 34.1 per cent identifying with the Conservative Party (40.4 per cent of the whole sample).

We should remember that we are talking only of respondents who sympathised with feminist values, only a few of whom were active members of women's groups. The 'spread' of such values outside the 'new middle class' is, however, also apparently characteristic of environmental values. Rohrschneider uses Eurobarometer data from 1986 (covering all member states of the then European Community) to investigate the social location of those sympathetic to the environmentalist cause.[21] He also finds that, while it is certainly true that the 'new middle class' is more supportive of environmental organisations than are the 'old middle class' or the working class, the differences between these social groupings are surprisingly small; he concludes that 'membership in the new middle class is largely unrelated to public support for environmental groups.'[22] It serves to remind us that the well educated and better-off may be disproportionately represented within social movements, but all movements do draw at least some support from other parts of the social spectrum.

We must maintain a distinction between attitudinal support and involvement, however; and such data as we have infers that, while the message of feminism and environmentalism may be getting through to more and more people across all sections of society, it is still the educated middle class who get *involved* with movements. Our data may be patchy, but the consistency with which the educated middle class predominate in the composition of social movements across time and in different countries cannot be ignored. Demographic factors, then, are relevant, but they cannot tell us the whole story. Education and occupation may predispose people to social movements, but it is far from a deterministic relationship. There are many among the well educated and better-off who are either apathetic or antagonistic towards social movements; what else, then, distinguishes those who get involved in movements from their uninvolved counterparts in the middle class?

POLITICAL ORIENTATION

Social movement supporters are clearly located on the left of the political spectrum. In some cases, it would be surprising if they were not. Peace movement supporters are unlikely to be drawn to the Conservative Party, given its relentless opposition to unilateral nuclear disarmament. Both the environmental and women's movements have strongly condemned what they see as the lack of progress in their areas by Conservative governments since 1979, and have been promised much by Labour. Having said that, we should not dismiss the possibility of those in the centre or on the right of the political spectrum becoming involved in social movements. The Conservative Party may have set its face against most of the beliefs of the peace movement, but it at least professes commitment to the general aims of the women's and environmental movements. Even if it did not, there is little reason why a habitual Conservative or Liberal/Liberal Democrat should not become engaged in one area or campaign which was at odds with their party. So, while we might expect those on the left to form a substantial proportion of movement supporters, we should not be surprised if we find a fair smattering of support from those with different ideological outlooks.

The data we have on the peace movement is predictable. Parkin's mid-sixties survey investigated in some detail respondents' attitudes on key issues such as the monarchy, the Church, private property and nationalisation, and found a clear preference for left-wing views.[23] The 1985 survey, looking at respondents' voting preferences, found 67 per cent supporting Labour, 15 per cent the then Liberal/Social Democrat Alliance and 10 per cent the Green Party; 25 per cent were members of the Labour Party. Harrison's 1991 survey showed, if anything, a slight drift to the left: in terms of voting preferences, 62 per cent indicated Labour, 7 per cent the Liberal Democrats and 20 per cent the Green Party; 38 per cent were members of the Labour Party, and 11 per cent the Green Party (3 per cent in 1985). As we have seen, the British Participation Study's 'green/peace' advocates, although a wider category, are not dissimilar, with over half being among the 25 per cent on the furthest left of the left–right scale.

The data on the environmental and women's movements is more interesting, given the less clear-cut relationship between movement aims and the professed stance of all the main parties. Cotgrove's study of environmentalists (Friends of the Earth and the more mainstream Conservation Society), undertaken in 1978, identified 55 per cent as being on the left of the spectrum, with 24 per cent in the centre and 21 per cent on or towards the right. Following Parkin, this study also investigated a number of issues to determine respondents' ideals and values, and discovered that, like Parkin's subjects, its respondents rejected the 'dominant' values of modern industrial society. More recent evidence from Europe offers further confirmation; an examination of support for environmental and other social movements in Western Europe in the mid-eighties found that the strongest support was from those with left-wing views.[24] Against this, however, the 'feminists' in the British Participation Study were more mixed: Labour supporters were 'over-represented' at 36.7 per cent, but 34.1 per cent were Conservatives.

In short, we have a similar picture for political orientation to the one we found with education and occupation. Left-wing views predominate among social movement supporters, and the relationship becomes stronger the more active a supporter is. Movements are not the exclusive preserve of those on the left, however, any more than they are of the humanistic middle class. Roughly speaking, about two-thirds of supporters do fall into these camps; we must not forget the one-third who do not.

GENDER

One other factor we should note about the composition of movements is that of gender. Relatively little work has been undertaken on the extent of, and reasons for, women's participation in movements. This is perhaps surprising as one of the more striking subjective impressions of movements (discounting the women's movement for obvious reasons) must surely be the relatively high profile of women within their ranks. Movement organisations like CND and Green Parties in the UK and abroad have made a point of electing women to leadership positions. It is hard to think of a major protest action in any sector of movement activity which has not involved women to a significant degree. Some, indeed, have gained a unique resonance precisely because of women's involvement. Ask the 'average person' at any time over the last ten years to mention two or three things that come to mind about CND, for example, and it is a fair bet that the Greenham Common women would be one of them. Before speculating upon the significance of this, let us see what evidence we have.

Information on the number of women involved with movements other than the women's movement is virtually non-existent. We do have data on CND; in both the 1982 and 1985 studies, the proportions of male and female supporters was just about 50/50; in the 1991 study, women were in a clear majority (62 per cent female, 38 per cent male). We have no comparable data for the environmental movement, although van Liere and Dunlap's survey of environmental concern found (admittedly on what they acknowledge to be limited evidence) that there were no significant differences between the numbers of male and female supporters.[25] Kriesi's study of the Dutch movements concluded that women were not less likely than men to support movements. He viewed this as significant, because he contrasted it with 'normal' political participation – it 'provides support for the idea that barriers to women's participation in New Social Movements are significantly lower than in traditional politics.'[26]

Something of a counter-argument is offered by Parry *et al.*, however. Analysing the gender composition of their 'green/peace' sub-set, they note that the percentage of women in the sub-set (59.9 per cent) is almost the same as that of the whole sample (56.6 per cent). Moreover, they make the point that, whereas it is common to find studies of participation in other countries which show quite clearly that men are more involved and active than women, this is not the case in the UK. Their evidence suggests that there is a 'gender gap' in British political participation, but it is 'a very modest one'.[27] What is more, when analysing the particular types of participation which lie outside the party political process (contacting politicians and officials, engaging in collective and direct action), they find that the gender gap remains small – 'there is no obvious *general* propensity for women to be more drawn than men to the world of "*ad hoc* politics" – of group-based issue politics or confrontational protest. Some are attracted to such activities . . . but, as a whole, we find that women are somewhat less attracted to them than men.'[28] They do note, however, that the very small number in their sample who were actually members of a feminist group (only 1.3 per cent of their female sample) were also highly participative in other areas – especially participation in the form of collective and direct action.

Our evidence is inconclusive, then. On the one hand we have some empirical data and subjective impressions that women play an important part in movement activity. On the other hand, we have little proof from studies of participation generally that women are particularly drawn towards movements. Despite this, there is still a widespread *feeling* that women have a particular sympathy for movements, partly because of *how* they go about campaigning and partly because of *what* they are advocating. As far as the *modus operandi* of movements is concerned, the premise is that women are less comfortable with the formalised, hierarchical and bureaucratic nature of conventional politics than are men (some commentators arguing that this is a product of women's different life experiences, others looking for more deep-rooted causes). Thus, the argument goes, women find the informal, non-hierarchical network-based world of movement politics a far more rewarding environment, and one in which they feel comfortable about taking high-profile roles. Some take this a stage further, arguing that there is something about the goals of movements which makes them particularly relevant for women. This is a school of thought which equates nuclear weapons and destruction of the environment with inherent male violence – as Lovenduski and Randall put it, 'more or less essentialist, pro-women theories which rejected as male (and therefore bad) science technology, rationalism, hierarchy and centralisation, and embraced as female (and therefore good) nature, low technology, nurturing, spirituality, ancient mythologies and the oppressed.'[29] These are ideas we will discuss further when looking at the women's movement.

AGE

One might expect social movements to attract younger people. Some of the theories we discussed earlier (those of Olson and the Resource Mobilisation school) draw attention to the problem of 'costs' associated with movement activism, ranging from giving up time to running the risk of arrest. Younger people tend to have less family commitments, and not to have established careers, and therefore may well have more disposable time and be less apprehensive about unconventional, possibly illegal tactics. On the other hand, we have other theoretical arguments (notably those of post-materialism) which suggest that a particular generation or cohort – those born in the era of economic growth in the fifties and sixties – have a particular set of values which predispose them towards movements; such values may not be shared by succeeding generations born in the seventies and eighties, when economic recession was more the norm. Let us examine the evidence.

As far as CND is concerned, the data fits neither theory precisely, but offers some support for both. On the one hand, younger people have certainly constituted a substantial proportion of supporters. Parkin's study in the sixties did not analyse the age distribution as such, but he recognised the importance of young people by including a separate sample group of those aged between 15 and 25 – indeed, over 55 per cent of his total sample came from this group of younger people. Similarly, the 1985 study found that just under half of the respondents were in the 25–40 age band, with a further 24 per cent being under 25; in all, 71 per cent of the sample were aged less than 40. On the other hand, the proportion aged less than 40 in the 1992 study dropped dramatically to some 29 per cent; only 6 per cent were aged 24 and under. The older age cohorts had increased; only 17 per cent of the 1985 sample were aged between 40 and 60, whereas some 43 per cent of the 1991 study fell into this band. As Harrison notes, CND in the early nineties was an ageing movement.[30] It was holding on to much of the support it garnered in the eighties, but was failing to attract younger participants. Obviously, one could view this as substantiating the post-materialist argument; those born during the fifties and sixties were and appeared still to be the backbone of the campaign. One has to be cautious with this data, however. It could be that young people in the late eighties and nineties were still attracted to movements to the same degree as their elders, but chose movements other than CND – Greenpeace, for example, has enjoyed a much higher media profile than CND in the nineties, and nuclear disarmament does not have the same potency as an issue as it had before the collapse of the Soviet Union.

Unfortunately, we do not have enough reliable data on the supporters of other movements to test this idea. Cotgrove's 1979 study of environmental groups found that around a third of his sample were aged 30 and under, with almost 60 per cent in total aged 40 and under, but we do not have comparable data for the nineties. We have some corroborating data for the seventies, however. Van Liere and Dunlap's review of American research on those who demonstrated 'environmental concern' casts a much wider net than any study of active movement supporters, but it confirms the thesis that the young are attracted to such issues – 'the predominant finding has been that age is negatively correlated with environmental concern'.[31] Kriesi's 1986 study of Dutch social movements reached the same conclusion – 'the younger one is, the larger one's mobilisation potential for New Social Movements'.[32] We have more recent data on Green voters, in the form of a study of the 1989 elections to the European Parliament (the high point of electoral success to date for Britain's Green Party).[33] This concludes that the main socio-demographic correlates of green voting are youth and education, of which youth is the marginally more important.

None of this, of course, tells us whether this is a case of young people *per se* being drawn to movements, or whether just a particular generation (who were young in the seventies and early eighties) were particularly active in movements. We know from more general studies of attitudes towards unconventional and/or direct action and protests that young people are more likely to be involved. Barnes and Kaase's 1979 study across five advanced industrialised societies (including the UK) confirmed this,[34] although we must remember that this was an investigation only of willingness to participate in varieties of direct action, not of actual participation – let alone active support of a movement. The work of Parry *et al.* in 1992 has the advantage of studying actual participation, and also concludes 'young adults in Britain . . . have an abiding attachment to direct action'.[35] Moreover, young people (aged 18–29) are the strongest supporters of green and feminist ideals among the age groups.[36] Again, however, this relates to Parry *et al.*'s whole sample. Interestingly, the age profiles of their 'green/peace' and 'feminist' supporters are not significantly different from the sample as a whole. Indeed, the proportion of young people among the strongest 'green/peace' advocates and feminists is actually slightly lower than their proportion in the sample as a whole.

The evidence is far from perfect, but what we have does not seem to contradict the impression that, while many young people agree with the *goals* of social movements, active *support* may well be concentrated among a particular generational cohort, those now aged between thirty and fifty. Recent work on the women's movement would seem to bear this out, suggesting that the young in the nineties agree with the idea of equality between the sexes, but have a distinctly negative image of the women's movement itself.[37] In short, we simply do not know enough to pronounce with certainty on the relationship between age and social movement support; but what we do know is that what data we have tends to confirm the post-materialist argument. Let us now take a closer look at this theory, and some of the criticisms which have been made of it.

EXPLANATIONS

It is one thing to identify some trends in the demographic composition of social movement supporters, but it is quite another to explore the cognitive dimension – that is to say, to try to get inside the heads of those who do become involved in movements and find out *why* they do this when others with similar backgrounds tend not to. As we noted in Chapter 4, one of the most influential explanations has come from Ronald Inglehart, who argues that some people in society have different values from the rest – 'post-material' values.

Inglehart's argument draws upon the earlier work of Maslow,[38] who developed a 'hierarchy of need' as his explanation of human motivation. Maslow argued that people are motivated by a succession of needs, starting with basic physiological needs like food and shelter, and working up through social needs (belonging, status, etc.) and culminating in self-actualisation needs (achieving one's full potential). The point to note in this context is that the process is sequential; only when one 'level' of needs has been satisfied do people move on to be motivated by the next level, because they value most what is in short supply. Inglehart has adapted this approach to the study of political motivation, his most influential work being based on a nine-nation European survey in 1973.[39] His starting point was to ask respondents to prioritise various issues – for example, defence, inflation, free speech and participation. Those who prioritised issues like fighting inflation or maintaining order in the nation were dubbed 'materialists', and those who prioritised areas like giving people more say in public decision-making were 'post-materialists'; later surveys incorporated questions on areas such as maintaining a high rate of economic growth and fighting crime (materialist), and making cities and the countryside more beautiful and moving towards a society in which ideas count for more than money (post-materialist).[40]

Having identified these post-materialists, Inglehart explains why their attitudes are different with his thesis that economic growth in advanced Western societies since the fifties has meant that the better-off in those societies have grown up in conditions of material well-being and security – not for them the experience of two world wars and the depression between those wars. As their material needs were thus satisfied and secure, they became less concerned about policies designed to increase economic growth and material security (for example, the fight against inflation), and more concerned with issues which were either the consequences of economic growth (for example, pollution) or to do with self-expression (for example, the opportunity to participate and to enjoy freedom of information). In this sense, the post-war generation 'moved on' to the next level of motivation, from 'materialism' to 'post-materialism'.

Inglehart points to the wave of student protest and the rise of the 'alternative' culture beginning in the mid-sixties as evidence of the spread of these new values. He terms it a 'silent revolution', in that such new values constituted a new political cleavage which was not at first apparent in the mainstream political system. Whereas the old cleavage consisted of left and right fighting over the distribution of the benefits of economic growth, a struggle expressed via the 'traditional' political parties and pressure groups (like trade unions), the new cleavage distinguishes between those of both left and right who prioritise material issues on the one hand, and those who espouse the post-material issues on the other. It was a silent revolution, in that traditional parties and groups did not express this division; parties and pressure groups, whether from business or organised labour, all accepted the necessity of economic growth. Hence post-materialists, who questioned the wisdom of prioritising growth given its attendant problems, or were more concerned with how politics was conducted than the end result, turned to less traditional forms of political organisation, like social movements, to make their views felt – as Inglehart puts it, post-materialists are the 'ideologues and core support' of social movements.[41]

One problem with this theory is that, while it might be credible for the 'summer of love' generation who reached adulthood in the mid-to-late sixties, who were raised in an era of steadily improving living standards, it does not seem to account for the persistence of post-materialist values and social movement activity during the economic downturn of the seventies and much of the eighties. As Flanagan has argued, one might expect post-materialists to revert to materialist values if their perception of how well off they are alters for the worse.[42] Inglehart has an answer for this, however. He has a second string to his argument, which is that socialisation during childhood years is particularly important, in that it is at this stage that basic and enduring values are formed. From this, he argues that those who developed post-material values in their childhood are likely to stick with those values during their adult years, even if the economic environment has once again become relatively insecure.

Inglehart's thesis has prompted much discussion, some empirical research, and not a little disagreement. There is certainly empirical evidence which appears to substantiate his argument. We have already noted the age distribution of social movement supporters, and the 'over-representation' of the 25–40-year-old cohort which we observed in fieldwork dating from the seventies and early eighties fits Inglehart's thesis. A review of empirical work on environmental movements (written in 1986) concluded that a variety of studies confirmed that post-materialists are more likely than materialists actively to support environmental, anti-nuclear and peace movements.[43] Inglehart's own data shows that people with professional occupations born before 1945 are much more materialist in their outlook than their counterparts born after 1945; moreover, young people (those aged below 25) at the end of the (economically less secure) seventies were less post-materialistic than their predecessors raised during the fifties and sixties.[44]

Inglehart's approach can, however, be questioned on a number of levels. A determined critic could argue that the delineation of an individual's 'value system' is a rather more complex undertaking than is suggested by Inglehart's technique of differentiating between respondents on the basis of their prioritising just a few issues. Another fundamental criticism would be to dispute the inevitability of the hierarchical progression argued by Maslow – that is to say, the assumption that people will always develop a concern with self-expression and participation once their material needs are satisfied. Sociologists might also dispute the assertion that childhood socialisation is such a strong influence that it imparts virtually immutable values for the rest of one's life. There is also the point that Inglehart (and, to be fair, those who have tested his assertions) have assumed that issues like environmentalism and anti-nuclear protest have been adopted by post-materialists purely as a result of their value orientations, when such issues may have emerged simply because of changes in the 'real world' – worsening pollution or new nuclear weapons. Rüdig and Lowe are particularly critical of this aspect. Looking at the rise of environmentalism, they argue that we must allow for the context in which activism does or does not occur; in other words, rather than making what they term 'sweeping generalisations about the connections between changes in attitudes towards general issues such as inflation and freedom of speech and concrete political developments',[45] we would be better advised to look for contextual factors (both specific environmental problems and the nature of the political system in question) as offering a convincing explanation.

Even if we set aside these methodological and theoretical problems, Inglehart's argument raises other questions. Let us assume his thesis is correct: people who experience material security prioritise non-material goals and issues, and pursue these via unconventional political groupings like social movements because all the conventional parties and interest groups are still overwhelmingly concerned with material issues. If this is so, three questions immediately arise. First, Inglehart is talking of society-wide developments, in the sense of advanced industrial societies enjoying periods of material well-being; why, then, do most of those who display post-materialist attitudes come from the middle class? The simple answer to that, of course, is that the middle class (and their children) have experienced relatively more economic security. Two further questions follow from this, however: why are there some among the middle class who have experienced this material security yet remain resolutely 'materialist' in their outlook; and why are there people active in social movements who have not experienced such security? We know from our review of the empirical data relating to Britain that such people exist; taking a broad brush approach, the empirical studies of social movements we have at our disposal suggest that as many as a third of movement supporters do not appear to fit the 'post-materialist' profile. Similarly, we have seen that the majority of the middle-aged middle class do not participate in social movements. From a cross-national perspective, the same kind of problem arises; Rüdig and Lowe, for example, note that support for post-materialist values rose steeply in Britain and Germany during the early eighties, while there was a decline in Belgium;[46] and yet Green parties were successful in Germany and Belgium but not in Britain. One could counter this with the argument that post-materialism does not necessarily have to be expressed by support for a green party; against this, however, Savage has conducted work which claims to show that, even within the ranks of post-materialists, it is possible to discern both left- and right-wing attitudes.[47] If Inglehart's thesis is correct, then other factors must be at work to explain this variance.

Some commentators stress adult rather than childhood experiences as causal factors, especially education and occupation. Eckersley, drawing on such distinguished analysts as Lipset, Galbraith and Gouldner, argues that higher education tends to have a radicalising effect; intellectuals often give a lead in criticising the existing order and suggesting alternatives.[48] Given this, and the rapid expansion of further and higher education post-war, Eckersley contends that, while childhood socialisation may well have some bearing on adult values and without claiming that higher education necessarily produces post-materialists, higher education is nevertheless a more important factor than socialisation. This is partly because of the radicalising effect of higher education generally, especially in the humanities and social sciences, but also because the better educated are more able to appreciate the scale of the problems produced by industrial society – 'higher education not only increases an individual's ability to acquire information, but also helps to cultivate the ability to think critically, question everyday assumptions, form an independent judgement and be less influenced by the judgement of others'.[49] It is an argument also advanced by Offe: 'higher education increases the capacity to think (and conceivably even to act) independently, and the preparedness to critically question received interpretations and theories about the world. In other words, educated people would not only be more competent to form their own judgement but also less bound by rigid reliance on the judgement of others.'[50] Knutsen's test of the post-materialist thesis in the Nordic context also concludes that education, rather than class or income, is the variable which is most strongly correlated with post-materialist values,[51] as does Betz's study of German Greens[52] and de Graaf and Evans's investigation of young people's values.[53]

One might question this assumption that only the highly educated are capable of perceiving new tensions in society, such as the burgeoning environmental crisis, especially because this does not take into account the huge expansion of electronic and other media since the sixties. It may have been the case that one needed a degree in the mid-sixties to appreciate the threat of global warning, but that certainly could not be said by the eighties, when television in particular was devoting large amounts of time and resources to explaining such matters as simply and directly as possible. The role of the media is a point to which we shall return. In the meantime, let us assume that the better educated are at least more likely to adopt a critical attitude towards some of the effects of economic growth and the pursuit of material happiness. This still does not explain why some who have received such education maintain resolutely materialist values, but both Eckersley and Offe have an answer for this. It is the combination of education and occupation, Eckersley argues, which produces the difference. Those who are employed in the 'non-productive' sector (e.g., welfare, health, education, the media) have less of a personal stake in the production process in industrialised societies, and are therefore much less constrained from taking a critical line. Offe has a similar line of argument, adding the point that, while Inglehart may be right to suggest a relationship between economic security and post-material values, it is the relative security of one's *present* economic position which is more important than any security enjoyed during formative years – and such economic security and relative prosperity is found among public-sector rather than private-sector employees. In short, both Eckersley and Offe accept the idea that it is occupations which are tangential to the production-oriented private sector which are most likely to produce social movement sympathisers and activists.

Offe takes this idea of distance from the productive process one stage further, arguing that one can identify at least two other groups in society who are significant sources of support for social movement. The first of these are certain elements of the 'old' middle class, principally the self-employed, the farmers and the shopkeepers. Offe argues that their support for social movements is not a function of 'distance', but instrumental, in that their immediate economic interests happen to coincide with the causes advanced by movements – for example, small retailers may have an interest in resisting large-scale urban renewal. Of more interest to us in this context are those who go to make up Offe's second category, the 'peripheral' or 'decommodified' in society. By this he means social groups 'whose members are not (presently) defined directly in their social situation by the labour market . . . examples include middle-class housewives, high school and university students, retired people, and unemployed or marginally employed youths.'[54] He makes the point that such people have either a lot of free time or, like their 'new middle class' counterparts, a relatively flexible time schedule; such available time becomes a 'resource' which can be devoted to a movement. This is an uncontroversial point, though it leaves open the question of why only some of these groups choose to become involved. More controversially, Offe argues that such groups in society are unusually constrained as a result of their economic and social situation; 'one common characteristic of these social categories is that their conditions of life and life chances are shaped by direct, highly visible and often highly authoritarian and restrictive mechanisms of supervision, exclusion and social control . . . they are in this sense "trapped", and this has often led them to engage in revolts against the bureaucratic or patriarchal regime of these institutions.'[55] It is difficult to understand the basis for such an argument; the idea that the lives of pensioners and students are, in comparison with those of the rest of the population, particularly restricted by authoritarian bureaucracies is, to say the least, counter-intuitive. There may be more force in the argument that the life chances and experiences of middle-class housewives are restricted by patriarchal attitudes, but this still does not explain why only some subscribe to movements. Nevertheless, if we set aside the particular argument about social control mechanisms, we are left with the fundamental point that social movements exercise a particular attraction for those who are in various ways 'distanced' from the production process in society.

Eckersley and Offe are not alone in stressing this point; most commentators accept that there must be some kind of deterministic relationship between occupation and social movement support which explains the predominance of those outside the private sector. Where they differ is in their identification of the causal factors at play. While Eckersley and Offe concentrate on the 'distance' of public-sector occupations from the productive process as providing the autonomy and sense of career security which lies behind the preponderance of the 'new middle class' in social movements, others take a different view. Burklin, for example, in his study of supporters of the German Green party, confirms the presence of a high proportion of the 'non-economic' professions among them, but argues it is insecurity which motivates them – in the sense that they have an interest in pressing for a more regulatory state and expansion of welfare services because this would improve their own career opportunities.[56] Frankel takes this a stage further, arguing that the self-interest of the 'new middle class' leads to a careful selection of causes which are endorsed – 'there are noticeably few cases where NSM organisations have pursued objectives in clear conflict with the income and jobs of "new class" members. The majority of peace activists, feminists, gays, environmentalists and animal liberationists have tended to focus their activities on capitalist enterprises and those state apparatuses (e.g., defence depts.) which do not necessarily threaten jobs in the "social wage" services of local and national state sectors.'[57]

These are arguments which emphasise the *instrumental* nature of 'new middle class' motivation; social movements are supported because they are arguing for policy changes and agendas which will ultimately benefit those whose 'capital' is in the form of knowledge rather than economic wealth. The implication is that post-material attitudes stem from occupational experience; the educated middle class employed outside the private-sector production process are seeking to bolster their own position by subscribing to different values and goals. Yet other commentators turn this on its head, arguing that values precede occupational experience. As we noted earlier, Parkin argues that an individual's values will largely determine career choice; accounting for the high proportion of those in the 'welfare and creative' professions among his sample, Parkin maintains that 'middle class radicals' are highly selective in their choice of occupation – 'the connection between these particular occupations and political radicalism is to be explained not in terms of the strains created by status inconsistency, nor as a result of individuals adopting the humanistic values generated within the professions, but rather as a result of the tendency for individuals who are already radical to enter these fields of employment rather than others.'[58] Others are more circumspect: Cotgrove and Duff, examining environmentalists, see value in both notions – that values acquired during pre-adult socialisation may well influence subsequent career choice, and that environmentalism is 'an expression of the interests of those whose class position in the "non-productive" sector locates them at the periphery of the institutions and processes of industrial capitalist societies.'[59]

CONCLUSIONS

Overall, then, what data we have (and it is important to remember that much of that data refers to sympathisers and attitudes among the general public, rather than activists) suggests two things:

- that social movements draw much of their support from the well educated post-war generation who work in occupations outside the mainstream of the production-oriented private sector;
- that values are formed young and persist over time; that the post-war generation underwent a qualitatively different socialisation experience from their predecessors and successors; that this inculcated a set of values which predisposed that generation both to pursue certain types of careers and to evince sympathy for social movement aims and methods because they reflect those distinctive values.

Although the empirical data we have is far from perfect, there is enough for us to accept the first of these, with one important proviso. That is, Offe's ideas on the 'decommodified' apart, we have little or no speculation on the sizeable minority (usually said to be about a third) of social movement supporters who do not fit into this category. This minority may well be of particular importance if one is looking at those who engage in protest and non-violent direct action; after all, it would be difficult to live up a tree for weeks on end in order to stop a road development if one was also holding down a 'new middle class' job. Having said that, the basic proposition that a disproportionate number of social movement adherents share a distinct socioeconomic background holds over time, different movements and different societies. The second proposition is more problematic. If one accepts the methods by which post-material values are defined, then there do seem to be valid grounds for arguing that a majority of those drawn to social movements do exhibit such values – but we still do not know why only some of the 'new middle class' subscribe to these values. Given the difficulties of generalising on the basis of data which is incomplete and not always comparable (some relating to those who agree with movement goals, others to actual supporters), perhaps the best way forward is to assess the evidence in the context of specific movements. This is the approach we shall adopt for the next few chapters. Rather than seeking to generalise about the aims, organisation and tactics of movements, we shall now look at each of these aspects in the context of particular movements.

6   CND and the peace movement

We turn now to a consideration of particular movements in recent British politics. We have seen from our discussion of theoretical viewpoints that public protest is arguably not the only significant aspect of movements, given the stress some commentators place on the 'private', interpersonal dimension of movements. All are agreed, however, that protest and political activism outside of the 'normal' channels of politics, even if only on a sporadic basis, is one of the defining features of movements. While there have been important changes in the nineties, the movement with the highest profile in Britain over the last thirty years when it comes to protest has been the peace movement.

Its marches and demonstrations have attracted more people on to the streets than any other movement. It has had a major impact upon Britain's political parties – almost splitting the Labour Party in the early sixties, playing an important part in the breaking away of senior Labour figures to form the Social Democrats in the early eighties, and seeing 'its' issue play a central part in the 1983 General Election, and remaining a significant factor in the General Election of 1987. To those born after 1979, the peace movement may have a relatively low profile. After all, in the mid-nineties it is Greenpeace which receives the lion's share of the media coverage of protest, and the peace movement has become almost invisible. Demonstrations which once attracted hundreds of thousands of people have now dwindled to a few thousand. Politicians, once anxious to parade their commitment to the movement, have either left or keep their support away from public attention. During the ten years between 1979 and 1989, however, the issue of nuclear disarmament was a regular source of bitter disagreement at Labour and Liberal/SDP/Liberal Democrat party conferences. The campaign's distinctive logo and badges were to be seen almost wherever one turned (even the Queen sported a CND badge – at least

TV's *Spitting Image* puppet of Her Majesty did!). Its media profile was high: barely a week passed when the peace movement was not in the news, with leading figures like Bruce Kent being probably better known than many Cabinet Ministers to the general public.

Having said this, compared with the women's and environmental movements, the peace movement's actual achievements seem minimal, if not non-existent. One of the movement's main targets in the eighties, Cruise missiles, have been removed, but few outside the movement would accept that this was a result of the movement's campaigning rather than the consequence of wider international developments. Britain's 'independent' nuclear deterrent, Trident, remains in place. In short, the peace movement seems to be a good place to start our examination of movements in British politics. Its example encourages us to ask such questions as why it has survived for so long, why it has experienced cycles of dramatic growth followed by decline, and what has been the relationship between its tactics and its apparent failure. It also offers a good opportunity to 'test' some of the theoretical ideas about movements, not least because much of its activity has been in the public rather than the private sphere, and has thus been clearly visible.

CND AND THE PEACE MOVEMENT

Before we go any further, we have to decide exactly what we mean by the term 'peace movement'. Where are its boundaries? A common assumption in the literature, and certainly in the media, is that the peace movement and its largest single organisation, the Campaign for Nuclear Disarmament (CND), are synonymous, yet this is not strictly true. During the eighties, at the height of the movement's popularity, there were many other organisations and groups. Some, such as the Freeze campaign and END (campaign for European Nuclear Disarmament) were British branches of international movements. Others, such as the Greenham Common women and the Cruisewatch network, included many CND supporters among their ranks, but were not formally part of CND itself. Many local peace groups sprang up which were affiliated to CND but often went their own way – in the mid-eighties, there were estimated to be some 250,000 people in such groups when CND's national organisation had some 100,000 members. Similarly, groups based upon professions or occupations were in evidence – for example, SANA (Scientists Against Nuclear Arms), JANE (Journalists Against Nuclear Extermination), Lawyers for Nuclear Disarmament and the Medical Campaign against Nuclear Weapons – and these also were affiliated to CND while retaining their own identity, as were a number of major trade unions. Many (Labour-controlled) local authorities formed close links with CND as part of the Campaign's Nuclear-Free Zones initiative. To confuse matters even further, CND itself had its own 'specialist sections' – Labour CND, Green CND, Liberal CND, Trade Union CND, Christian CND and Youth CND. Having said this, I think it is fair to concentrate upon CND. Groups such as the Freeze movement and END were numerically very small, and – as with local peace groups – little is known about their supporters. Most of the others were affiliated to CND in one way or another, and a discussion of CND's tactics and behaviour will incorporate their salient features. Only the Greenham Common women established an identity and agenda which was qualitatively different from that of CND.

THE STIMULUS FOR REVIVAL

The Campaign's fortunes have fluctuated. We have already noted that the first phase of CND's prominence in British politics effectively ended in the mid-sixties. This was due to a combination of domestic and international developments. Domestically, Labour was in power and – at least initially – Harold Wilson was viewed by the left of his party as being much more 'one of their own' than Hugh Gaitskell had been, which gave Wilson more scope to prevaricate upon the question of nuclear disarmament. It quickly became clear that the Wilson Government had no serious intention of pursuing unilateral disarmament, withdrawal from NATO, or change in the 'special relationship' with America. By then, however, the Labour left had more pressing concerns – those perennial problems of post-war Labour governments, cut-backs in public expenditure and perceived attacks upon the trade union movement. Internationally, although the Cuban missile crisis of 1962 had provoked very real fears of nuclear conflict between the superpowers, its eventual resolution also suggested that, when it came to the crunch, they would back off. The international agreement to ban nuclear tests in the atmosphere, reached in 1963, strengthened the feeling that multilateral rather than unilateral action was a viable option.

Between 1964 and 1979, CND dwindled into almost complete obscurity. Anti-imperialist and pacifist sentiment was channelled into the protest over the Vietnam War. The domestic agenda was largely dominated by economic affairs, particularly the role of trade unions, and – towards the end of the seventies – by resurgent nationalism within the UK. CND stayed alive, but only just – partly because it had a formal organisation, and partly through the support of two groups in particular, the Communist Party of Great Britain and the Quakers. The former were attracted by CND's apparent opposition to nuclear alliances (i.e., to NATO), a contentious point within the Campaign to which we shall return. The latter saw in CND an expression of their commitment to pacifism – again, something which was subsequently to cause internal dissent. Even with the support of these two groups, CND only managed to limp along with a membership of between 2,000 and 4,000, and virtually no media exposure; unilateral nuclear disarmament was simply not on the agenda of national politics.

The Campaign underwent a dramatic re-birth from 1979 onwards. As Table 6.1 shows, the rate of growth in the early eighties was little short of remarkable. These figures[1] relate only to national CND – during the eighties, CND used to claim that there were probably at least two local group members for every national member.

As before, it was a combination of international and domestic developments which prompted this pattern of growth and relative decline. Internationally, the single most important factor was NATO's decision to introduce new nuclear-capable missile systems into Europe – Cruise and Pershing. The crucial point about these new missiles was that they were short-range. Although Cruise could also be air- and sea-based, all the land-based sites would be in the UK, Belgium, Holland and Italy; Pershing would be sited in Germany. Often implicitly, sometimes explicitly, peace movements throughout Europe portrayed the decision to deploy Cruise as an example of American domination. In fact, it was the European partners in NATO who pressed for deployment, precisely because they were becoming fearful that the apparent rapprochement between America and the Soviet Union would weaken America's commitment to the defence of Europe. The Soviet Union was deploying a new generation of intermediate-range missiles

Table 6.1 Membership of national CND

1970	2,120	1979	4,287	1988	72,000
1971	2,047	1980	9,000	1989	62,000
1972	2,389	1981	20,000	1990	62,000
1973	2,367	1982	50,000	1991	60,000
1974	2,350	1983	75,000	1992	57,000
1975	2,536	1984	100,000	1993	52,000
1976	3,220	1985	92,000	1994	47,000
1977	4,287	1986	84,000	1995	47,700
1978	3,220	1987	75,000		

(for example, the SS-20), yet strategic arms limitation agreements being reached between the superpowers were excluding Soviet missiles targeted on Europe. The Europeans' aim was two-fold: to counter the threat of new Soviet weapon systems by deploying their own, and then offering to reach a multilateral agreement to remove all such weapons from Europe (the 'twin-track' strategy); and, by declining America's offer of joint US–European control over the new weapons (the 'dual key' option), inextricably to tie the Americans into any nuclear confrontation fought on European soil.

Despite this, NATO's announcement sparked off protest throughout Western Europe. It was argued that the new weapons represented an escalation of the arms race, by virtue of their unprecedented accuracy and the potential thereby created for 'limited' nuclear war – a war for which the UK and continental Europe would become the battlefield. Such discontent might have been limited to a small minority had it not been for the rapidly changing climate of world politics at the beginning of the eighties. 1979 saw the Soviet invasion of Afghanistan; with the eighties came the Reagan administration and its rhetoric of the 'evil empire'. Superpower talks aimed at abolishing intermediate weapons like Cruise and SS-20 from Europe finally ground to a halt in 1983 without reaching agreement, and NATO went ahead with its deployment of Cruise and Pershing in December of 1983. European governments were probably relieved. The Reagan administration had announced its Strategic Defense Initiative (SDI – popularly known as 'Star Wars'), conceptualising an impenetrable defensive system erected over the United States. Such thinking only worsened European fears that, when it came to the crunch, America would leave Europe to see to its own defence. The deployment of Cruise and Pershing, however, prompted the Soviet Union to declare that, as these new weapons were targeted on the Soviet homeland, they would be seen as no different from America's intercontinental missiles. Their use would trigger a retaliatory strike against America itself – precisely the link between American and European security that NATO's European partners wanted.

Domestically, the new Thatcher-led Conservative Government announced its decision to update Britain's own nuclear deterrent. The ageing Polaris was to be replaced by the new Trident missile system from America. Opposition to Trident (popularly dubbed 'the Rolls-Royce of missile systems') spread beyond just those who objected to all nuclear weapons. Many who agreed with Britain having a nuclear deterrent questioned the wisdom of a minor world power such as the UK acquiring what was seen as a very sophisticated and expensive superpower weapon. As I have argued elsewhere,[2] given that such decisions on the 'core' of Britain's independent nuclear deterrent are only made every twenty years or so, the Trident decision inevitably had a high political profile. It is hard to imagine, however, that such events taking place under a Labour government would have sparked quite the scale of response that they did under the new Conservative administration. The Labour governments of the sixties and seventies had maintained and updated Britain's nuclear deterrent at considerable cost, and remained committed members of NATO, without inspiring much in the way of protest. In the early eighties, however, these developments were taking place in a political context where Labour and its strongest power-bases were under fierce attack from a Conservative Government determined to impose the discipline of the market. The trade unions, local authorities, public-sector workers – all were under intense pressure to change. In such an environment, support for CND was a highly attractive option for those who wished to register their protest against Thatcherism. Whether convinced by the moral arguments about the evil of weapons of mass destruction, or the more pragmatic argument that such nuclear capabilities were incommensurate with Britain's role in the world and only served to decrease national security by making the UK a primary target, unilateral nuclear disarmament once again became a rallying point for those with left-wing sympathies who wished to demonstrate their distaste for what they saw as the belligerent nationalism of the new Conservative Government.

The year 1979, then, marked the re-birth of CND. Our discussion of its experiences since then will be in two parts: a narrative, outlining the development of CND over the last sixteen years; and a consideration of how useful the main theoretical perspectives are in helping us to understand what has happened and why.

CONTEMPORARY CND: ORGANISATION

One of the most striking differences between CND and the 'typical' social movement is that it has a formal organisational structure. In this respect, it bears a closer resemblance to conventional political parties (especially Labour and the Liberal Democrats) than it does to other movements. In addition to the specialist sections and affiliated groups mentioned earlier, there is a network of local groups. These are coordinated in a structure of national, regional and area organisations. All these different elements have representation at an Annual Conference. Unusually, there is also provision for individual members to attend and have voting rights at the Conference. Few people attend as individuals (normally around 250); only about half the local groups, on average, send delegates. The Annual Conference is the ultimate arbiter of policy, but in practice much decision-making is devolved to the National Council. This body comprises some 100 people, around a quarter of whom are elected by the Annual Conference, the remainder being delegates from national, regional and area organisations and the specialised sections. It meets four times a year. The day-to-day running of the Campaign (and, some within the Campaign argue, most of the real policy-making) is in turn devolved to Committees of the National Council – the most important being the National Executive Committee, while others are function-based, such as Finance, Projects, etc. The parallels with the way in which the Labour Party is organised are clear. As with the Labour Party, a federal structure almost invites sectional disputes; as we shall see, CND has had its fair share of such disagreements.

CONTEMPORARY CND: ISSUES AND TACTICS

CND's aims have remained unchanged since its inception. As a relatively formalised organisation, CND has a written constitution which spells these aims out:

> The aim of the Campaign for Nuclear Disarmament is the unilateral abandonment by Britain of nuclear weapons, nuclear bases and nuclear alliances as a prerequisite for a British foreign policy which has the world-wide abolition of nuclear, chemical and biological weapons leading to general and complete disarmament as its prime objective.

Broad aims are one thing; how they are put into practice, particularly in terms of what is prioritised and what is paid little more than lip-service, can be quite another matter. CND's campaigning since 1979 has been multi-faceted, but I think it can be summarised under a number of headings, distinguishing between issues and tactics. Each requires further consideration, not least because most have provoked disagreement within the Campaign. The following is not an exhaustive list; there have been many other issues on which CND has adopted a particular stance from time to time, but these are the issues and tactics which have been an enduring part of CND's campaigning since 1979.

Issues

Unilateralism the argument being that the UK should set an example to the rest of the world by unilaterally renouncing nuclear weapons, and the main target being the Polaris/Trident systems; the (minority) counter-argument from some within the Campaign being that CND should try to widen its support base by attracting people who opposed Trident or Cruise, but did not believe in complete and unilateral nuclear disarmament.

Nuclear bases the arguments being that the UK should not only rid itself of its 'own' nuclear weapons, but should also remove American nuclear bases from British soil (not least because even a unilaterally-disarmed UK would remain a target if American nuclear bases remained on British soil), and the target being Cruise; generally accepted within the Campaign, although there was a counter-argument from a minority that the Campaign should concentrate upon British weapons.

Nuclear alliances the argument being that the UK should not participate in any international alliance which includes among its capabilities a nuclear option, and the target being British membership of NATO and, to a lesser extent, the very existence of NATO and the then Warsaw Pact. Of all CND's campaigning issues, this has been the most contentious, provoking at least two strong counter-arguments: first, that CND should not prioritise anti-NATO campaigning, but should devote equal attention to both NATO and the then Warsaw Pact, as both were nuclear-based alliances which had failed to take any unilateral action towards disarmament (such arguments coming mainly from supporters of END, and preceding the Gorbachev initiatives); second (a counter-argument often put by the leadership of the Campaign), while accepting that the Campaign should seek to educate the public about the undesirability of a nuclear-armed NATO, there was a necessity for pragmatism since, given that withdrawal from NATO was unpopular with both the electorate and all the main parties, to make it a non-negotiable, top campaigning priority would be self-defeating.

A non-nuclear defence policy the argument being that CND should develop or endorse a defence policy based upon conventional weaponry, as this would enhance the Campaign's credibility with the middle ground of the electorate, most of whom appeared to be convinced by the Conservatives' argument that unilateral nuclear disarmament would leave Britain 'defenceless'; the counter-argument being that CND was not a political party, and so had no need to develop or endorse such policies, but should restrict itself to persuading parties and voters that the nuclear option should be closed off (and the sub-text being that any such development or endorsement would be bitterly resisted by the 40–50 per cent of the Campaign who espoused pacifist principles).

Conventional weapons, warfare and pacifism   the argument being that CND should become a fully-fledged peace movement, and thus campaign against any UK involvement in conventional conflict (e.g., the Falklands, the Gulf War) or the manufacture and export of conventional weapons; the counter-argument being that CND should continue to focus upon the nuclear dimension, and any move towards outright pacifism would be unpopular with both the electorate and potentially sympathetic political parties.

Civil defence   the argument being that there is no effective method of protecting the civilian population from the effects of nuclear war, and the targets being to convince the general public of the misleading and complacent nature of the government's civil defence programme, and to persuade as many local authorities as possible to declare themselves 'Nuclear-Free Zones'; accepted by virtually all within the Campaign.

Development and the third world   the argument being that less developed countries are not only exploited for the raw materials necessary for the manufacture of nuclear weapons (and as testing sites for those weapons), but they also suffer in the sense that resources devoted to nuclear weapons and the arms race generally should be diverted towards providing aid to these countries; the counter-argument being that any 'peace dividend' should be directed towards domestic problems.

Nuclear energy   the argument being that the development of nuclear energy inevitably leads to the proliferation of nuclear weapons, as more and more states have the facilities and expertise to manufacture their own weapons; the counter-argument being that other groups and movements are already campaigning in this area (and the sub-text being opposition from some trade unions supporting the Campaign, who were apprehensive about the effects of opposition to nuclear energy upon the job security of their members).

Tactics

The Campaign's supporters have used many different kinds of tactics to communicate their beliefs, at both national and local levels. While disagreements over issues have been relatively visible, being argued out at Annual Conferences and within CND's own publications, dissent over the best and most appropriate campaigning tactics has not always been so apparent. Given the loose relationship between national and local groups, CND's leadership has been able to respond to any criticism over choice of tactics by pointing out that it was not directive; if local groups wished to adopt different tactics, then they were perfectly free to do so. Nevertheless, disagreements have surfaced quite regularly, usually stemming from decisions over the allocation of funding and resources between unconventional and more conventional actions. Standing back from the details, at least three broad categories of tactics can be identified.

Unconventional – NVDA (non-violent direct action) the argument being that, despite the risk inherent in breaking the law, people have a moral obligation (and thus a justification) to protest when the policy at stake is itself fundamentally immoral and not open to much in the way of democratic input or control; the actions ranging from mass demonstrations to specific protests at nuclear bases.

Conventional – education and persuasion the argument being that the moral claims of the campaign should be reinforced by the dissemination of as much specialised knowledge as possible on different weapons systems, problems of proliferation and the awesome consequences of any nuclear conflict; the outputs ranging from glossy magazines and books to detailed scientific arguments, and aimed at both the 'layman' and those with more expertise.

Conventional – lobbying the argument being that desired changes could only be effected by government and established political parties, who should therefore be constantly reminded of the Campaign's thinking; the methods ranging from networks of volunteers who monitored their local MPs' attitudes and participation in Parliament on the nuclear issue, to proselytising by the Campaign's own specialised sections within parties, unions and local authorities.

As one can tell from the above, CND might have the outward appearance of a tightly focused single-issue campaign, but it has cast its net somewhat wider than 'Britain's Bomb'. It has also had to react to changing circumstances, not just in the international arena, but also in the domestic political context. Its experiences along the way are relevant to many of the theoretical points we have looked at – has it compromised to make itself more acceptable to political parties, do its supporters have instrumental or expressive motivations, has its relatively structured organisation made it easier or harder to handle internal disagreement, and so on. We shall seek to address these questions by looking in more detail at the main issues, and the tactics employed to pursue them.

UNILATERALISM AND BRITAIN'S BOMB: A NON-NEGOTIABLE PRINCIPLE?

Unilateralism – getting rid of Britain's 'own' nuclear weapons, Polaris and Trident, without insisting upon any other countries getting rid of some of theirs – could be said to be CND's *raison d'être*. One might reasonably expect unanimity among the campaign's supporters; surely all would agree on the desirability of unilateral nuclear disarmament? In many ways, the answer is 'yes, they did and still do' – even though this core belief has been questioned by leading figures within the Campaign, and decisively rejected by most of Britain's political parties and voters.

Throughout the seventies, Britain's possession of an independent deterrent (Polaris) was condemned upon both moral and more pragmatic grounds. Morally, it was argued that the *use* of such weapons of mass destruction could not be contemplated; no human being with any shred of moral integrity could unleash a weapon which would have such devastating results. Pragmatically, it was argued that their *possession* simply made Britain more of a target. Even if there were no American weapons based upon UK soil, the then Soviet Union would still target the UK in the event of nuclear war, simply because it would not take the chance that the UK would not use its weapons in support of the Americans (and, presumably, of NATO). To such charges, the acquisition of Trident added a strong financial element. Its initial estimated cost[3] gave CND the opportunity to highlight other ways in which such money could be spent – even to the point of arguing that it would have a detrimental effect upon the country's conventional forces.

Tactically, there was also broad agreement. It was accepted that both conventional and unconventional tactics had a role to play. Unlike Cruise, campaigning on Trident did not raise awkward questions about the UK's role in NATO. While leading politicians and the main parties were obviously reluctant to pursue any option which rested upon British withdrawal from NATO, let alone the idea of formal neutrality, there was at least some scope for trying to persuade them to do something about Britain's 'own' nuclear weapons. Protest was not the only option, therefore; Conservative governments might not be interested, but there were grounds for being optimistic that other established members of the polity might be persuaded to endorse the unilateralist option. Consequently, considerable effort and resources went into publicity material aimed at the general public, and more targeted briefing of sympathetic MPs and lobbying of the less sympathetic, and this caused few waves within the Campaign.

Similarly, the need to supplement such conventional tactics with more unconventional protest was generally accepted. In theory, there was scope for 'actions' – that is, for NVDA at particular sites (usually military bases), undertaken by relatively few people but often involving trespass and/or damage, with the attendant risk of prosecution. The shipyards at Barrow building Trident, the Polaris/Trident bases in Scotland (Faslane) and the warhead storage site at Coulport were all possible targets for such actions. In practice, protest over Trident was centred upon the tactic of mass demonstration. While 'actions' could lead to squabbles within the Campaign, mass demonstrations were much less problematic. 'Actions' tended to be the province of the die-hard NVDA enthusiasts, who simultaneously thrilled the less committed with their daring while exasperating the more conventional by providing the Campaign's opponents with yet more media exposure of the movement as outsiders. As we shall see when we look at Cruise, the desirability of 'actions' as a campaigning tactic was the subject of heated debate within the Campaign. Mass demonstrations, on the other hand, were a long-established feature in the Campaign's tactical repertoire, seemed popular with the Campaign's supporters, and – as long as they were big enough – were guaranteed high-profile media coverage. CND staged some remarkably successful demonstrations in the early eighties – 80,000 turning out in 1980, 250,000 in 1981, 400,000 in 1982 and 300,000 in 1983.[4] All these were held in London, however. There were some rumblings within the Campaign that, because the bases and facilities associated with Polaris/Trident were mainly in Scotland, local groups in Scotland were being left to carry the burden of protest on Trident, with money and resources being diverted to the English groups focusing on Cruise in the south and east of England. When CND responded to this by holding the 1984 demonstration at Barrow, turnout dropped to some 25,000, which silenced much of the criticism.

In the early eighties, then, there was broad agreement on both the aims of unilateralism and opposition to Polaris/Trident, and the means adopted to further those aims. The Freeze movement, which argued for a halt to new weapons while pursuing multilateral disarmament negotiations, made some headway in America around this time, but never took off as a serious challenger to CND's more radical stance in the UK. Between 1979 and 1983, everything went well; the Campaign's support increased dramatically without leading to internal dissent or the formation of factions, and opposition parties responded favourably to CND's arguments. In the latter part of the eighties, however, some tensions did arise – as Britain's opposition parties followed the electorate's lead away from the unilateralist option.

Labour was the party which moved the most. After almost twenty years in which multilateralism was an accepted party policy, Labour's Annual Conference passed resolutions supporting the unilateralist case in 1980 and 1981. The formation of the Social Democratic Party in 1981 saw most of Labour's leading multilateralists leave the party. In 1982, unilateralism was endorsed by the two-thirds majority necessary to ensure that it became part of Labour's official party policy, the Conference committing the party not only to cancellation of Trident and Cruise, but also to the removal of all nuclear bases from the UK. Significantly, however, a resolution calling for withdrawal from NATO was heavily defeated, as similar resolutions had been in the previous years. Labour fought the 1983 General Election on a manifesto which, to put it charitably, was somewhat ambiguous on nuclear weapons, bases and alliances. On the one hand, there was a commitment that, within five years, a Labour government would institute a non-nuclear defence policy (which presumably meant no Polaris/Trident) and the removal of all nuclear bases from UK soil (which presumably meant no nuclear-equipped Cruise). On the other hand, there was a continued commitment to UK membership of NATO, and Polaris was to be included in multilateral global disarmament negotiations. If this was not enough to cause confusion, senior figures in the party (notably James Callaghan and Denis Healey) openly questioned the wisdom of unilaterally abandoning Polaris, arguing that multilateral negotiation was much the better tactic. Labour's leader, Michael Foot, although a long-serving supporter of CND, was unwilling or unable to unite at least the Parliamentary party around a unilateralist policy.

For a Conservative government pursuing some unpopular economic and social reforms but still basking in the rosy afterglow of popular approval over the culmination of the Falklands dispute, such ambiguity and confusion on the issue of defence was an electoral gift from heaven. They had already decided that the growing popularity of the peace movement and the impact its message was having on opposition parties was such that it could no longer be ignored. Michael Heseltine had been appointed Minister of Defence at the beginning of 1983, and in the months leading up to the election he had gone on to the offensive with CND as his prime target, claiming that the Campaign was dominated by extreme left-wingers.[5] Having set the context, the charge of left-wing irresponsibility which would leave the country 'defenceless' was then repeatedly levelled against Labour during the 1983 campaign – with good effect, it would seem, as the salience of defence as an issue in the election shot up from previous years – with most voters questioned by pollsters backing the Government's line.

The year 1983 was a watershed for CND and unilateralism. Unlike in the early sixties, Labour was persuaded to fight an election with at least a lukewarm commitment to unilateral nuclear disarmament – and had suffered its worst defeat in post-war history, with polling evidence suggesting that the nuclear issue had been significant if not decisive.[6] The Conservatives saw the result as a vindication of their defence policies, and diminished their efforts publicly to counter the unilateralist message. Cruise and Pershing were deployed in Europe. CND took some comfort from the election of another long-time CND supporter, Neil Kinnock, as Labour's leader.[7] Labour duly confirmed its commitment to cancel Trident and remove Cruise and nuclear bases at its 1984 Conference, but also made explicit its intention to remain within NATO. Between 1984 and 1986, Kinnock placed increasing stress upon the need to boost spending on conventional weaponry in an attempt to counter the 'defenceless' charge still being levelled by the Conservative Government. Nevertheless, Labour still went into the 1987 election committed to cancelling Trident and (in the longer term) getting rid of Polaris. Yet again, the polls strongly suggested that the stance was a vote-loser. By 1989, Kinnock was defending a multilateral approach to disarmament at Labour's Annual Conference.

There was disappointment but little surprise within CND when, by the time of the 1992 election, Labour had moved back to a clear commitment to multilateral rather than unilateral disarmament. The context was very different from that of the eighties. Gorbachev and the Reagan/Bush administrations had agreed to remove Cruise from Europe, the Soviet Union had disintegrated, and the Cold War had effectively ended. Yet Labour was no longer prepared to countenance unilateral action on Britain's nuclear deterrent. Arguing that no money would now be saved by cancellation (as the Trident construction programme was well under way), Labour was willing to negotiate with other countries on reductions in nuclear arms, but would maintain the nuclear deterrent in the meantime – albeit with a promise of 'no first use', and with fewer warheads. The only substantive difference between Labour and the Conservatives on the nuclear deterrent was whether there would be three (Labour) or four (Conservatives) Trident submarines – and even on that issue, Labour was hedging its decision to go for one fewer submarine, given the employment consequences of cancellation. As an ex-Chair of CND, Joan Ruddock (by then a Labour MP), put it, 'Labour must abandon unilateralism because otherwise it will lose the election.'[8] John Smith continued to advocate multilateralism while leader and, despite Annual Conference votes in favour of scrapping Trident in 1993 and 1994, Tony Blair has also rejected the unilateralist option.

Labour was not the only party affected by the unilateralist issue in the eighties. It was an important factor in the pre-merger relationship between the Liberals and the Social Democrats. The Liberals had a long history of combining a pro-NATO, multilateralist stance with opposition to an independent British nuclear deterrent. The new SDP, however, laid considerable stress upon the need to maintain a credible deterrent, although even they thought Trident was too expensive and sophisticated for the UK's needs. Overturning a Liberal Assembly vote against the deployment of Cruise in 1982, David Steel, the Liberal leader, agreed a joint manifesto with the SDP for the 1983 election which committed the two parties to scrapping Trident, but taking no unilateral action on Polaris. Steel was rejected by his own activists again in 1984 when, despite an unprecedented appeal by Steel, the Liberal Assembly again called for the removal of Cruise – but voted to maintain Polaris. Prior to the 1987 election, the two parties established a joint commission on defence policy, which again endorsed the cancellation of Trident. It was agreed that, pending multilateral disarmament, the ageing Polaris should be maintained, but the question of any replacement for Polaris was left open. David Owen, the SDP's leader, rejected this, arguing that either the Liberal–SDP Alliance or the SDP alone should enter into a clear commitment to replace Polaris, even if it was with some cheaper alternative than Trident. The Alliance went into the 1987 election with a manifesto commitment to cancel Trident, but also to replace it with a 'minimum British deterrent'. In the aftermath of that election, the two parties decided to merge. Owen resisted this, citing what he saw as a dangerous tendency among Liberal activists to flirt with unilateralist thinking as one of his grounds for opposition. By the time of the 1992 election, the new Liberal Democrats mirrored Labour's thinking that it was now too late in the day to view cancellation of Trident as a sensible option. Their manifesto promised to keep Trident, but limit the number of warheads deployed to the same level as Polaris (192 rather than the 512 planned by the Conservatives), which is still their policy in 1996.

How, then, did CND react to this change in fortunes? It had seen unilateralism make unprecedented headway between 1979 and 1983, but was then faced with a retreat from unilateralism by all the main opposition parties after the mid-eighties. There are two points of interest in the Campaign's reaction. First, there is the fact that a single-issue campaign like CND did make an attempt to compromise on unilateralism. The 1985 Annual Conference of the Campaign saw a formal attempt (supported by one of the Campaign's best-known figures, Bruce Kent) to amend its constitution, seeking to replace the explicit commitment to unilateralism with an endorsement of a non-nuclear defence policy. Second, there is the fact that this move was defeated then and has not recurred since, despite the attitude of the main parties over the last decade. Both the 1985 and 1991 surveys of CND's national membership found strong support for unilateralism – 89 per cent and 71 per cent respectively. Even by 1991, only some 14 per cent agreed that CND should modify its stance on unilateralism – and almost all of those were relatively recent members of the Campaign. As Bruce Kent himself has put it,

> Within CND there is a hard core of absolute fundamentalism, which I see as a parallel with religion. . . . I don't understand those people at all – nice people, but complete fundamentalists. . . . They are the lifeblood, but that obsession with unilateralism . . . how much other lifeblood might there be if we actually opened it up to people who weren't hung up on that word.[9]

Given that CND's campaigning during the eighties concentrated upon Trident and Cruise, as distinct from Polaris, and combined with the anti-unilateralist stance of the parties after 1983, the continuing commitment to unilateralism by the Campaign's supporters is indicative of some principles being non-negotiable, even if there seems little or no chance of those principles receiving endorsement by established members of the polity.

CRUISE AND NATO

If the Campaign's position on unilateral action over 'Britain's Bomb' was relatively straightforward and immutable, the twin issues of Cruise and NATO represent the other end of the extreme. Opposition to Cruise was virtually unanimous. Even those who argued that the Campaign (especially in England) devoted too much attention to Cruise and not enough to Polaris/Trident were only questioning the balance between the two; there was never any real question of not opposing the deployment of Cruise. The problems came with the tactics, with several clashes between proponents of NVDA and the Campaign's leadership. NATO, on the other hand, was the source of quite serious dissent on a policy level. It was an issue on which the Campaign could make little or no progress with either the established members of the polity or the electorate. Yet any argument that, for politically pragmatic reasons, the Campaign should at least downplay its stance on withdrawal from NATO (if not drop it) was met with vociferous opposition. From both a tactical and ideological perspective, Cruise and NATO are issues which lay bare the internal politics of the Campaign.

Cruise was a more attractive target for 'actions' than was Polaris/Trident. The latter were submarine-based weapons, operating out of established military bases. Cruise in the UK was to be land-based, at Greenham Common (an established American base) and Molesworth (under-developed, and effectively still a green-field site). This, combined with the fact that the Campaign had several years' warning before the missiles were actually deployed, opened the way for protest and disruption at both sites – the aim being to prevent the missiles ever arriving. The first problems arose with Greenham. The Greenham Peace Camp was established in 1981, when some forty women, men and children completed a protest march from Cardiff to Greenham. Deciding to establish a camp outside the base, the women voted in 1982 to exclude the small number of men involved in the action. Drawing on feminist theory, they rejected the idea of any kind of formal structure or hierarchy, which was equated with patriarchy – as, indeed, were nuclear weapons themselves. They also argued that a women-only action had the added advantage of accentuating the disparity between female peace protesters and the male military and civil authorities. The Camp burgeoned over the next few years, as women from the UK and abroad came to participate. Tactics varied. There were some large-scale demonstrations (30,000 women 'embracing the base' in 1983, 40,000 in 1984), but the real strength of the Camp was its persistent use of smaller-scale actions, usually involving breaking into the base to paint slogans or leave reminders of their presence. We shall have more to say on the feminist perspective of Greenham when we look at the women's movement. There can be no doubt as to the media impact of the Greenham women, however; Greenham attracted as much attention as anything else the much larger CND was doing at the time.

Greenham did not become problematic for the wider Campaign until the first missiles were due to arrive at the end of 1983. Male advocates of NVDA were insistent that the arrival of the missiles had to be marked by a show of physical (but peaceful) resistance. The Greenham women, however, were just as adamant that they wished to preserve their women-only strategy, and did not want to join in any action with men. The argument was taken up at CND's National Council. An attempt at compromise was sought – the women to mount their own action at the base, with a mixed demonstration nearby. The Greenham women refused this. Eventually, national CND gave way, and accepted the women's veto. One of the reasons for this was the standing the Greenham women had quickly developed among the Campaign's mass membership. They were seen as the real heroines of the campaign, the ones who were permanently on the front line of the struggle, refusing to give in despite continual harassment from both the civil and military authorities. Whenever Greenham women spoke at CND's Annual Conferences, they received the kind of ecstatic reception that a Labour Party Conference would give someone like Nelson Mandela. One also has to bear in mind that 50 per cent of the Campaign's national membership were women, and the Campaign's leaders were only too well aware of the dangers of appearing to be misogynist.

Dissent over NVDA did not go away, however. 1984 saw the creation of Action '84, a 'campaign within the Campaign' of activists encouraging local groups to both engage in direct action and pressurise the Campaign's national leadership to put more effort and resources into unconventional rather than conventional protest. With some 150 local groups endorsing the Action '84 agenda, national CND quickly endorsed a strategy of direct action at the other Cruise site, Molesworth. Construction work had yet to start, so the base was wideopen to disruptive direct action. The tactic adopted was to mount a continuous protest, with each region of the Campaign organising volunteers to be present on a rota basis. Just five days before the protest was to start, several thousand men from the army and police were drafted in by the Government to erect a seven-mile fence around the base – accompanied by Michael Heseltine looking particularly dashing in an army flakjacket. Overnight, much of the point of the Molesworth strategy was lost. Unable to intervene directly, protest was limited to vigils outside the base, and came mainly from protesters who lived near the base. Despite this, CND remained formally committed to the strategy for some time, precisely because the leadership did not want to risk yet another bruising open disagreement with their NVDA enthusiasts. As with the issue of unilateralism, the price of holding the Campaign together was observing parameters set by significant minorities within it.

One can discern a similar process taking place over the issue of the Campaign's stance on Britain's membership of NATO. Here was an issue on which it seemed clear that there was little or no chance of persuading either the main parties or most of the electorate to agree with the idea of withdrawal from a nuclear-based NATO. Pragmatists within the Campaign argued that more progress might be made on Polaris/Trident and Cruise if the Campaign were to concentrate its resources on these specific issues, if not drop its opposition to NATO altogether. A related argument came from those who were also active in END, who did not question the principle of opposition to NATO, but argued that just as much effort should be put into campaigning against the then Warsaw Pact. Both viewpoints were opposed, most notably by Labour CND, which saw NATO as an instrument of American imperialism. There were repeated arguments at annual conferences during the eighties, as more militant elements argued for more resources to be devoted to campaigning on NATO, and END and most of the leadership advocated a lower-profile strategy. The 1985 survey indicated that such differences of opinion were spread throughout the Campaign. Just under half the respondents agreed that the UK should withdraw from NATO, a quarter were unsure and no less than 26 per cent actually disagreed. The problem for the pragmatists was that opposition to NATO was strongest among the more active in the Campaign; those who believed the Campaign should move closer to the political centre ground by dropping its anti-NATO stance tended to participate only infrequently in both campaigning activities and annual conferences. Modifying the position on NATO might have had advantages in terms of focusing attention on 'Britain's Bomb' and nullifying some of the damaging consequences of the charge of advocating a 'defenceless' policy, but it was another instance of a significant minority within the Campaign insisting that opposition to NATO was a non-negotiable principle.

AREAS OF AGREEMENT

This is not to suggest that everything the Campaign has undertaken has caused disputes between supporters. There has been debate over the stance the Campaign should take with respect to development issues, but it has never occupied centre stage. Were Trident to be scrapped, then the issue of a 'peace dividend' and how it should be spent would come to the fore. As it is, we merely note the differences of opinion it has caused, reflecting an 'internationalist' and 'domestic' focus to be found among the Campaign's supporters, and move on.[10] Similarly, the Campaign's position on nuclear energy is not without interest, not least because it illustrates the problems which can arise when a movement begins to attract support from 'established' members of the polity, in this case the trade unions. Had important trade unions not been affiliated to the Campaign, then the Campaign's supporters – as 'outsiders' who did not have to take account of the stances or interests of others – would not have been inhibited from full-blooded opposition to nuclear power. It is also interesting because, had they done so, they would have effectively been in competition with other groups and movements like Friends of the Earth and Greenpeace which have opposition to nuclear energy at the heart of their beliefs. As it is, we can again note this and move on, because by the time the issue arose within CND (in the mid-eighties), FOE and Greenpeace were already so popular that there seemed little point in duplicating their efforts.

The issue of civil defence has also been relatively uncontroversial. It was one of the issues, together with Trident and Cruise, which kick-started the rebirth of the Campaign. The Conservative Government published its pamphlet 'Protect and Survive' in 1980, setting out the Government's advice to the public upon enhancing the chances of survival in the event of nuclear attack. The pamphlet rested upon such useful stratagems as taping up windows to prevent being showered with broken glass, and, if caught outdoors, lying down. It presented the Campaign with a golden opportunity to hammer home the message that not only was such advice useless, but that people should voice their concerns, and led to the publication of CND's own view of civil defence, 'Protest and Survive' – which argued that there was no effective means of civil defence against a nuclear attack, and that the only 'true' defence was to rid Britain of nuclear weapons (thus making it less of a priority target for other nuclear powers) and set an example to those other powers by such unilateral action. It also gave the Campaign the opportunity to highlight what were seen as the implicit authoritarian and elitist assumptions underlying government policy – the emergency powers which would be granted to the police and armed forces in the event of a crisis, and the bunkers which would shelter leading politicians and civil servants while the rest of the populace would be lying down behind whitewashed windows with their eyes closed and their fingers in their ears. Not surprisingly, the issue received a good airing in the media, with the Government (yet to develop its riposte that unilateralism equated with 'defencelessness') on the back foot.

One other aspect of the civil defence issue which we should note has been the tactics employed. Unlike weapons systems or international alliances, where both the formulation and implementation of policy was firmly in the hands of central government, this was an area in which a crucial implementation role was played by sub-national political institutions, the local authorities. CND seized upon this opportunity with its campaign to persuade local authorities to declare themselves 'Nuclear-Free Zones' – opposed to nuclear weapons, the dumping of nuclear waste and the transportation of nuclear materials in their area; and refusing to participate in the Government's civil defence planning and exercises. At its height in the early eighties, almost 200 local authorities (predominantly Labour-controlled) had been persuaded to adopt a Nuclear-Free Zone policy. Here, then, was an instance of a movement engaging with established members of the polity and apparently achieving some concrete results. Success was short-lived and largely symbolic, however. The Government simply responded on the civil defence front by introducing new regulations which imposed upon local authorities the duty to participate in all civil defence planning and exercises – regulations which, given the unitary nature of the British system, could not be challenged in law. Any objections to the location of nuclear waste could be overcome via the planning process, in which central government ministers had the final say, and movements of nuclear materials were a matter of national security. CND was able to enlist the support of some democratically-elected political authorities, but they were effectively powerless to translate their support into concrete action. It is a point to which we shall return when discussing the relationship between political opportunity structure and the object of CND's campaigning.

7 The women's movement[1]

The women's movement is in many ways diametrically opposed to the peace movement. They share many supporters and a distaste for machismo and militarism, the peace movement in particular being 'feminised'. While the peace movement made its name through public protest and mass demonstration, however, the women's movement has operated as much on the 'private' or 'personal' plane as on the public. Britain's peace movement stands out from other peace movements because it is dominated by one single organisation. The British women's movement is distinguished from its counterparts in most other countries (especially America) because it has no single, over-arching organisation – indeed, little in the way of any formal national organisation at all. The peace movement has targeted the public authorities on one particular issue, and lost. The women's movement has targeted many, many different aspects of both public policy and interpersonal relationships. Given the gender inequalities which remain in contemporary Britain, one could hardly say the women's movement had 'won', but equally no-one could deny the immense impact that feminist attitudes have had on public and private attitudes and practices over the last thirty years. From an American perspective, the British women's movement is admired for its ideological purity, but admonished for its failure to buckle down and 'organise'. From a European perspective, the women's movement is about as close as you can get to a 'pure' social movement in Britain.

Before we look at the actual movement, we should say a few words on the subject of feminism. One of the distinctive features of the women's movement has been the amount of attention it has paid to the constant examination and redefinition of the meaning of its central organising idea, feminism. The issues raised by the peace and environmental movements have given rise to some discussion within the academic community, but feminism has become something of an academic industry, such is the interest it has inspired. Today, one can talk of many different varieties of feminism – from equal rights feminism, to radical feminism, to postmodern and deconstructionist feminism. It is not our intention here to analyse every nuance of such theorising, although the interplay between ideas and action is so marked in the case of the women's movement that we do have to understand the basic differences, and how they developed over time. We need a starting point, however. Given the different viewpoints over what constitutes 'feminism', and the diffuse nature of the movement itself, this is inevitably somewhat arbitrary. I am using definitions advanced by Dahlerup, Lovenduski and Randall: taking 'feminism' to mean those 'ideologies, activities and policies whose goal is to remove discrimination against women and to break down the male domination of society',[2] and 'women's movement' to mean 'all those individuals, networks, organisations, ideas and practices that espouse feminist values and goals'.[3]

The women's movement in Britain has a history which precedes the last thirty years, of course. Women's rights, opportunities and status have been on and off the agenda of British politics throughout this century. Sometimes they have been on the agenda largely because those in power have perceived a particular need for women's active involvement in economic and social life (as, for example, during the Second World War). At other times, however, women themselves have forced their concerns on to the agenda. There have been 'waves' of such political mobilisation by women. The 'first wave' of activity was the suffragette movement, which peaked between 1900 and 1914. The suffragettes' concern was with equality, particularly of course representational equality in the form of the franchise. It is the 'second wave' which concerns us here, dating from the late sixties to the present day. This second wave still encompasses those who equate feminism with equal opportunities and parity of representation in established institutions; but it also includes those who go beyond equality, believing the central concern to be the struggle against patriarchy (in both its public and private manifestations) and the recognition of 'difference' rather than just 'equality' in contemporary society.

Hopefully, the social movement theory we have already outlined will help us to understand the phenomenon of second-wave feminism, as applying conventional pressure group theory to the women's movement raises more questions than answers. For example, there have been important legislative changes over the last three decades, abortion reform, equal pay, employment protection, the creation of the Equal Opportunities Commission and the Sex Discrimination Act being

among the most important. Over the last decade both Labour and the
Liberal Democrats have made commitments which (if realised) will
make far-reaching changes to the presence and impact of women in
national Parliamentary politics. As important, the issues and questions
raised by feminist analysis and prescriptions have entered into virtually
all aspects of political, economic and social life. This is not to argue
that everyone has accepted the arguments advanced by feminism, but it
is hard to imagine circumstances in which anyone is not aware of at
least some of the basic issues raised by feminists – in short, there has
been substantial *cultural* as well as *political* change. Establishing
causality is a notoriously difficult undertaking, but from the perspective of conventional pressure group theory, it is tempting to assume
that there must be some kind of direct causal relationship between
these two developments. On the one hand we have a significant (verging
on dramatic) upturn since the sixties in both the scope and variety of
collective action on the part of women, and on the other we have
significant political and cultural changes. Yet the relationship is
ambiguous. In broad terms, the seventies was an era in which women
created the loosely linked network of activities and ideas which became
known as the Women's Liberation Movement – but, as we shall see, this
movement devoted most of its energies to activities inside the
movement rather than outside lobbying, and in any case some of the
most significant legislative milestones actually preceded the time when
this movement was at its most vibrant. During the eighties and into the
nineties, the commonly accepted picture is one of this movement
disintegrating and fragmenting, and yet this is the time when women
have made a real impact upon the mainstream politics of political
parties, trade unions and local authorities. The answer lies in the fact
that the women's movement differs from more conventional collective
action. Let us attempt to trace the development of the movement and
its ideas.

THE SEVENTIES: SISTERHOOD

The second wave of feminism in Britain grew out of the upsurge of
interest in revolutionary socialism and libertarianism in the late sixties
that centred upon the Vietnam War and is now referred to in shorthand
terms as the 'student movement'. The women's movement became
visible in Britain at a national level in 1970 with the first National
Women's Liberation Movement Conference, at which four basic
demands were agreed – equal pay, equal education and opportunity,
extensive nursery provision, and free contraception and abortion on

demand.[4] From the outset, however, such nationally coordinated mobilisation was the exception rather than the norm. Instead, the movement developed through small groups, based on locality, occupation or existing political allegiances. Although many of the early activists were also active in left-wing politics, ranging from the Labour Party and trade unions to the revolutionary left groups, and sought to impart a feminist perspective into these, their message fell largely on barren ground. Notwithstanding some successes within the trade union movement (on issues like equal pay and conditions of work), the Labour Party was locked in internal struggle over the best strategic response to a Conservative Government and, in any case, was perceived as too bureaucratic to be a very attractive prospect to those whose prior political experiences were in the libertarian left. The more extreme left organisations not only tended to view feminism as something of a distraction from the fight against capitalism, but were, if anything, even more prone to sectarianism and rigidly formalised processes of internal democracy and decision-making. Women turned instead to starting their own autonomous groups and organisations.

In the early years of the women's movement in Britain, simply coming together as women within their own 'spaces', be these local groups in mainly urban areas or groups within institutions and professions, was the key ingredient in developing a feminist consciousness. Although it was not to last long, in the early to mid-seventies 'sisterhood' – taking this to mean a recognition that all women were to varying degrees the victims of oppression and a determination to remedy this – was a sufficiently exciting and engaging ideology to mask any disagreements over how and why such oppression occurred. There is little in the way of precise data, but hundreds of local groups sprang up during the seventies, with many of them establishing women's centres which not only provided a meeting place but also often published local newsletters, organised artistic and cultural activities, and generally acted as a resource base for local activists. Little attempt was made to establish national coordination, although communication between groups was certainly facilitated by the launch of *Spare Rib* magazine in 1972.

Out of this plethora of small groups came initiatives and campaigns on single issues such as domestic violence, rape, abortion and health. Some took the form of creating a physical space – for example, the creation of refuges for victims of domestic violence (a British innovation which later spread to America). These multiplied to the extent that, in 1975, a National Women's Aid Federation was established to act as a coordinating body; by 1977 there were almost two hundred refuges in the UK, and they have survived the vicissitudes of fragmentation in the women's movement since, with there being the same number in England alone by the nineties.[5] Rape Crisis Centres started to emerge at a local level from the mid-seventies onwards (offering victims telephone counselling and support groups); they also have survived into the nineties. The issue of abortion did not give rise to much activity at the local level, because the legislative changes of 1967,[6] although falling short of 'abortion on demand', were sufficient to make other issues seem more pressing; although there were marked variations between different regions of the NHS, the 1967 Act was implemented more liberally than might have been expected, with some 14 per cent of pregnancies being terminated in 1972.[7] When the 1967 changes were threatened, however, in the form of another Private Member's Bill in 1975,[8] the women's movement responded with one of its relatively few instances of nationally-organised protest. The National Abortion Campaign (NAC) was created, drawing together not just existing local women's groups, but also establishing its own network of groups within the Labour Party and trade unions as well as the urban areas. As well as lobbying within these institutions and encouraging supporters to put pressure on their constituency MPs, the Campaign mounted a national demonstration which attracted some 20,000 people – relatively small in comparison to some of the demonstrations organised by CND in the eighties, but nevertheless 'the biggest demonstration on a women's issue since the suffragettes.'[9] When the provisions of the 1967 Act were again threatened, this time by the Corrie Bill in 1979,[10] the NAC (in conjunction with the TUC) mounted a protest march with some 100,000 participants. While this kind of mobilisation was taking place at the national level, women involved in local groups made the connection between reproductive rights and preventive health care for women, and began creating local self-help groups aimed at providing an alternative to the male-dominated view of women's health needs emanating from the established medical profession. Many of these followed the American example, and evolved into 'well-woman' clinics in the eighties; they also set the context within which loosely-knit groups within the medical profession (such as Women in Medicine and the Association of Radical Midwives) emerged, determined to put the feminist perspective upon the agenda of the medical community. By the beginning of the eighties, there were estimated to be some 10,000 committed activists and a further 20,000 active on a more intermittent basis.[11]

THE EIGHTIES: FISSION IN THE MOVEMENT

Although it was certainly making its point of view heard, the movement was facing two problems. One was that – precisely because it engaged in such a variety of activities, from women's theatre groups and the creation of women's studies courses in higher education to conventional lobbying of local and national politicians and protest demonstrations – its impact on British society was arguably more marked in the cultural sphere than the political. Feminism was certainly on the agenda in terms of causing people to question popular attitudes and values, but (with the exception of some trade unions) it had yet to make its mark on the mainstream political parties and major interest groups. We shall return subsequently to the question of whether this was a failing or not. The other problem was that the movement itself was undergoing some major internal disagreements over ideology and tactics. Different viewpoints had been evident within the women's movement from its inception. To adopt the commonly used terminology, there were at least three different perspectives by the mid-seventies – 'Liberal' (or 'Equal Rights'), 'Socialist' and 'Radical'. Such differences were easily tolerated in the early years: as Wilson has observed, 'in the beginning all socialist–feminists were radical feminists and all radical feminists were socialist–feminists; or rather the two strands had not yet separated out as distinct currents.'[12] Things changed in the eighties, however, as the movement became more factionalised. It is worth noting that this rarely affected the smaller groups, located outside the major conurbations; in most of these, tolerance persisted throughout the seventies and into the eighties. In the larger groups, however, disagreements became bitter to the point that the WLM held no more national conferences after 1978. What, then, lay behind these different viewpoints?

Liberal feminists argued that equality of opportunity between the sexes was the important goal. Inequalities were seen to stem from both public and private barriers to women's progress. Although prejudice on a personal level was part of the problem, liberal feminists believed that the key lay in the public sphere. If women could be given equal rights and equal opportunities, particularly in the worlds of politics and the workplace, then their advances in these areas would sooner or later produce changes in personal attitudes. Hence liberal feminists had a representational strategy; their aim was to get more women into positions of power and responsibility in both the workplace and Britain's democratic institutions. Consequently, much of their attention was centred upon the public rather than the private sphere; they were particularly active in the political parties, the professions and the more conventional women's organisations. For them, new laws like the Sex Discrimination Act and promises to increase the number of women in Parliament were significant victories. For others in the feminist movement, however, such a strategy was flawed, not least because it could be argued that it rested upon women becoming more like men. As Bradley has argued, the liberal feminist standpoint 'does little to question the gendered cultural assumptions which underlie prevailing social arrangements – for example, that it is more socially valuable to go out to work than to stay at home and look after children, or that some kinds of work, like management and money-making should be more highly rewarded than others like cooking and cleaning.'[13] Moreover, there were suspicions that the liberal strategy might well benefit educated middle-class (usually white) women, but be of distinctly less utility to other women less well equipped to join men at their own game – especially if the new female MPs or female corporate managers were using other, poorer women to look after their children and clean their houses while they were out breaking through the glass ceilings of public life.

The potential exploitation of women by other women as well as by men was highlighted by the second of our different feminist perspectives, socialist feminism. Like liberal feminists, socialist feminists were also concerned with the poor deal that women received in the workplace and public life. They argued, however, that this was not just the result of legal and institutional blockages to women's progress, but rather part of a wider problem – the oppression which was an integral feature of capitalism. Women's inequality, not just in economic terms like lower pay or lower-status occupations, but also in wider terms like preserving traditional family structures, was seen as functional within the capitalist system – along with class inequalities, it helped to keep the capitalist system going. The tactical implications of such an analysis were that the fight to improve the position of women in society was only part of a broader struggle to replace capitalism with socialism – because the advent of socialism would inevitably mean the end of inequality between the sexes.

Consequently, socialist feminists argued that women had to work with other exploited sections of society, and placed particular stress on mobilisation among working-class women (usually through the Labour Party and the trade union movement). This analysis and strategy received at least as much criticism from within the wider women's movement as did the liberal viewpoint. Defending it cannot have been an easy task; as Bradley notes, 'gender divisions were shown by comparative and historical study to be characteristic of all societies, not just capitalist or even class-divided societies, and to be marked in the Soviet bloc where capitalism had been rejected.'[14]

Although there were these analytical and tactical differences (and, if only implicitly, often class differences) between liberal and socialist feminists, both could agree that there was nothing inherently wrong with cooperating with men to achieve their aims. Radical feminists, in contrast, took a more fundamental view. They saw patriarchy rather than class or institutional barriers as the cause of women's disadvantage. Indeed, radical feminism was rightly named, in that it offered an analysis which went much wider than even socialist feminism, let alone liberal feminism. Patriarchy, originally 'rule of the father' but now taken to mean rule by men, was the foundation stone of inequality – it produced the gender inequality that 'was the primary source of social division from which all others evolved.'[15] The argument rested on an assertion of difference rather than equality. Women were different from men; men had power over women and would continue to exercise that power because it benefited them – unless women (and only women) mobilised to fight against the patriarchal attitudes which permeated British society.

The differences were both ideological and tactical, with the radical feminists arguing that political separatism was the only way forward. Seeking representational advances within mainstream political institutions, as prioritised by liberal feminists and seen as part of a wider struggle by socialist feminists, was not part of their tactical repertoire. For them, such parties and institutions were hopelessly imbued with male values and interests. The answer lay instead in interpersonal and women-only group activities rather than the institutional sphere; it was the radical feminists who, more than anyone else, took the women's movement out of the 'public' sphere and firmly into those areas which had until then been viewed as 'private'. While liberal feminists were agitating for more women in public life, and socialist feminists for more equality in the workplace, radical feminists were moving firmly into the area of sexuality – not just questioning traditional institutions like marriage, but also arguing that reproduction was a source of repression. Most disconcerting for men, radical feminists asserted that all men were potentially capable of violence towards women, and that things like rape and pornography were manifestations of patriarchy which, in the final analysis, rested on a bedrock of male force.

It was because of such thinking that radical feminists took a different tactical route. Preferring self-help to agitation within mainstream institutions, they prioritised such activities as Rape Crisis Centres and women's refuges. Theory and practice became self-reinforcing, as such activism increased their concern with male violence; as Lovenduski and Randall note, the focus of radical feminists 'shifted steadily from an assertion of women's equality to a preoccupation with male sexual behaviour and to an increasing certainty of the need for separatist strategies of liberation ... This shift was accompanied by an analysis that implicated heterosexuality as the means of men's domination of women'.[16] The result was a strong current of opinion among radical feminists that lesbianism was the mark of a 'true' feminist. The move from political to sexual separatism split the women's movement; some simply left, and those who remained were unable to agree on strategies of action.

Nor was this the only division. Towards the end of the seventies, black women began to articulate a dissatisfaction with the wider women's movement. Their argument was that feminism, as conceptualised by all three of the strands we have looked at, was essentially a white women's movement (and, indeed, well educated, middle-class white women at that). Black women argued that they faced problems their white sisters did not – ranging from discrimination in employment, to immigration and (especially in the Asian community) a hostile reaction from members of their own community when it came to questioning traditional family relationships. Indeed, the whole role of the family was argued to be qualitatively different – 'while white feminists tended to view the family as an agent of patriarchal domination, black women argued that for them the family was a source of solidarity against the racism and subordination they experienced in white-dominated society.'[17] The Organisation of Women of African and Asian Descent (OWAAD) was created in 1978, but by 1982 even this had split as women of Afro-Caribbean and Asian descent could not agree upon priorities and tactics.[18] The emergence of a black lesbian grouping in the early eighties produced yet more divisions.

TACTICS AND ACTIVITIES

By the beginning of the eighties, the movement no longer had a single core. This did not mean that it was paralysed, however; activists may have been unable to agree on a unified strategy or analysis, but this did not stop them from pursuing their own different strategies for empowerment. Although, as we shall see, many women turned to interaction with established political institutions during the eighties and nineties, protest and associated 'unconventional' political activities did continue. One of the best known was the Greenham Women's Peace Camp which was discussed in Chapter 6, which, while it certainly reflected the ethos of radical feminism, also attracted women from throughout the movement and mobilised many new supporters. Of course, it can be argued that the Peace Camp was not specifically a 'feminist' project, in the sense of being concerned solely with women's rights, but it was a powerful symbol of women's determination to act autonomously, and there are many anecdotal accounts of the powerful consciousness-raising impact it had upon those who participated. It may have acted as something of a spur for another instance of mass collective action by women in the eighties, Women against Pit Closures.[19] Taking place in the context of the 1984/5 Miners' Strike, this took the form of women mobilising in support of their male relatives – ranging from mass demonstrations attracting around 10,000 women to a network of support groups and rallies at the local level. The movement petered out with the ending of the strike, though it was revived to some extent following the 1992 decision to close many of the UK's major pits. Like Greenham, however, its significance in this context was not so much the impact (or, rather, the lack of it) on the specific policy issue involved, as in the reinvigoration it gave to women's belief in their capacity for autonomous direct action. As Lovenduski and Randall note, commenting on research conducted in the early nineties, 'when we interviewed feminist activists – in different cities and involved in different issues (health, women's refuges and so forth) – we regularly found that they had played some active part in supporting Greenham or the miners' wives, in some cases both, and that this had affected them quite deeply.'[20]

Confirmation that direct action remained part of the women's movement's tactical repertoire can be seen in the strategies adopted by the various groups campaigning on the issue of pornography since the mid-eighties. Inspired by the Labour MP Clare Short's Indecent Displays Bill in 1986, the anti-pornography campaign has utilised both 'conventional' tactics, such as lobbying of Parliament and the media, and direct action in the form of demonstrations and picketing of retailers which stock pornographic magazines. This has been in spite of the ideological difficulties which the whole issue of pornography has raised within the movement. Radical feminists have taken the view that 'pornography is society's most significant means of subordinating women and that violent pornography reveals men's true sexuality'.[21] As such, they have little difficulty with the idea of censorship of pornography, even though it does entail taking common ground with those on the right of the political spectrum. Some liberal and socialist feminists, however, fear that state-imposed censorship on pornography could easily spread into the realm of artistic expression, and consequently actually campaign against such censorship. In practice, the radical viewpoint has received far more attention in the media, and would seem to have attracted substantially more support within the movement as a whole than the anti-censorship argument.

Further evidence that the movement was capable of burying its ideological disagreements and organising direct action on a national scale came in 1987 when the issue of abortion arose again. The pro-choice movement had split in the early eighties, as some women became disenchanted with what they saw as the National Abortion Campaign's preoccupation with 'the practical concerns of middle-class white women'.[22] Abortion, it was argued, was only one aspect of the broader area of reproductive rights; there were other important aspects, like forced sterilisation in some third world countries or the reproductive rights of lesbians. There was also some unhappiness with the involvement of men in NAC. This led to the creation of breakaway groups, most notably the Women's Reproductive Rights Campaign in 1984. Initially there was tension between the two groups, if not bitterness.[23]

When MP David Alton tried in 1987 to gain Parliamentary approval for a Private Member's Bill reducing the twenty-eight week limit on abortion to eighteen weeks, however, differences were set aside. The National Abortion Campaign immediately joined forces with the Women's Reproductive Rights Campaign (and the Abortion Law Reform Association) to form the Fight the Alton Bill (FAB) campaign. At its height, FAB had over 150 local branches and groups throughout Britain,[24] and was able to mount a national demonstration to coincide with the second reading of the Bill in the House of Commons (which subsequently fell[25]), even though this was on a significantly smaller scale than the demonstrations of the seventies. It was left to the NAC to take the lead two years later, however, when the Thatcher Government successfully proposed a reduction in the time limit for abortions from twenty-eight weeks to twenty-four[26] – a decision hailed as a victory by the pro-life organisations, but seen as little more than a confirmation of the *status quo* by their pro-choice counterparts.[27]

Direct action, then, remained a characteristic of the women's movement during the eighties, but the largest mobilisations were of women protesting about issues which were wider than those articulated by the women's movement of the seventies; gender-specific issues did not inspire 'unconventional' protest and action in the way they had during the previous decade. One reason for this may well have been simply a reflection of a degree of success; attitudes had changed since the inception of the second wave of feminism – as the British Social Attitudes Survey concluded in 1988, 'Britain seems to be much more egalitarian now on women's issues than it was twenty years ago'[28] – reducing the sense of urgency evident in the seventies. Another reason, on the other hand, was that it was clear by the eighties that institutional and legislative innovations like the Sex Discrimination Act and the Equal Opportunities Commission were falling far short of delivering equal rights and opportunities for women. An implementation gap was evident, and that was something best addressed from within the system rather than from outside. In short (and to oversimplify), if the seventies was a decade of getting women's issues on to the political agenda of the mainstream established political institutions, the eighties was one in which the issues were pursued within those institutions.

One area that was of particular importance was the development of Women's Committees in local authorities. Although these originated largely as the result of pressure by socialist feminists active in the Labour Party and the trade unions, radical and liberal feminists were also involved, and the Committees saw their task as facilitating the mobilisation of women from all wings of the movement. The first full Committee to be formed (as distinct from informal working groups) was the Greater London Council (GLC) Women's Committee in 1982 – control of the GLC having fallen to the Labour group under the leadership of Ken Livingstone the previous year. Others soon followed, although it should be noted that they were virtually all found in Labour-controlled authorities, and only around a quarter of those at that.[29] These Committees sought to impact not only upon the internal practices of local authorities (for example, conditions of service and appointment procedures) but also upon the provision of services such as child care and initiatives in the area of women's health issues, and liaison with police authorities over domestic and other threats of violence to women. Many have not survived into the nineties, not least because of high profile criticism from both the Conservative Party and the media over decisions to fund lesbian groups, but their emergence marked the engagement of what had been an autonomous liberation movement with mainstream institutions of the state. The Committees themselves were, of course, to some extent a reflection of increasing engagement with the Labour Party and trade union movement. It was during the eighties that the Labour Women's Action Committee (LWAC) was formed, which campaigned within the Labour Party partly to give some real power to the women's organisations which had existed for over sixty years[30] but only operated under the sufferance of the party's National Executive Committee, and partly to introduce new initiatives, such as the compulsory inclusion of women candidates on all Parliamentary candidate selection shortlists. A similar process took place within the unions, as women both pressed for (and achieved) a change of attitude towards the TUC Women's Conference, persuading their male colleagues to treat this as a serious political forum, and mobilised within individual unions, resulting in many unions adopting new policies in such areas as equal rights, maternity provision and sexual harassment in the workplace. Indicative of their success was the creation of an Equal Rights Department by the TUC in 1988.

Such advances were facilitated by factors outside the Labour and trade union movement, not least the commitment of the newly-formed Social Democrats in 1981 to equal opportunities policies and compulsory shortlisting of women Parliamentary candidates (both of which survived the subsequent cooperation and merger with the Liberals); given the potential electoral threat Labour perceived the Liberal/Social Democrat Alliance to represent in the mid-eighties, this was clearly a spur to action on the part of the Labour movement. The process was somewhat delayed by internal party politics, as the LWAC was perceived by the party leadership to be closely associated with the Hard Left (especially Militant Tendency) within the party – who were, of course, the prime target of the leadership between 1983 and 1987. It was only towards the end of the decade, when the leadership was clearly winning its battle with Militant Tendency, that it was prepared to respond to demands from the feminists within its ranks. Its response then, however, verged on the dramatic. A Shadow Ministry for Women was established in 1989. The 1990 Annual Conference agreed that within the next ten years the party would have women comprising at least 40 per cent of all representatives on all the party's important policy-making bodies, including the NEC and the new National Policy Forum, as well as a target of at least half of all Labour MPs being women. To this end, it was agreed in 1990 that henceforth all ballot papers cast by members of the PLP in elections for the Shadow Cabinet had to include votes for at least three women, or they would be rejected as invalid – and, despite some rumblings of discontent within the PLP, this number was increased to four in 1993. At constituency level, it was agreed in 1988 that henceforth the selection of Parliamentary candidates would be subject to the requirement that all shortlists had to include at least one woman. The 1993 Annual Conference took this one stage further, deciding that there would be women-only candidate shortlists in half of the party's 'winnable' seats – that is, marginals and those where an incumbent Labour MP retires – and this was confirmed at the 1994 Annual Conference after an extensive debate.

The leadership changes during the early nineties have not impeded this process, although there are some doubts about the depth of New Labour's commitment. John Smith was known to be sympathetic to the idea of increasing women's representation within the party, and upgraded the post of Women's Officer towards this end. Tony Blair has reaffirmed his commitment, but was considered to be wary of the possible electoral consequences of women-only shortlists. In the event, the problem has been solved for him by an industrial tribunal ruling that women-only shortlists are in contravention of the Sex Discrimination Act. Although Blair and his colleagues were considering an appeal, they decided in February 1996 to take their lawyers' advice against such a course. The policy is now in abeyance, although this has not affected the 35 constituencies which have already selected women candidates. Labour is hoping to see some 90 female Labour MPs after the next election. Many of these candidates are receiving assistance from an organisation known as Emily's List; set up by Barbara Follett to emulate the American organisation of the same name, which has been instrumental in tripling the number of female Democrats in Congress, Emily's List offers women candidates some financial assistance and training. As with so many other areas of New Labour policy in 1996, it is hard to be sure how any future Labour Government will act in practice, but Blair has made a point of promoting new women MPs to his front-bench team.

Even the Conservative Party has made some response to pressure from the women's movement; a ministerial group was established in 1986 with the task of considering the effect of all proposals for legislative change on women, and Prime Minister John Major upgraded the status of this group to a Cabinet Committee in 1992. Beyond that, however, it has to be said that the Government's response has been limited to protestations of support for equality of opportunity, with little in the way of concrete action. While it may not have been a deliberate outcome, a number of commentators have noted that one effect of the Conservative drive to replace direct service provision by the public sector with contracting-out services to the private sector has been to diminish the impact of equal opportunities policies.[31]

There is much to suggest that such progress within the political parties is reflecting rather than leading public opinion. As we saw in Chapter Five, the major study of participation in Britain undertaken by Parry *et al.*[32] in the mid-eighties found overwhelming agreement with the proposition that women should enjoy equal opportunities, and almost half the respondents in favour of relaxing restrictions on abortion. Altogether, 46 per cent of their sample could be regarded as having pro-feminist values. Moreover, this study suggests that support for such values is relatively dispersed among the population. More were from the working class than from the salariat; almost a third were men; almost 90 per cent were not graduates; their age profile matched that of the total sample. Nor are such outlooks found only on the left of the political spectrum; although over 14 per cent were on the 'far left', and 36.7 per cent identified with the Labour Party, there was also a strong contingent from the centre and the right of the political spectrum, with 34.1 per cent identifying with the Conservative Party. The British Social Attitudes surveys produce a similar picture; while just over half the respondents in 1984 agreed with the idea that a husband's role was to earn the money and a wife's to look after the home, by 1989 only a quarter agreed and over half disagreed; around 90 per cent thought that the job of a Councillor or MP was equally suitable for men and women.[33] Having said this, attitudinal change is not necessarily synonymous with behavioural change. The same Social Attitudes surveys show that only around half of those who agree that 'domestic' responsibilities should be equally shared actually practise this. Nor should we forget just how much progress has yet to be made in the public sphere; at the beginning of 1995, for example, women accounted for 50 per cent of the workforce, but only 9 per cent of MPs, 7 per cent of the senior judiciary, 9 per cent of the senior civil service, 3 per cent of company directors and 5 per cent of university professors.[34]

If the women's movement can take heart from the progress made to date, there is clearly a long way to go before its objectives could be said to have been fully achieved. Yet, on the face of it, the movement has significantly declined during the nineties. *Spare Rib* ceased publication in 1993. Lovenduski and Randall's impression at the end of the eighties – 'everywhere we went, except Scotland, we encountered a sense that numbers of activists were falling, local women's newsletters were folding, old networks were breaking down'[35] – is confirmed by more recent surveys which suggest that, despite widespread agreement with the aims of the women's movement, the younger generation born since the seventies tends to see the movement as 'extreme, man-hating and separatist'.[36] This gives rise to two questions: did the women's movement of the seventies and eighties set about its task of changing British politics and society in the 'right' or 'best' way; and what are the prospects for the future?

PURITY OR PRAGMATISM?

Even disregarding those who disagree with its aims, the women's movement has certainly not lacked its critics. We have already noted the internal divisions within the movement between those adopting radical, socialist and liberal perspectives, each of whom has been ready to criticise the others. More detached criticism has come from sympathisers outside the movement, particularly those whose experience has been in the American women's movement. At least some of those who have both been active in the American movement, and have analysed it, have argued that it has suffered from internal splits resulting from ideological disputes. Ryan is a good example, her study of the American movement noting the repeated instances during the movement's early years of 'trashing', whereby ideological disagreements were, in effect, closer to character assassinations and occurred in all sectors of the movement.[37] 'Within the women's movement, disputes over theory turned into disputes over who was the most feminist or who was the right kind of feminist . . . when feminists could have focused their efforts on issues of concern to poor and working-class women, they were fragmented and fighting over labels.'[38]

From an American perspective, their own women's movement is usually perceived as having managed to nullify most of the negative effects of such factionalism, not least because of the creation of a genuinely national organisation in the form of the National Organisation for Women (NOW). The British women's movement, however, still comes in for some quite trenchant criticism. It tends to be seen as being commendable for the degree of commitment it has inspired, but regrettably insistent upon ideological purity at the expense of coalition-building which would result in pragmatic gains. Gelb's observations are characteristic: she has argued that the failure of the British women's movement to construct a national organisation which could then engage in dialogue with policy-makers at the national level has resulted in 'a strangely limited vision of feminist goals and ideals which, in fact, produces less societal change than might be expected.'[39] To be fair, Gelb stresses that any movement can only be assessed within the context of its 'political opportunity structure', the concept we discussed in Chapter Four. She notes that the British system is much more closed and inflexible than the American, and that there are consequently less opportunities to forge alliances with parties which have stronger ideological imperatives than their American counterparts, or to influence administrators who operate in a centralised system rather the multi-level openings which are a feature of the

American federal system. Moreover, her view of the British women's movement reflects the generally-held view among American commentators on social movements that movements 'mature' by becoming more formally organised over time, and that this increases their chance of influencing public policy. Nevertheless, the point remains: if the British women's movement had been less concerned with developing theoretical analyses of the causes of their subordination, and more prepared to bury their differences and work together (and, at least in the case of radical feminists, work more closely with male sympathisers), might not the movement have achieved more in the way of concrete change and done less to apparently alienate the younger generation?

A counter-argument is provided by continental European commentators, who, as we have seen, tend to assess social movements not so much by their impact upon political institutions and public policy as upon culture and ideas in society. They make the point that social movements may well have instrumental motives, as in seeking to achieve legislative change, but they also have non-instrumental goals which are concerned with 'living out' the cause. Melucci's argument that it may be necessary to analyse the 'visible' aspects of movements but one should also take into account what happens at the 'invisible' level of social interaction, for example, is clearly relevant in this context.[40]

The women's movement may well have inhibited its impact upon mainstream institutions by choosing to remain localised rather than national; non-hierarchical rather than bureaucratic; loosely networked rather than coordinated by a 'peak' organisation performing an aggregative function; and purist rather than pragmatic. However, this strategy is not without its advantages. The very lack of a structure meant that the movement was able to survive the disputes of the late seventies, which a more conventional organisation almost certainly would not have done, because there was no hierarchy within which to pursue them. Fragmentation is a disadvantage if one views the goal as impacting directly upon mainstream political institutions; but if, following Melucci, one views the *raison d'être* of a social movement as challenging the dominant values and cultural codes in society, then such fragmentation enriches a movement. It is the sign of a movement preoccupied with identity. The women's movement has been, and is still, trying to create a new identity in society – Eyerman and Jamison's concept of 'cognitive praxis' which they derived from the experience of the ecological movement would also apply to the women's movement in this context[41] – and getting the rest of society to accept this.

Fragmentation is understandable in a movement centred upon claims to a different identity and experience, as distinct from a particular policy or issue. Once women started to assert their difference from men, the way was open for women to assert their differences from each other. Identity politics may militate against coalition-building within the movement, and between the movement and established actors in the political process, but it expands the ideological parameters of the movement. The more women moved from a concern with 'equality' to the assertion of 'difference', the less radical (and thus more acceptable to the mainstream) arguments for equality appear.

The American analysis emphasises the visible, quasi-formal interactions between the movement and the established political authorities, and it is true that ideological disagreements have divided the movement, and rendered the development of such connections more difficult. The European analysis stresses the importance of new meanings of social reality being developed and expressed in 'private' as well as public life, as it is out of this that widespread challenges to dominant cultural values emerge, and it is equally true that the multifarious disagreements within the women's movement over the last twenty years have given it an intellectual dynamism and vitality not found in other movements which stress policy change rather than identity. The American perspective can be criticised for concentrating upon how the movement interacts with political authorities, and overlooking why the movement exists at all – where it is coming from. Similarly, the European perspective directs our attention to the underlying source of visible mobilisation, but has little to say on where it is going. There is, however, an element of common ground between the two, and it lies in the concept of collective identity. What is sometimes lost sight of in discussions of social movements is that, in comparison with the peace or environmental movements, the women's movement has the potential to develop a strong sense of self-interest, as distinct from more altruistic motives. If the consciousness of a collective identity can be formed, then women's awareness of their common interests as women, rather than as members of a class or ethnic group, may well influence their political behaviour and partisan loyalties. If so, then established institutions like political parties and unions will move towards accommodation of women's issues almost regardless of how fragmented the movement is. Identity-centred politics has split the movement, and introduced sometimes bitter divisions; but it has also widened the parameters of the debate such that what was formerly contestable – the claim to equality – is now common ground. Women have argued with each other, but this has acted as a catalyst for the creation of a strong self-interest in demand-ing at least the lowest common denominator of agreement, equality of opportunity and treatment. The activists of the last twenty years have failed to act in concert but, by their constant striving to question their own ideology, they have changed the consciousness of the vast majority of women in the UK, and not a few men, and this is now reflected in the promises held out by what is likely to be the next government.

The worrying aspect for the movement is that such argument may have been stimulating, but it appears to have communicated a negative image to the younger generation. If, as seems the case, the autonomous women's movement has largely disappeared, and the succeeding generation does not wish to revive something they see as unnecessarily strident and separatist, then from where will the driving force come to ensure that the agenda continues to expand and that such promises are kept? Social movements are like icebergs – the visible 10 per cent is important, but without the underlying 90 per cent they will melt away. The identity-centred politics of the women's movement has put equality firmly upon the political agenda; out of the disputes between radical, socialist, black and lesbian definitions of feminism has come a core of agreement, a collective identity centred upon women's rights to equality. It has not been cost-free, however; with the exception of solidarity on the basis of sexual orientation,[42] the foundations of the movement are withering. Without the stimulus of women coming together in autonomous groups to push forward arguments about the higher ground of difference and the need to recognise it, it might be easier for parties and governments to come to view the lower slopes of equality as too much of an uphill struggle to pursue.

8   The green movement

Of all the issues raised by social movements over the last thirty years, 'environmentalism' has had the greatest impact, permeating many diverse areas of social, economic and political life not only domestically, but also on a global scale. Even the women's movement, which has also been a genuinely global phenomenon, has not attracted the same degree of attention. The issue has had a particularly strong profile in Western democracies, with virtually all now having a Department or Ministry focused on environmental issues; transnational bodies such as the European Union and the United Nations also have agencies specifically devoted to the area, not to mention the creation of Global Environmental Summits in recent years.

Within a European context, Britain has been in the forefront of this explosion of interest, at least in the sense that many of the well-known campaigning organisations developed in the UK before they did so in continental Europe. In comparison with the rest of Europe, however, Britain is something of a paradox; it is generally acknowledged to have more of its citizens involved in environmental groups of various kinds than any other state in Europe, and it was the first European state to have a Green Party enter the electoral arena – yet that party is one of the weakest in Europe, the British government has a poor reputation internationally on green issues, and the green message has yet to be taken on board in substance rather than rhetoric by the major political parties. The answer to this conundrum lies partly in the variety of groups and viewpoints which are commonly subsumed under the general heading of 'environmentalism', and partly in the nature of the British political system itself.

The term 'environmentalism' covers a wide range of concerns and tactics: from conventional lobbying over rare species, to direct action over road-building and pollution; from concerned citizens taking their old newspapers to supermarkets for recycling and localised schemes to replace money with systems of barter, to life-threatening manoeuvres on the high seas. It is also a long-established interest of British society; although, like feminism, it has enjoyed a 'second wave' from the late sixties on, environmentalism first became popular in the nineteenth century. To understand its development, it is necessary to draw a distinction between two broad types of environmentalism. On the one hand, there is what we shall call the *conservation* aspect of environmentalism, and on the other what we shall term its *ecological* aspect.[1]

The conservation orientation is one which stresses the protection and preservation of flora, fauna and habitats perceived to be under threat. Although it may deprecate industrialisation for the pressures on the environment it produces, the ideology of conservationism is not anti-industrial or anti-technocratic as such; it is reformist rather than radical or revolutionary, because it seeks only to achieve certain specific aims within the overall confines of the existing socioeconomic system. As Richardson has argued,[2] the conservationist philosophy is anthropocentric, in that it argues for the preservation of certain features of the environment essentially for the people's enjoyment. With some exceptions, it generally pursues such aims within the existing mainstream political institutions, and without recourse to unconventional political action. Conservationist groups first emerged in Britain in the latter half of the nineteenth century. Indeed, as Young notes,[3] the Commons, Open Spaces and Footpaths Preservation Society – founded in 1865 – is usually cited as the first environmental group in the world. The Royal Society for the Protection of Birds, which is today by far the largest conservation group in the UK with a membership of over 400,000, was founded in 1889; another group which has become highly successful (with over a million members in the 1990s, although its interests extend beyond conservation as such) is the National Trust, which was formed in 1895. The Garden Cities Association (which subsequently became the Town and Country Planning Association) originated in 1899, the Society for the Promotion of Nature Preserves (subsequently the Royal Society for Nature Conservation) in 1912, and the Council for the Preservation (subsequently Protection) of Rural England, in 1926. For the middle and upper classes in Victorian Britain, conservation was a popular issue and attracted the support of such leading intellectual figures as Ruskin and John Stuart Mill. It rode on a tide of opinion which also found expression in the formation of groups dedicated to animal welfare: the Society for Prevention of Cruelty to Animals was founded in 1824 (receiving royal approbation in 1840), the National Anti-Vivisection Society in 1875, and the British Union for the Abolition of

Vivisection in 1898. It was a trend reflected in continental Europe in the early 1900s, as major conservation groups were founded in Germany, Holland and France, even if some had their own rather distinctive view of the purpose of such preservation – the French National Society for the Protection of Nature, for example, marked its annual meetings with a dinner at which exotic game was consumed.[4]

The ecological orientation, in contrast, has a much wider focus of concern and employs a much greater variety of tactics, both conventional and unconventional. The ecological movement is what Richardson terms 'biocentric', in that it rests upon a holistic theory which sees humankind as just one part of a greater natural system, the planet. The argument is that all the living organisms of the earth are interconnected, and humans have to learn to coexist with other lifeforms, not dominate and exploit them, if the whole system is to survive. It is from this view of the world that the ecological movement derives its radical ideology, one which not only argues the necessity of fundamental political, economic and social change but is also reflected in the movement's own tactics and organisation. As may be clear from this, it is the ecological movement which is of prime concern to us, as it embodies the defining features of a social movement, while the conservationist groups are much more akin to conventional 'cause' or 'promotional' interest groups.

It was not until the beginning of the 1970s that new forces began to emerge. When they did, however, it marked the beginning of a qualitatively different approach to environmental campaigning. As with the women's movement, some of the initial impetus came from North America. Friends of the Earth (FOE) was founded in San Francisco in 1969, arriving in the UK in 1970/71; Greenpeace was first established in Canada in the early seventies and opened a London office in 1977; the radical direct action group Earth First! was formed in America in the early eighties, and a British offshoot was established in 1991. Others were home-grown: the Conservation Society was created in 1966, and the Green Party in 1973 – the first such party in Europe, preceded in the world only by Australia and New Zealand (formed 1972). Dalton[5] makes the point that at least one of the reasons for the emergence of this new wave of environmental activism was the work emanating from the scientific and educational network created by the existing conservationist groups, a prominent example being the publication in 1962 of *The Silent Spring* by Rachel Carson which made a powerful argument against the widespread use of pesticides. Ten years later, an international grouping of scientists and industrialists calling themselves the Club of Rome published *The Limits to Growth*, which took Carson's questioning of scientific and economic orthodoxy much further by arguing that the planet could not indefinitely satisfy the patterns of consumption which were a hallmark of 'developed' societies, and became a much-quoted source in subsequent ecological texts. Such intellectual inputs obviously had a significant role to play; what really tipped the balance towards a new wave, however, was the conjunction of such new knowledge with the cultural shift which took place in Western societies during the late sixties. The student movement and other liberationist movements, which we have already discussed, seized upon the ecological argument as an apposite instance of their criticism of the materialist society and conventional politics they so disliked. In Britain, France, Germany, Holland and Belgium between 1966 and 1970, young people in particular saw in ecology a critique of industrialised society and the centralised state that transcended old-style Left–Right politics. Their enthusiasm for this new approach was not restricted to groups advocating an ecological stance. Conservation groups expanded dramatically during the seventies with, for example, the membership of the RSPB in the UK growing from some 30,000 at the end of the sixties to 200,000 in 1975 and over 400,000 by the mid-eighties. Nevertheless, it was the ecological dimension which produced a new type of environmental politics, in terms of ideology, organisation and tactics, and it is to such groups that we now turn.

FRIENDS OF THE EARTH

Friends of the Earth (FOE) was originally formed in San Francisco in 1969. As is by no means uncommon in the field of environmental groups, its founder (David Brower) was already active in environmental campaigning, but was motivated by a sense of frustration. Working with the Sierra Club,[6] he failed to persuade his fellow members of the pressing need to add a strong element of direct action to their existing conventional lobbying, and branched out on his own. A UK wing was founded in 1970 (FOE-UK), making it the first such ecological group in Britain. The organisation has since flourished. In the UK, membership rose from around 15,000 at the end of the seventies to some 39,000 in 1988; there was a massive increase in 1989 to 125,000, rising to 190,000 in 1990 with an annual income of around £4.5 million.[7] Worldwide, FOE had organisations in 52 countries in 1995, and claims to be 'the largest international network of environmental groups in the world'.

From the outset, FOE changed both the focus and the nature of environmental campaigning. There were three distinct elements: the scope of the target, the causal analysis and the tactical repertoire. FOE dramatically expanded the focus of environmental campaigning, particularly by highlighting issues like pollution and the perceived threat of nuclear power; for FOE, merely conserving an endangered species or preserving an area of natural beauty – although desirable – was not enough. If the longer-standing conservation groups had been concerned with the effects of early industrialisation, FOE was focused firmly on the problems it saw as being inextricably linked with advanced industrial society. Its argument was that the pursuit of economic growth was producing more and more material goods, the consequences of which were the depletion of finite resources, the introduction of potentially dangerous technology, air- and waterborne pollution, and toxic waste – problems which affected everybody in society, not just those with an interest in conservation.

FOE also broke decisively with the pattern set by conservation groups by adding a new, political dimension to the debate, arguing that environmental problems stemmed largely from the attitudes and practices of large industrial and corporate interests and the political systems which tolerated them. From the outset, then, FOE's analysis of the environmental problem was one which stressed the perceived underlying causes of environmental degradation – an economic and political system which is based upon economic growth. Consequently, fundamental changes to the way in which society operated were necessary, not just in terms of actions which had a specific effect upon the environment, but also in the way in which democracy itself was organised. 'Big Government' was as much of a problem as 'Big Business'; only decentralisation and a concomitant increase in democratic input could produce both the awareness that sustainability rather than growth was the way forward, and the opportunity for this to be put into practice.

FOE's ideology did not just expand the agenda from one concerned primarily with conservation to one which questioned the whole structure and dynamic of Western industrialised societies; it also included an explicit commitment to participatory democracy, on the ground that only a major expansion of democratic participation could deliver the necessary commitment to effect a change to sustainable development. This ideological stress upon participation is reflected in FOE's views on the appropriate role and behaviour of its supporters. FOE has always argued that the scale and immediacy of the environmental crisis was, and is, such as both to justify and necessitate direct action; while, as we shall see, not solely or even primarily a protest group, FOE has consistently encouraged its supporters to mount non-violent demonstrations and actions, particularly on a local level. Its own structure is decentralised; each national organisation is effectively autonomous, and within the national organisations (and this is particularly so of FOE-UK) local groups are equally autonomous, controlling their own budgets and deciding upon their own activities – the role of the national office being to advise and offer assistance. There is also an expectation that supporters will 'live out the cause' in their personal lives. FOE stresses the necessity for change on both a societal and individual level; fundamental changes in public policy are needed, but individuals themselves can make a difference by modifying their own lifestyles – for example, by using public transport, or by recycling waste materials.

The ideology of FOE has remained unchanged over the last twenty-five years; its 1995 Mission Statement[8] defines its aims:

- to protect the earth against further deterioration and restore damage inflicted upon the environment by human activities and negligence;
- to preserve the earth's ecological, cultural and ethnic diversity;
- to increase public participation and democratic decision-making. Greater democracy is both an end in itself and is vital to the protection of the environment and the sound management of natural resources;
- to achieve social, economic and political justice and equal access to resources and opportunities for men and women on the local, national, regional and international levels;
- to promote environmentally sustainable development on local, national, regional and global levels.

The message remains the same: diversity is important in both an ecological and sociological sense. In this recognition of the positive benefits of recognising 'difference' in society, FOE has much in common with at least the radical feminist wing of the women's movement and the liberationist movements of the late sixties.

This is not coincidental; FOE grew out of the student and allied movements, and consciously modelled its loose, decentralised structure on that of the student movement. Thus, decision-making in local groups (of which there are some 250 in the UK in the nineties) is achieved via consensus and voluntary input rather than by any hierarchical structure. Similarly, the relationship between the national organisation and local groups is based upon the formation of informal consensus rather than on any formal, bottom-up representational structure or top-down instruction. FOE-UK has no written constitution as such, and no means of disciplining local groups (although the national organisation retains control over the use of the name 'FOE'). FOE-UK organises regular workshops and conferences which bring together local activists and coordinators, but participation is voluntary, and there is no question of local groups electing 'delegates' to attend such gatherings, nor is there the equivalent of an Annual Conference which determines strategy. This is not to say that there is no guidance from the national/international level; Annual General Meetings of FOE International adopt packages of activities and campaigning issues, which national organisations and their local groups are encouraged to follow, but it is left very much open at both the national and local level for activists to substitute their own priorities if local circumstances seem to justify this.

In practice, as one might expect, this has led to a wide variety of campaigns and tactics, such that it would be impossible in this context to provide an exhaustive list of them. FOE activities can be subsumed under two broad headings: direct action and more conventional lobbying. The former has always been a part of the repertoire, though it is noticeable that it has become a less frequent occurrence as FOE has matured. FOE-UK first came to public attention with a piece of direct action, highlighting what it saw as the unnecessary waste of non-returnable bottles by dumping 1,500 of them on the doorstep of the London HQ of the soft-drink firm Schweppes; the action received wide attention in the media and resulted in a boom in membership. On a local level, activists have taken direct action, either in the form of demonstration and/or protest or in terms of establishing self-help initiatives such as recycling depots, over numerous local issues. As we shall see, groups like FOE and Greenpeace have been somewhat upstaged in the nineties by more radical direct-action groups, but – although we do not have definitive data – there is strong impressionistic evidence to suggest that many individual FOE members are also active in these more recent campaigns. In short, direct action has been a consistent feature of FOE's tactical repertoire, although more often it has been in the form of suggesting and agitating for (if not actually organising) local alternatives to environmentally-unfriendly practices than of street-based protest.

Not all of FOE's campaigning is as confrontational as this. Over the last ten years, FOE has moved into the area of consultancy, working with private companies to advise on how to conduct environmental audits and cope with environmental problems. Although tangential in direct-action terms, FOE has been in the forefront of the 'green consumerism' campaign, trying with some success to persuade consumers to use their purchasing power to influence manufacturers and retailers; it took the lead in the eighties over the issue of chloro-fluorocarbons (CFCs) in aerosols, packaging and refrigerants, resulting in the consumption of CFCs being halved in the UK during the eighties.

As FOE has grown, however, conventional lobbying has become more and more central to its activities. This should not be taken as a sign of atrophy or battle-weariness on the part of FOE activists. On the contrary, as the justification for direct action was part of the founding philosophy, so too was an equally strong insistence that FOE would always seek to base its campaigning on the firmest possible foundation of rigorous scientific and ecological research. Indicative of this, as Pearce notes,[9] the first Director of FOE (Graham Searle) imposed a rule in the early days of the campaign that no member of FOE staff could talk publicly on any subject until they had first spent six months researching that subject. The emphasis upon providing authoritative data has continued since, much of it being obtained from official sources. In some cases, the information is used in a relatively unfocused manner, the aim being media exposure; thus, to take a recent example, in 1993 FOE pointed out that the British Government, in its attempts to comply with EU criteria on measuring emissions from car exhausts, had established just seven monitoring stations (compared with over 200 in Germany), only one of which was sited in an area of heavy traffic. Following critical comment in the media, the Government gave way and rapidly established nine more stations. In other cases, FOE targets its research more directly, and has shown itself both willing and able to exploit any opportunity offered by mainstream institutions in the judicial as well as the political field, and internationally as well as nationally. Thus, for example, where FOE can make use of the law, it will; when it discovered in 1993 that scores of British firms were still breaching limits on the discharge of pollutants into rivers, set by the new National Rivers Authority some four years earlier, it did not only publicise this, it also threatened the directors of fourteen major companies that private prosecutions would be brought against them if they failed to remedy the problem. It has also challenged the UK Government at the European Court of Justice in attempts to ensure that EU regulations and directives have been implemented.

Similarly, FOE has sought to take full advantage of the quasi-judicial forum of Public Inquiries, agitating for them to be established in areas like the development of the nuclear energy industry or the road-building programme, and participating when such inquiries do take place. One of the earliest instances was the inquiry into the development of a nuclear fuel reprocessing facility at Windscale (now known as Sellafield) in 1977. FOE received positive coverage in the media for its well presented and researched objections, and its participation has been seen by one academic commentator as 'the single most important turning point in FOE's credibility'.[10] Such input has continued – FOE's participation (together with CND and the CPRE) in the three-year-long inquiry into the proposal to build a pressurised water nuclear reactor at Sizewell in the mid-eighties, and the similar Hinckley C inquiry in the late eighties, are cases in point, as are the numerous inquiries relating to motorway developments in the nineties; although in the case of nuclear reprocessing FOE has failed to change government policy, there have been successes in the campaign against the building of more roads.

The presence of full-time staff at the national level enables FOE not simply to protest, but also to offer authoritative alternatives. When it objected to the Government's proposed new crossing of the Thames by road in East London in 1993, for example, FOE did not just publicise the environmental damage it said would result, but also produced its own plan for a £300 million underground rail link as an alternative. The breadth as well as the depth of FOE's research gives it greater authority. For example, FOE preceded the Chancellor of the Exchequer's 1994 Budget with a report which, drawing on research and evidence from across the industrialised world, produced a comprehensive argument that changes in industrial, transport and energy policy towards a more environmental perspective would not only transform the quality of life, but also produce some 700,000 new jobs and save some three billion pounds in unemployment benefits. This is a good example of the kind of constructive protest FOE favours; not merely objecting, but also offering alternatives. Such expertise gives FOE a significant advantage when lobbying, particularly with sympathetic backbench MPs who cannot resort to the civil service for information. FOE has successfully persuaded MPs on several occasions to adopt FOE-drafted proposals for legislation as Private Member's Bills, and claims to have drafted three major environmental acts passed by Parliament.

Nor are their horizons limited to the national level; particularly since the UK's accession to the European Union, FOE can and does take advantage of its sister organisations internationally to bring pressure to bear domestically. Thus, for example, FOE was active in lobbying the EU to introduce directives on standards for drinking and bathing water in the early nineties; when the directives were withdrawn after pressure from Britain and France in the Council of Ministers,

FOE responded by saying it would mobilise support in more sympathetic member states who would then bring pressure to bear on the British government at the European level. FOE-UK is also, of course, active in international campaigns, as part of the global FOE network.

Much of the above relates to FOE at the national level, and there is no doubt that, at this level, FOE has succeeded in establishing itself as a reliable purveyor of an authoritative alternative perspective. It is rare, in the nineties, to find any media report on an environmental topic which does not include at least a brief reaction from FOE. Nor are FOE's views today ridiculed as the outpourings of a bunch of hopelessly unrealistic hippies, which was certainly their fate in the organisation's earlier years. As we shall see, such scorn tends to fall on the Green Party instead, but even without such an alternative, it is hard to imagine such treatment being meted out to FOE given its record of careful research, low-key direct action and willingness to work with polluters in educational programmes. None of this, however, should obscure the importance to FOE of local activities. Here, research and direct action are much more likely to go hand-in-hand, although even the direct action is more often than not of the self-help variety, rather than sheer protest. Local FOE groups are encouraged to participate in national campaigns, but they are also free to undertake their own campaigns at the local level. This may well involve protest, as, for example, in small-scale demonstrations or organising petitions; it is also likely to involve some input designed to have a direct impact upon the problem. Activities undertaken by the 250 local groups are too diverse to summarise, but a hypothetical example may help; if development of an unspoilt piece of land was proposed, the local FOE group would probably use both conventional tactics (lobbying local councillors, contacting the local media, etc.) and more unconventional tactics (demonstrating, petitioning, leafleting, etc.) – but would also probably organise volunteers to clear the land of litter, undertake a study of flora and fauna on the land in conjunction with local schools, and so on. Members of FOE are expected to be active members, not just passive supporters.

The pressure to be active is only moral, of course, but the expectation exists, and it extends to participation in the local group's decision-making as well as its actions. Although FOE has undoubtedly benefited from some high-profile individuals at the national level – Jonathon Porritt, director of Friends of the Earth from 1984 to 1990, adviser to Prince Charles and dubbed by *The Times* as 'the acceptable face of green activism', is the best-known example – they do not exercise effective central control. There is a very clear distinction here between FOE and Greenpeace. The latter does not really have a conception of internal democracy in the sense of mass participation; the mass membership is there to provide support, not direction. In FOE, the stress is upon individual commitment and activity. It is indicative that FOE activists were instrumental in the creation of the Green Party. Impressionistic evidence suggests that many of those active in more radical groups such as Earth First are past activists in FOE. Involvement in FOE socialises people into *doing* things as well as professing certain beliefs. Given this, and the parlous state of the Green Party electorally, FOE offers the only real chance for the ecologically-minded to participate in actions which often produce concrete results at the local level, and yet stop short of illegal activities. 'Green' individuals can vote for the Green Party (if there is a candidate), but they know this is essentially a symbolic gesture; they can subscribe to Greenpeace, but most of Greenpeace's activities are at the national/international level; or they can become involved with FOE and look for local solutions to local problems, as well as feeling they are part of a process which impacts at the national level. These are not exclusive alternatives, of course; what evidence we have suggests that most 'greens' do all three. The point remains, however, that FOE represents the core of local activism among the UK's green movement.

GREENPEACE

The ideology may be much the same, but when it comes to organisation and decision-making, FOE and Greenpeace could hardly be more different. Greenpeace is the best-known environmental group in the world. FOE may claim to have the largest network of greens on a global scale, but it is Greenpeace which grabs the headlines – precisely because of its chosen *modus operandi*. Greenpeace has an organisational structure not dissimilar from that of a private-sector company, and a command and decision-making system which is almost military in nature. This is not meant to be pejorative, but to emphasise the point that Greenpeace has a strong conception of staff and line. It has supporters, whose input is to provide money and moral support, and it has its 'front-line troops', whose function is to get out there and carry out the 'actions'. The actions are deliberately targeted at obtaining maximum exposure from the media and – while the coverage may not always have been as positive as Greenpeace would like – there can be no doubt that they have been very successful in getting that media exposure.

Greenpeace was formed in 1971, when protesters against nuclear testing off Alaska (the 'Don't Make A Wave' Committee, based in Vancouver) renamed their group; the UK branch was established in 1978. From the outset, the emphasis was on public direct action, the first protest taking the form of a dozen activists sailing a small boat into the American nuclear testing zone in the sea off Alaska. Although their tactical repertoire has since expanded into more conventional areas, this kind of potentially hazardous direct action has always been at the core of their thinking. As Greenpeace itself has expressed it, 'determined individuals can alter the actions and purposes of even the most powerful by "bearing witness"; that is, by drawing attention to an abuse of the environment through their unwavering presence at the scene, whatever the risk'.[11] There have been occasions when this has meant activists coming under attack, but Greenpeace is firmly committed to the principle of non-violence, rejecting attacks on either people or property. As with FOE and CND, Greenpeace argues that direct action is necessary, but not sufficient; research, analysis and conventional lobbying are seen as important. As with CND, the balance between conventional and less conventional tactics has been the source of serious internal disagreement.

Greenpeace grew steadily in the seventies, its number of supporters around the world rising to some 30,000 by 1979. The eighties was a period of explosive growth, support reaching the million mark by 1985 and peaking at around five million by 1990.[12] It was during the eighties that Greenpeace became a genuinely international organisation, with supporters drawn from over 150 countries, and 49 offices established in 32 countries. The organisation has always been strongest in the advanced industrialised societies of the West – which Greenpeace sees as only right: 'it is they who should bear the burden of cleaning up the environment, having been largely responsible for polluting it in the first place'.[13] There has been some decline in the nineties. In 1996, there are 43 offices in 30 countries employing some 1,300 staff, with support put at just over three million. Supporters in Britain number about 411,000; their subscriptions and revenue from the sale of T-shirts, badges, etc. generate an annual income of £9 million – approximately 10 per cent of Greenpeace's global income – although the recent decline in membership has meant a reduction in paid staff from around 80 to 60.

As one might expect, Greenpeace's campaigning priorities tend to fluctuate over time, often in response to specific events like nuclear testing. Overall, however, there have been a number of persistent themes:

- the 'greenhouse effect' and climate change;
- the dangers of nuclear energy and problems of disposal of nuclear waste (especially highlighting the UK's role in international disposal);
- opposition to nuclear weapons (using arguments which stress the possibility of accidents and dangers of transportation rather than adopt the moral tone of CND's thinking); exposure of links between civil and military nuclear programmes; opposition to the international trade in plutonium which, it is argued, leads to nuclear weapons proliferation;
- ocean ecology (concentrating partly on threatened species, especially whales, and partly on pollution, especially toxic waste);
- terrestrial ecology (campaigning to preserve rain forests and against ecologically unsound agriculture; highlighting the role of governments, banks, and aid agencies in encouraging what are seen as undesirable practices in both these areas);
- toxic materials – argued to be the most prevalent form of pollution (campaigning in the developed world ultimately to end the production of such toxic materials, and warning third world countries against accepting first world toxic waste).

As with FOE, the tactics Greenpeace employs in pursuit of these campaigning priorities are a mixture of the conventional and unconventional, with the difference that Greenpeace's activities are often international in scope. They are best known, of course, for their direct action, particularly at sea – where the international nature of Greenpeace is an obvious advantage. Although still active in such areas as campaigning to save the whale or prevent the culling of baby seals, Greenpeace now spends much of its time fighting multi-national corporations and governments. At the time of writing (1996), Greenpeace International owns some eight ships, thirty inflatables and a helicopter; they also charter other vessels when circumstances demand. Given the variety of activities undertaken, it is hard to provide a watertight classification, but broadly they are used for two types of action – intervention and monitoring. Intervention typically takes the form of placing vessels and activists in prohibited zones – the classic examples being, of course, the protests against French nuclear testing at Mururoa. This was one of the first actions ever undertaken by Greenpeace when, in 1972, David McTaggart, one of the founding members of Greenpeace, took his yacht into the area and was rammed by French warships before having the yacht seized and impounded by the French authorities. The tactic has been used at least seven times since, most notably in 1985 (when the *Rainbow Warrior* was bombed by agents of the French Secret Service in Auckland, resulting in the death of a Greenpeace photographer) and again in 1995 – when the campaign received massive publicity worldwide with 160 governments registering a protest, and which arguably contributed to the French decision to mount only six tests rather than the eight originally planned. The tactic has also been used to protest against Soviet testing at Novaya Zemlya in 1990, and Chinese testing in 1996. Monitoring, normally of pollution of one form or another, does not usually enjoy such a high profile – although the discovery that a Russian tanker was dumping liquid nuclear waste into the sea off Japan in 1993 was a notable exception.

In all these cases, Greenpeace has become highly skilled at exploiting media coverage to the full. This is an area in which the UK arm of Greenpeace is important, as it is home to Greenpeace Communications, with 29 staff and a budget in 1995 of some $1.5 million. Greenpeace Communications maintains an international contact base of freelance photographers and cameramen, has its own editing facilities, and runs on a 24-hour basis. Their photographs and video footage are transmitted by satellite to the London office and then distributed to international TV and print news agencies free of charge. More often than not, this means that such agencies are dependent upon Greenpeace for footage – something which has caused disquiet among both the news organisations and Greenpeace's targets. ITN, for example, wanted to put its own cameraman on the Greenpeace boats heading for Mururoa in 1995. Greenpeace allowed an ITN correspondent to sail with them, but insisted that all video footage would be provided by themselves. The first thing the French did on boarding the new *Rainbow Warrior* during this action was to destroy the vessel's satellite links.

It was an issue which came to the fore during the 1995 campaign to prevent Shell from dumping its Brent Spar oil installation into the North Sea. As well as occupying the rig, Greenpeace ensured that dramatic video footage was made available. Greenpeace's own estimates of the direct costs of this particular operation amounted to some £350,000 (out of a total campaign cost of around £1.4 million). As a BBC news editor commented, this was far more than the BBC could have afforded: 'this particular David is not armed with a slingshot so much as an AK47'.[14] A Channel Four executive voiced generally-held concerns among the media establishment over this and other Greenpeace actions: 'On Brent Spar we were bounced . . . we all took great pains to represent Shell's side of the argument. By the time the broadcasters tried to intervene on the scientific analysis, the story had long since been spun far, far into Greenpeace's direction. When we attempted to pull the story back, the pictures provided to us showed plucky helicopters riding into a fusillade of water cannons.'[15] Greenpeace's campaign led to consumer boycotts in Germany, Holland and Denmark which forced Shell's main board into reversing its British company's decision to dump – much to the fury of the British government. Despite the embarrassment of having subsequently to apologise publicly to Shell because they had wrongly estimated the pollution risk posed by the oil installation, Greenpeace hails this as one of its most significant victories – and it is certainly an excellent example of the organisation's skilful use of the media on a transnational scale.

Greenpeace does not just rely upon high-profile actions, it also expends considerable effort upon more conventional means of exercising pressure. In the UK context, this ranges from publicising the extent of 'legal' pollution of Britain's rivers and seas, to issuing reports upon the safety records of British nuclear establishments, and to commissioning opinion polls on the extent to which the British electorate prioritises environmental issues when it comes to voting in general elections. The basis for much of this is the scientific expertise Greenpeace can draw upon from its own staff and sympathetic outsiders. This ensures that Greenpeace can attempt to take on the 'official' scientific establishment on its own terms. It was seen to good effect in the longstanding campaign against the establishment of the Thorp nuclear re-processing plant at Sellafield.[16] Although Greenpeace did mount some direct action over this issue, most of its efforts were expended upon a battle through the courts. British Nuclear Fuels disputed the right of Greenpeace to bring a case against them. In a decision which could well have significant implications for other campaigns in the future, Greenpeace was granted the right to do so (*locus standi* – the right to appear). In the event, the battle was finally lost, but not before Greenpeace was able both to present its own evidence in court and to question that of BNFL.

Greenpeace UK makes a significant input to the overall effort to substantiate the international organisation's arguments with a strong scientific basis. It is the UK arm which spearheads the questioning of the interface between science and public policy, as Greenpeace UK has assembled a critique of the risk assessment methodology commonly used by decision-makers and the scientific establishment. Greenpeace advocates a precautionary approach to environmental protection, in contrast to what it argues is the prevailing notion that industry should continue to produce whatever it wishes unless there is absolute proof that a given substance is causing environmental harm. Such general arguments are then applied to specific campaigns which change over time; in the mid-nineties, for example, Greenpeace UK is particularly concerned with what it sees as the seriously underestimated problem of hormone-disrupting chemicals, while other national Greenpeace organisations will apply the same general thinking to other perceived problems.

Between the two extremes of dramatic direct action and scientific argument, Greenpeace also becomes involved in many aspects of current public policy, when it often uses conventional methods of applying pressure. Greenpeace UK, for example, leads the way in advocating the use of solar power, and exhorts its supporters not only to install their own solar panels but also to engage in the conventional lobbying of MPs and electricity companies. In the mid-nineties it has struck an alliance with much of the UK's fishing industry in opposition to what it dubs 'industrial over-fishing' by other nations; while the British fishermen are concerned with their livelihoods, Greenpeace is concerned with maintaining biodiversity. As we shall see, it has (eventually) become involved in the spate of anti-road-building campaigning which has swept the UK in recent years. Sometimes its ideology can lead it into apparently unpopular stances. The Conservative Government's decision in 1993 to impose VAT on domestic fuel was widely condemned across the political spectrum, but Greenpeace (together with FOE) felt obliged to support the change – as it would encourage greater energy efficiency and conservation, and reflected Greenpeace's thinking on the need to bring home to people the true cost of energy use. They were careful, however, to accompany this stance with a demand that low-income households be compensated via the social security system for higher domestic fuel prices, and pointed out that any extra revenue should go towards more public investment in energy conservation and efficiency.

One can appreciate, then, that Greenpeace has always pursued a multi-faceted tactical approach in its campaigning. Equally clear is that, whatever the arguments about its concrete gains in changing public policies, it has been remarkably successful in terms of attracting media coverage and supporters on a global scale. As long as the organisation was growing throughout the seventies and eighties, any internal dissent over tactics was muted. In the nineties, however, the organisation has had to cope with a relative decline in support. This in turn has brought into the open some disquiet over what Greenpeace does. Perhaps surprisingly, however, there has been little dispute over how it runs itself. Let us look at this latter aspect first.

As mentioned above, decision-making in Greenpeace is quite unlike that in any of the other movements and organisations which we are looking at. At the international level, Greenpeace is run by a Council. Each national Greenpeace office – and it is significant that they are termed 'offices' rather than organisations or movements – appoints a representative to this Council, which then makes decisions upon the overall direction, policy and budget allocations. Each national office is an autonomous entity, but decides upon its specific campaigning priorities within these parameters. National offices have their own Boards of Directors and Executive Directors. In the case of Greenpeace UK, the Executive Director is Lord Melchett, a former junior minister in the last Labour Government. He is assisted by five other directors, covering the areas of Campaigns and Programmes, Communications, Legal matters (which includes the Investigations and Solutions Unit that seeks to identify environmental offenders), Resources, and Marketing. This relatively centralised, corporate-like structure has not evolved over time as Greenpeace has grown, but has been part of its ethos since its inception. David McTaggart (one of the founders and, today, honorary international chairman) has always emphasised the benefits of strong leadership, arguing that consensus is not the way to build a massive international movement. This appears to have been accepted by supporters, although it is hard to say for sure, given that they have no way of voicing dissent other than by ceasing to support the organisation.

There has, however, been dissent at both the international and national level over what Greenpeace has chosen to do during the nineties. At the international level, this has been stimulated by the decline in support and hence the reduced revenue. Since 1994, Greenpeace International has been struggling to impose budget cuts of almost 20 per cent. The decision has been taken to cut the number of salaried staff and campaigners, while protecting the organisation's capital assets, especially its marine fleet. This has impacted upon Greenpeace UK, which is planning to reduce its staff by up to a quarter. At the time of writing, Greenpeace intends to move Greenpeace Communications from London to Amsterdam as part of the process of centralising the organisation and cutting costs – a decision which has led most of the affected staff to resign in protest. Such problems of 'downsizing' are not our main concern, however; of more interest has been dissatisfaction with Greenpeace (and other 'established' environmental groups) at the national level, which has led to a variety of more radical direct action.

ENVIRONMENTAL PROTEST AND 'DISORGANISATIONS'

The environmental movement is so wide-ranging it would be impossible to detail here all the different campaigns that have taken place in the UK in recent years. Many have been purely localised actions, in which members and supporters of the larger environmental organisations have been active without the organisation itself becoming directly involved. Others are single-issue organisations which have grown from local roots to quite sizeable groups – one example would be Surfers Against Sewage, which has grown from a small group of surfers based primarily in Cornwall to an organisation claiming some 23,000 supporters in 1996. Analysis of all these various activities would require a book in itself. There have been two particular areas that have attracted considerable interest, however, especially in the nineties. These are protests against the building of new roads and campaigns based upon the idea of animal rights. One thing they have in common is that each has inspired protest significantly more radical than that associated with the main environmental groups (extending as far as terrorism in one case) and yet also managed to secure 'respectable' middle-class support.

Such a combination is perhaps less surprising in the case of the anti-roads protests which have become increasingly common during the nineties. In common with other planning issues, proposals to build new motorways and by-passes have often provoked local protests in the past, leading to the coining of the term NIMBY-ism (Not In My Back Yard). What has differentiated the most recent wave of protests has been the introduction of direct action – non-violent, in the sense of violence against people, but also entailing considerable damage to property. Between 1993 and 1996, there have been such protests across the whole of the UK – at, for example, Twyford Down, the M11 extension in East London, Bath (Solsbury Hill), Exeter, Glasgow, Lancashire, Lincolnshire, Manchester, Newcastle, Newbury, Norfolk and Somerset. When the campaigns first started, they tended to use conventional tactics. Friends of the Earth, for example, which has been particularly active in the Twyford Down protest, pursued a strategy of campaigning in the media, lobbying at both Westminster and Brussels and restricting its NVDA to peaceful demonstrations and vigils at the construction sites. The new element came with the involvement of the

British arm of Earth First!, an organisation first established in America.

Set up in the UK in 1991, Earth First! claims 63 autonomous local groups in the UK in 1996, and is active in thirteen countries across the world. Given the lack of formal membership, its actual size is hard to estimate, and in any case almost certainly fluctuates; nevertheless, some 3,000 activists attended a gathering in 1996 to assess their campaigning to date and their future direction.[17] In terms of its ideology, tactics and organisation, it quite deliberately distances itself from the more established groupings like FOE and Greenpeace – it does not take much imagination to work out to whom they are referring in their publicity material when they pose the question: 'are you tired of namby-pamby environmental groups that are more worried about their image than saving wilderness?' It makes great play of the fact that it is not an organisation, but a movement; it has no members as such, no central office, no paid officers, and no decision-making boards. It champions biocentric or 'deep green' views, and is almost entirely oriented towards direct action. Its activists do not believe in compromise; so, for example, they do not respond to new road projects by suggesting alternative routes, but rather they campaign for no road at all. As the UK arm of Earth First! puts it, 'Earth Firsters quite often have to break the law to achieve their ends, but this is not a drawback, it's fun!'[18] – although they stress that how far people go is entirely a matter of personal choice. As far as one can tell, Earth First! supporters have been in the forefront of the more radical tactics employed by anti-roads protesters in recent years – everything from living in trees scheduled for felling, to sabotaging bulldozers and blockading roads, and to declaring part of East London the Republic of Wanstonia. They have been joined by other anti-roads groups in the mid-nineties, some of them purely localised but others more wide-spread. A good example of the latter is Reclaim the Streets, which grew out of the Twyford and M11 protests and is another grouping which emphasises that it is a 'disorganisation' – in other words, a network of activists, in this case 'committed to ending the rule of the car'. As with Earth First!, much stress is laid by Reclaim the Streets activists on the differences between themselves and groups such as Greenpeace: 'we are not a send-a-donation/get-the-mag/sit-in-your-armchair organisation. We are about getting involved and changing things through our own actions'.[19] By mid-1996, Reclaim the Streets had organised some fifteen 'parties' in which main roads were blocked; one in London attracted an estimated 8,000 participants.[20]

Such networks are to Britain in the nineties what the hard-line NVDA activists of Greenham and Cruisewatch were in the eighties. They have been much more successful in enlisting support among the local communities in which they campaign, however; probably because of the specifically local nature of much of their protest. There have been many media reports drawing attention to the unusual spectacle of pillars of the local community voicing sympathy with their actions and even joining in themselves. Their example may also be argued to have been instrumental in some re-ordering of priorities by FOE. Although always opposed to major programmes of new road-building, FOE did not seem to give much priority to the issue in the early nineties. By 1995, however, FOE had moved anti-roads campaigning to the top of its domestic agenda, taking a prominent role in the Newbury protest in particular. Greenpeace has remained somewhat aloof, rejecting criticism from the anti-roads campaigners that it should become more involved by arguing that each organisation and movement should do its own thing. The differing responses of the established environmental groups to this new outbreak of NVDA reinforces the point we made earlier about the nature of decision-making in each of them. Greenpeace can decide to maintain a certain distance between itself and groups such as Earth First!; if its supporters disagree with this, then realistically their only option is to cease supporting Greenpeace. This was the case with some of Earth First!'s founders – they left Greenpeace because they were disillusioned with what they saw as its inadequate commitment to direct action in exactly the same way that Greenpeace was founded by those dissatisfied with the tactics of such organisations as the Sierra Club. Such fission is common when organisations have top-down decision-making processes. FOE, on the other hand, with its strong principle of local autonomy and individual participation in decision-making, has no option but to respond to the wishes of its supporters on the ground.

ANIMAL RIGHTS

There are some parallels here with the way in which protest over animal rights has evolved, but the context is rather different. The established groups which are concerned with animals have a much longer history than FOE or Greenpeace. The Society for the Prevention of Cruelty to Animals was established in 1824 (becoming the royal society – RSPCA – in 1840). It has seen its membership decline in recent years, falling from over 40,000 at the beginning of the eighties to just over 21,000 in the mid-nineties, but is estimated to have a further

500,000 supporters producing an annual income in the region of £20 million. The Royal Society for the Protection of Birds [RSPB] is much larger; its membership of some 770,000 makes it one of the largest voluntary associations in the UK, producing a income similar to that of the RSPCA. Both have always acted like traditional cause groups, concentrating upon conventional lobbying rather than direct action. However, the RSPCA in particular – because it is the best known and covers all aspects of animal welfare – has always had its fair share of internal dissent stemming from those who advocated more direct action. It was such pressure during the seventies and eighties, for example, that finally persuaded the RSPCA to adopt an anti-hunting policy, as well as policies on acceptable use of animals, but it is still far from being an 'animal rights' group.[21]

Predictably, the tension between conventional and more action-oriented, unconventional tactics has also led to fission, resulting in many new groups springing up over the last twenty years. There are at least three different strands to the animal rights movement, each of which contains a mixture of conventional and unconventional groupings.

There are groups which prioritise opposition to hunting. The League Against Cruel Sports (with a 1995 membership of around 40,000) was founded in 1924 by former RSPCA members who objected to society's pro-hunting stance. It has remained committed to conventional tactics, such as lobbying and providing free legal advice for farmers and landowners who object to hunting on their land. In turn it suffered mass defection in 1964, with the formation of the Hunt Saboteurs Association. Direct action, in the form of non-violent protest and diversionary interventions, are the *raison d'être* of the HSA. There are over 140 local hunt saboteur groups in the UK in 1996, and the HSA claims that all of them are active at least once a week against their local hunts and shoots – averaging some 200 events a week.

Then there is a wider category of groups which prioritise the linked issues of farming practices and the export of live animals. A good example is Animal Aid, founded in 1977, which has some 100 local voluntary groups in Britain. Although endorsing NVDA, much of its work is more conventional, although still interventionist – for example, investigating conditions in livestock markets, factory farms, zoos and circuses, or launching large public campaigns such as the Living Without Cruelty campaign in 1985, which argued that 'food, household goods, medicines and to some extent clothing and entertainment are all dependent upon causing pain and misery to other living creatures'. The groups which have captured most of the media coverage in recent years, however, have been Compassion in World Farming (established in 1967 by a farmer concerned at the use of intensive farming methods, and with a current membership of some 10,000) and Respect for Animals (established in 1993 when the anti-fur-trade group Lynx was forced to disband following an unsuccessful libel case). They were the moving forces behind a series of demonstrations against the exportation of live animals held at British ports and airports (most notably at Shoreham, Brightlingsea and Coventry) during 1995. These attracted considerable attention, not just because of the telegenic attractions of such actions, but because they attracted considerable local support – and, as in the case of some anti-roads protests, much of that support was from the middle class and middle-aged members of the local community. The Brightlingsea protest in particular caught the media's attention, producing such headlines as 'Grandmothers versus the police in the Battle of Brightlingsea', and the issue hit the front pages when in February 1995 Jill Phipps, a 31-year-old single mother and veteran animal rights protester, was killed after falling under a lorry carrying calves to Coventry Airport.

It is in the third main strand of the animal rights movement that direct action has become the most notorious, however. This strand comprises those who prioritise concerns over the use of animals in medical and scientific research. The longest-established groups are the National Anti-Vivisection Society (founded 1875) and the British Union for the Abolition of Vivisection (founded 1898). These use advertising and lobbying to encourage public concern about scientific experiments, but are firmly opposed to any kind of violent protest. This is in contrast to a more recent arrival on the scene, the Animal Liberation Front (ALF). Founded in 1976, the ALF itself grew out of a group of Hunt Saboteurs who decided in 1972 to start using direct action against vehicles operated by hunt members. By 1973, this had escalated into arson attacks on laboratories which used animals for experimentation, action which resulted in the imprisonment of some activists who then formed the ALF upon their release. The ALF began by breaking into laboratories and factory farms to remove animals, but then moved on to bombing the cars of laboratory staff (there are some 18,000 British researchers licensed to carry out experiments on animals) and arson attacks – on both laboratories and retail stores such as Harrods and McDonalds. ALF was estimated by police in 1992 to have been responsible for over 400 incendiary attacks. In a further escalation, a group known as the Justice Department has emerged; in 1993, this group claimed responsibility for a bombing campaign in which 32 bombs were planted, injuring 7 people. It also claims to have sent thirteen parcel bombs containing empty syringes to animal researchers, threatening to send them full of HIV-infected blood next time. The ALF says it does not know the identities of members of the Justice Department, but issues press releases on their behalf. The ALF itself has no members as such – just a number of local cells which, for security purposes, remain self-contained; any activist is allowed to attribute an attack to the ALF, so long as the operation is in keeping with the group's objectives. The ALF claims some 2,500 in its Supporters Group, producing an annual income of around £60,000. Its activists claim there are 2,000 among them who would attack shops; of those, 1,000 would be prepared to rescue animals from farms; of those, maybe 200 would be prepared to commit arson; police estimate there to be a 'hard core' of about 60 activists involved in the most serious offences.[22] The police were sufficiently concerned by such activities to form a special unit at Scotland Yard in 1985, the Animal Rights National Index, which recorded over 3,000 crimes between 1990 and 1992. Moreover, the Anti-Terrorist Squad has since been involved, partly as a result of lobbying of the Home Secretary by the scientific community which argues that such activists should be treated as terrorists.

The Green Party

If the ALF represents one extreme of the environmental movement, another is the only group to attempt to engage directly with the political system by participating fully as a political party, Britain's Green Party. The Green Party is certainly far removed from the likes of the ALF (it 'does not remotely approve of guerrilla tactics of the sort used by animal rights bombers'[23]), yet it is in many ways much more akin to a social movement than a conventional political party. Its record to date certainly presents us with a conundrum. It started before any of the other green parties in Europe, it operates in a society which has a greater proportion of its population enlisted as members and supporters of environmental groups than any other in Europe – and yet it has been stunningly unsuccessful. The explanations lie in the interplay between the party's ideology and organisation and the British political system. Let us start by examining its progress to date, and then consider these explanations.

The Green Party started its life as the People Party (a local initiative in Coventry in 1973), changed its name to the Ecology Party in 1975, and finally became the Green Party in 1985. It fought its first General

Election in February 1974, but did not become a significant factor on the electoral scene until 1979, when it fielded sufficient candidates to qualify for its first party political broadcast on television. As Table 8.1 shows, with one exception its has signally failed to attract the British electorate ever since.

It is not alone in this, of course, as green parties throughout Europe have all struggled to attract mass electoral support. Nevertheless, while the German Greens scored over 7 per cent in the 1994 all-Germany elections (as did the French Greens in their 1993 election), and (along with Luxembourg and Ireland) boosted that to some 10 per cent in the 1994 European elections, the British Green Party's record of averaging around 1.3 per cent in national elections and (1989 apart) around 3 per cent in European elections is pretty poor. Of course, part of the answer lies in the British first-past-the-post electoral system, which squeezes out well established parties like the Liberal Democrats, let alone much smaller parties. Even as a repository for 'protest votes', the Green Party faces stiff competition – not just from the Liberal Democrats, but also the nationalist parties of Scotland and Wales.

The Green Party has scored one apparent success, achieving 15 per cent of the vote in the 1989 European elections (in which it came second, ahead of Labour, in six seats), the highest percentage of the national vote ever won by a green party in any European state – though it should be remembered this was on the basis of a low turn-out of some 36 per cent of the electorate. Rootes has argued that this aberrant result can be explained by a unique set of electoral circumstances.[24] Margaret Thatcher's 1988 speech to the Royal Society, in which she made clear that she had become convinced of the need to address key environmental issues like global warming, and the spate of environmentalist motions presented to the subsequent Conservative Party Conference, helped to move Green issues nearer the top of the political agenda. By the time of the 1989 European election, the Conservatives

Table 8.1. Green Party electoral record

British General Election	Number of candidates	Average percent of vote won by candidates	European Parliament Election	Number of candidates	Average percent of vote won by candidates
Feb 1974	5	1.8	1979	3	3.6
Oct 1974	4	0.7	1984	16	2.6
1979	50	1.5	1989	all seats	15
1983	106	1.0	1994	all seats	3.2
1987	133	1.4			
1992	256	1.3			

were electorally unpopular, not least because they had just introduced the Poll Tax. Labour was still in the throes of modernisation, and had recently alienated some on its own left wing by dashing all realistic chance of returning to its stance of unilateral nuclear disarmament. The Liberal Democrats had only recently completed the bruising merger between the former Liberals and the Social Democrats. In other words, there was a great number of potentially disaffected voters around in 1989 and – especially as it was a European, rather than a national, election – quite a few were prepared to shift their allegiance to the Greens. It was only a temporary shift, however. Almost all of them returned to their various folds in 1992, leaving the Greens to fall back on the tiny percentage of the electorate they have been able to attract at all other times. In a society which seems to boast such a large number of citizens who are sufficiently interested in environmental issues to support voluntary groups and campaigns, such a lack of success cannot be attributed to the electoral system alone; other factors must be involved.

One of those is undoubtedly ideology. All of Europe's green parties have disagreements over ideology, being pulled between those who advocate an uncompromising, 'deep green' approach (the 'fundamentalists') and those who favour a more accommodating approach (the 'realists'). It brings us back to Richardson's distinction between biocentric and anthropocentric values.[25] In terms of green parties, the distinction is usually drawn between ecological (biocentric) and environmental (anthropocentric) ideologies. An ecological ideology stresses the 'rights' of the planet just as much as the rights of people; it is firmly opposed to economic growth; and it has a strong commitment to participatory values which make it suspicious of 'leadership'. An environmental ideology, while sharing with the deep greens the overall view of a conserver society rather than a consumer one, emphasises those aspects which are specifically to the benefit of humans, and is far more pragmatic both in terms of how parties should be run and organised, and in striking compromises in order to cooperate with other, more mainstream, parties. The British Green Party is viewed with a mixture of admiration and exasperation by other, more successful, European green parties, as it started with an uncompromising ecological ideology and has stayed with that ever since. Its ideology is radical and wide-ranging, but three main components can be identified.

First, there are the kind of commitments one might expect from any European Socialist party, especially in terms of political reform and international relations. On the domestic political front, the Greens not surprisingly favour a change in the electoral system to one based upon proportional representation, and would introduce a Bill of Rights and a Freedom of Information Act. Devolution is advocated, not just to Scotland and Wales, but also to the English regions – although it is not clear how this commitment to decentralisation squares with the challenge of actually implementing many of the Party's more fundamental policies, which would seem to require national or supranational action.[26] On the international front, there is outright opposition to nuclear weaponry. Moreover, a Green government would not only cancel Trident and make significant reductions in military spending overall, but would also leave NATO. While it would remain in, and would favour enlargement of, the EU, it would campaign to have Europe's Council of Ministers abolished and the European Parliament assume the supreme role. Aid to the third world would be increased, and the Party would campaign for the cancellation of third world debt, but a Green government would only support sustainable aid projects.

Second, there is the range of policies one would expect from any environmental party. A strong opposition to the use of nuclear energy is complemented by a commitment to move to renewable energy sources. Using less energy would be a priority. Penalties and incentives to encourage dramatic increases in energy conservation would include a complete overhaul of the taxation system, the aim being to shift the tax burden away from the proceeds of people's work (income tax, national insurance, VAT) and towards taxes on energy, pollution and raw materials. There would be a massive shift in public investment away from road-building and towards public transport – revitalising the canal system and expanding cycle paths, as well as the rail and bus systems. Planning laws would encourage the location of shops and workplaces close to centres of population rather than out of town. Recycling, more organic agriculture, and so on – are all part of what one might describe as a typical environmental policy agenda.

Third, however, there is also a distinctly ecological agenda which makes Britain's Green Party stand out as being rather more purist than most others in Europe. There is a flat acceptance that the pursuit of economic growth would have to come to an end. One effect of this would be a major restructuring of the pattern of trade. Gone would be the days of Britain as a major international trading nation; while accepting that some international trade is necessary, the British Greens believe that present levels of international trade are unnecessarily high, and are thus wasteful of energy and resources. Hence they are opposed to GATT (the General Agreement on Tariffs and Trade), or indeed any supranational organisation with the power to challenge a domestic policy which is seen as a 'barrier to trade' – which leads one to suspect that a Green government would not remain in the EU for very long. Given the Greens' hostile attitude towards multi-national companies, which they characterise as unaccountable bodies which cause massive environmental damage, one might also surmise that inward investment in the UK would decline dramatically. None of this is in the slightest way problematic for the Greens, as they favour a move to an entirely different kind of economic system, in which small is definitely beautiful. They wish to see the development of strong *local* economies; communities which have their own banks to provide local investment, people living and working locally – in short, an interlocking system of small communities, 'each as self-sufficient as possible'. They would encourage the growth of barter, via Local Exchange and Trading Schemes (LETS[27]). There is even a long-term aim of reducing the UK's population; although wary now of putting figures to this, the party used to talk in terms of a cut from 56 million to around 40 million.

This vision of smaller, more self-sufficient units, be they nations or local communities, producing more of what they need themselves and thus using less energy and resources, lies at the heart of Green economic thinking. It is part of a wider philosophical approach which emphasises cooperation rather than competition, which guides the party's firm endorsement of women's rights, gay rights, racial equality, social justice and a general recognition of 'difference' in society. It is clear that what is being offered is not just an amelioration of some of the less desirable effects of the industrial and consumer society, but a fundamentally different way of conducting our lives and assessing our self-worth. It is summed up in the Party's declaration on the first pages of its manifesto at the time of the 1992 general election: 'we need to stop building on the quicksand of materialism, patriarchy, competition and aggression'; and epitomised in its practice of preceding its conference debates with a few minutes silence in which delegates 'attune' themselves before beginning their work. This is a very different kind of politics.

The difference extends to the way in which the Party organises itself. Although it has a national framework, its strong belief in decentralisation is reflected in a structure in which local party organisations have much more autonomy than their counterparts in the main parties. Indeed, national officers are often unaware of what is happening at the local level, let alone in control of it. Voting at the annual conference is open to any member who attends, not just to official delegates. The stress upon participative processes and structures is, of course, facilitated by the relatively small size of the party. Membership for much of the eighties was around 5,000; it peaked at nearly 20,000 at the end of the eighties, but fell to 6,500 by 1992, and 4,500 by 1993. It has remained at this kind of level since. The membership is an articulate group of people; a survey of members at the beginning of the nineties found that two-thirds were graduates or students and nearly half were employed in professional or technical occupations, with a notable concentration in teaching and caring professions.[28]

Some within the Party are clearly very happy with this mix of a radical ideological agenda and a *modus operandi* which is lightyears away from the internal politics of the mainstream parties. Others, however, have their doubts, on the organisational front if not the ideological. The disagreement has come to a head over the question of leadership. The Party has always resisted the idea of a single national leader, insisting instead that it should be guided by a collective leadership (usually two or three individuals). Some have become increasingly impatient with this, primarily because they feel the British electorate will never take the Party seriously or even be stimulated to consider its arguments unless there is a single leader who can personify the Party in the media and the public eye. They are also convinced of the need to streamline the Party's rather nebulous decision-making system, introducing what they see as a necessary degree of centralisation in the form of an authoritative National Executive. Arguing that the urgency of the looming environmental crisis is so great that they had to aim for government within 20 years, this faction within the Party (variously dubbed the 'realists' or 'electoralists') launched the Green 2000 campaign in 1990, aimed in part at internal reorganisation. They won their battle initially, when the 1991 Conference voted to create a National Executive to provide day-to-day direction of the Party's affairs, and elected a clear majority of 'realists' to it. It was a short-lived victory, however, as not only was the new Executive counter-balanced by a Regional Council dominated by the ideologically-pure 'fundamentalists', but at the 1992 conference the decentralists swept the elections for the Executive.

This reversal led to the resignation of one of the Party's better-known figures, former chairwoman Sara Parkin, who complained that the Party's reluctance to streamline and to some extent to formalise the way in which it ran itself would lead to it becoming 'a rump with no relevance to British politics in the foreseeable future'.[29] Any doubts that the Party might yet place electoral pragmatism before ideological purity were dispensed with two years later, when Parkin's departure was followed by that of the single best-known figure, Jonathon Porritt. One of the party's founders, Porritt was suspended for recommending that a fellow member support a Plaid Cymru candidate in the 1994 European Elections, rather than the Green Party candidate. Porritt defended himself by pointing to a past history of cooperation between the Greens and the Welsh Nationalists, and the advantages of tactical voting in this particular instance (Plaid Cymru stood a good chance of overtaking Labour). Such pragmatic considerations cut no ice with the Party's fundamentalists, however. Porritt left more in sorrow than in anger – 'I admit I was never hot on constitutional matters, but my crime (endorsing a Plaid Cymru candidate . . . on the grounds that he was both green and could well get elected, whereas the Green Party's Euro candidate was truly, madly, deeply green, but unlikely to save his deposit) seems a little out of proportion to the punishment – if common sense is your measure'.[30] Nevertheless, he was not the only one within the Party to equate 'deep' greenness with electoral insanity.

Overall, it is hardly surprising that the Green Party has found itself marginalised in the party political battle, and indeed it is still unsure as to whether it even wants to be in the fight. Its highly participatory style of organisation and decision-making makes even New Labour's much-hyped transition to a one-member-one-vote system of decision-making seem elitist and staid. There is certainly no chance of the Greens adopting New Labour's philosophy of a strong leadership and an acceptance of the market in its ideology in order to secure electoral gains. Nor does the Green Party's ideology sit comfortably with the prevailing consensus in British politics. The Greens take the long view, whereas the rest of Britain's political parties – and, indeed, political culture itself – is firmly geared to a much shorter-term perspective. Take an example like organic farming. In conventional economic terms, it is 'inefficient'; Greens, however, argue that we don't need methods which are less labour intensive, but methods which are, if anything, more labour intensive, in an era when unemployment is a problem. Moreover, from a long-term perspective, a move to organic methods should bring about reductions in the disease and illness associated with the chemicals used in inorganically farmed food. The more fundamentalist, or 'deeper', greens go even further, and talk about the spiritual benefits of closer relationship with nature, which they feel will bring about a consequent reduction in mental illness. All these arguments tend to be longer in time scale than normal, and thus uncomfortable in a financial system like that of the UK, notorious for its City financial institutions driven by short-termism. The same applies to energy conservation: the private sector and financial institutions are reluctant to invest in the development of such schemes given the known short-term costs, but only potential long-term benefits. When one combines these factors with the situation in which most of the longer-established environmental pressure groups will not ally themselves with the Green Party – partly because they do not wish to jeopardise the consultative status they have won with Government departments, and partly because of the apparently hopeless electoral position of the Greens – the future does not look bright for the Party.

This is why, on several different levels, it is tempting to view the British Green Party more as part of a social movement than a proper political party. Its members are clearly primarily motivated by their beliefs, rather than the pursuit of power, and both its ideology and its organisation are at odds with the prevailing values of the political system and culture – the classic traits of a social movement. For the fundamentalists within the Party, this is evidence of their integrity, in contrast to the hypocrisy they associate with conventional, 'grey' politics. For the few pragmatists left in the Party, one suspects it is a case of '*c'est magnifique, mais ce n'est pas la guerre*'.

9 Conclusions

It is no easy matter to summarise social movements in Britain. As we have seen, the very idea of what constitutes a social movement is contested. Even if we can settle on a working definition of what constitutes such a movement, then what those movements do is highly varied. We are trying to explain and understand a form of politics which extends from formal organisations with all the paraphernalia of national conferences and managing boards, to autonomous networks of activists who may not even know each other exists; a politics which stretches from conventional lobbying all the way through to sabotage and criminal damage; a politics whose objectives range from changing one particular public policy to revolutionising the way in which we think about economic and social life; and a politics which takes place within the mainstream political institutions, and on the streets, and in people's everyday 'private' lives. Little wonder, then, that theorising about social movements tends towards sweeping generalisations – any theory which purports to explain all this has a lot of ground to cover.

We noted earlier, when reviewing the theoretical literature, that there were a number of different propositions advanced as to why people become involved with movements and how movements develop. Although the dividing line is not clear, we have argued that these differences can be summarised under the headings of an American and a European approach. The American approach concentrates upon questions of mobilisation, organisation and relationships with established political institutions and organisations. It seeks to explain why one person rather than another becomes active – either because they have grievances which they cannot pursue through conventional channels, or because they are 'entrepreneurs' mobilising resources to push themselves into the political mainstream. It is also interested in why and how movements change their aims and tactics over time. There is an implicit assumption that movements are outsiders whose ultimate aim is to become insiders, to become part of the 'normal' process of American pluralist politics, and that they will moderate their aims and tactics in order to achieve this. The European approach also has views on why people become involved, but thereafter it is much more interested in questions of ideology than organisation or tactics. For the Europeans, a social movement is something which poses a *fundamental* ideological challenge, in the sense that its aims could not possibly be achieved without a complete restructuring of the way in which we conduct our economic, social and political lives. There is a strong emphasis on the cultural dimension, an interest in how *values* are adopted, whereas the American approach is much more concerned with the political, how changes come about in public policy.

As we have already argued, if there is a problem with the American approach, it is that it sees almost any incidence of public protest as evidence of a movement at work. Equally, the European theorists tend to assume that, if a challenging idea emerges in society, this is evidence of the existence of a movement even if it is not visible to the naked eye. If you want to be cynical, then you could argue that the American approach is coloured by a belief in the openness of the American political system; there is a predisposition to look for evidence of movements trying to become part of this system, rather than rejecting it. Similarly, you can argue that the European approach is itself coloured by an almost desperate search to find the revolutionary force in society which the industrialised working class have so signally failed to become. They are competing schools of thought, then, but they rarely meet head-on; each has different preoccupations.

I think it is possible to mesh the two together, and thus use the insights each has to offer. We can only do this, however, by acknowledging two things – that the concept of a social movement needs to be broken down into more specific categories, and that within movements we find elements that need to be differentiated. While I am reluctant to add to the plethora of models and concepts in this area, it does not seem unreasonable to draw some distinctions within a scale of political behaviour which stretches from doing little more than merely subscribing to an organisation, through to developing a new identity which impacts upon 'personal' as well as public behaviour and/or engaging in potentially hazardous protest. Before we start re-defining just what is and is not a 'social movement', however, let us draw out some of the differences which exist within what are normally described as social movements in Britain.

DIFFERENCES WITHIN MOVEMENTS

When we look at the particular experiences of movements in Britain, it quickly becomes apparent that we have also to make some distinctions within them. The American perspective on social movements, for example, predicts that they will 'mature'. Starting as 'outsiders', they will tone down their aims and formalise their organisations in order to retain their supporters, forge alliances with more mainstream political organisations and eventually become 'insiders'. One could argue that such a process can be seen in the experiences of the liberal and socialist wings of the women's movement or in the development of Greenpeace and perhaps even FOE, though we shall be arguing that there are other factors at work here. Radical feminists and the Green Party, however – let alone groupings like Earth First! – do not fit this mould. Similarly, while the European perspective, resting upon a concept of social movements as challenging the established political and cultural order, does perhaps hold true for radical feminism or 'deep' greens, it is less applicable to CND, 'light' greens or liberal feminists.

One way of looking at these differences is to revise our table in Chapter Two to incorporate significant differences between movements. If we take into account what we have learnt about the aims and activities of the peace, women's and environmental movements in Britain, I would suggest that the differences shown in Table 9.1 can be noted.

Table 9.1.   Collective political action re-visited

	Ideology	*Organisation*	*Tactics*
Political Parties	reformist	formal	conventional
Protectional Interest Groups	reformist	formal	conventional (excluding strikes)
Promotional Interest Groups	reformist	formal/informal	usually conventional
Peace Movement	reformist	formal	conventional and unconventional
Women's Movement	reformist and radical	informal	conventional and personal, with sporadic use of unconventional
Environmental Movement	reformist and radical	some formal; mostly informal	conventional, unconventional, with some emphasis upon the personal
Riots	usually radical	informal	unconventional

We have to disaggregate our three movements if we are to appreciate the variety of forms of political mobilisation that are at work here. Although the peace movement is relatively homogeneous, both the women's movement and the environmental movement contain diverse groupings. The aims and tactics of liberal feminists are significantly different from those of radical feminists, for example. The environmental movement is particularly problematic, encompassing as it does groups which have similar aims but very different tactics (FOE and Greenpeace), let alone the ideological gulf between mainstream conservation organisations and the 'deep' green vision of many in the Green Party. Given this, I think we can identify at least seven different groupings or organisations – CND within the peace movement, liberal/socialist and radical feminists within the women's movement, and Greenpeace, FOE, Earth First!/ALF and the Green Party within the environmental movement.

Let us explore these differences in more detail by returning to the summary of theoretical conjectures concerning motivation, organisation, tactics and so on that we outlined earlier, and relating them to the movements we have examined. People become involved with social movements, we are told, for one of two reasons: either because they have grievances which, being politically disadvantaged, they pursue through social movements, or because they have different values from preceding generations, which are expressed in both the aims and methods of social movements. The idea of outsiders with a grievance turning to a social-movement-type of activism to pursue their aims does seem to have some relevance to the early days of the women's movement in the UK. The mainstream political institutions – Parliament, the main parties, trade unions and so on – were hostile to the idea of greater representation for women. It took women coming together, as women, outside of those institutions for the collective consciousness to grow, which then underpinned their subsequent battle for better representation within the mainstream, and made the parties and unions more receptive. This only really applies to the liberal and socialist wings of the women's movement, however. The implicit assumption of the 'grievance model' that the ultimate aim is acceptance by and incorporation into the political mainstream does not apply to the radical feminist wing, which never had any interest in such a strategy. CND certainly had a grievance, in the sense of bitter disagreement with the cross-party consensus on nuclear weapons, but one could hardly call their well educated, articulate and politically active supporters 'disadvantaged'. Nor were they seeking inclusion – they simply wanted change in one particular area of public policy. The

Greens want change on a much wider and deeper scale, but again they have not turned to social movement structures and tactics because they are excluded, but simply because they are impatient with conventional ways of conducting politics and believe the urgency of the issue they are addressing necessitates a more focused approach.

Similarly, the 'different values' thesis is true for some but not others. It is most relevant to the Greens, in the sense that they have embraced an ideology which is fundamentally different from the mainstream consensus. Even so, the post-materialist argument seems flawed in their case, in that the green movement is the one which attracts considerable support from today's younger generations, rather than just those in the 35–45 age bracket. Post-material values are also relevant to radical feminism, given the stress they place upon the recognition and acceptance of 'difference' rather than equality. One can hardly argue, however, that the representational strategy of the liberal and socialist feminists constitutes the advent of a new value system when one takes into account the 'first wave' of the women's movement, the suffragettes. The same applies to CND; its 'first wave' preceded the birth of the contemporary women's and green movements by almost a decade, and its ideology and tactics during the eighties were broadly similar to those it adopted at the end of the fifties.

Theoretical thinking on the aims of social movements falls clearly into American and European perspectives. Europeans stress the combination of cultural as well as political objectives, arguing that social movements represent a fundamental challenge to the dominant norms of advanced industrialised societies. This is clearly applicable, at least to the 'deep' greens in the environmental movement and to the radical feminist. In both cases, adherents are arguing for a completely different approach to economic, social and political life. The idea of a fundamental challenge is, however, much less germane when one considers the conservationist (or 'light' green) wing of the environmental movement, the liberal/socialist feminists and the peace movement. All are pursuing aims which are sufficiently radical to present some difficulties to the mainstream parties, but equally all could be adopted and implemented without a recasting of the entire economic and social system. They are, therefore, closer to the American conception of social movement aims, which stresses the political dimension rather than the cultural, and acknowledges that such aims may well be piecemeal rather than across the board. The American perspective, however, also argues that such aims will be subject to adaptation if that would help to preserve the social movement organisation. This is demonstrably not the case as far as

CND is concerned; we have seen how several attempts to modify the Campaign's objectives have been consistently rejected. The American perspective assumes that social movement aims will take second place to social movement survival. Our evidence from the British context suggests that, even for those parts of movements which are more interested in specific policy changes and a reformist rather than a revolutionary ideology, certain stances are effectively non-negotiable – whatever the consequences for the movement organisations. Non-negotiability is a point to which we shall return.

British social movements also fail to conform with the ideas about organisational form which have been advanced. This is not an aspect which has attracted much attention from European theorists, but it is one to which American analysts have devoted considerable attention. The American perspective argues that movements are likely either to become more formalised over time, as they engage with mainstream political institutions, or to remain informal, because this is more effective. There is little or no evidence of either of these propositions holding true in the British context. There are certainly movements, or, more accurately, parts of movements, which have 'engaged' with mainstream institutions. CND is an obvious example, and much the same can be said of Greenpeace, FOE, the Green Party and the liberal/socialist wings of the women's movement. Some of these do, indeed, have a formal organisation. CND has one, but it has had this since its inception, and has not changed it. Greenpeace does not have a formal democratic structure, but again has kept its corporate structure intact since its formation. The liberal and socialist wings of the women's movement have become progressively more engaged with the parties and trade unions, but have not formed some kind of national organisation in order to facilitate this. FOE is as happy to participate in formal planning enquiries and lobbying the main parties as it is to protest and demonstrate, yet it has remained firmly committed to a very decentralised, informal form of organisation. Most striking of all, the Green Party has 'engaged' more than any other social movement organisation, yet has resolutely refused to make its organisation more like those found in mainstream organisations – whatever the electoral cost. Similarly, there is little evidence that the Green Party, FOE and so on, as well as those like the radical feminists and the less conventional 'deep' greens, have maintained their preference for informal networks because they judge such a structure to be more effective. In some cases, loosely connected networks have been adopted for what one might term 'security' reasons – those who have good reason to be apprehensive of attempts by the state authorities to curtail their activities, like the ALF today or Cruisewatch in the eighties, are well aware of the advantages of having no head which could be lopped off. Otherwise, however, all the evidence we have suggests that informal networks are utilised because this is the kind of organisational form supporters and members want and are most comfortable with. Ideology and organisation overlap and interact: those who have become involved in British social movements have done so not just because they want to see certain changes in society, but also because they want to pursue those changes in a manner and organisational context which is far removed from conventional politics. This is something which continental European analysts are happy to acknowledge, but the instrumentality which is a hallmark of the American approach is not to be found in the British context.

The tactics employed by movements in Britain are also closer to the continental European diagnosis than that offered by the American school of thought. European commentators argue that, while movements may well include conventional activities in their tactical repertoire, unconventional tactics and direct action will always be present as well. American analysts argue that, over time, tactics will become progressively more conventional – partly because this makes it easier for movements to persuade more mainstream bodies and institutions of their case, and partly because it enables movements to retain their supporters by asking them to undertake less risky activities. For some in the British context, the question has never even arisen: for those at the forefront of direct action on environmental issues, like Earth First! or the ALF, personal risk and commitment are part of the package. For the others, one can discern efforts to follow the American line of argument. CND, for example, has had its share of internal pressure to moderate tactics in order to present a more 'respectable' image, but this pressure has always been successfully resisted. Greenpeace has had to face a lot of criticism from some of its own supporters that it has become too obsessed with protecting its assets and wary of direct action which might place them at risk. Some, indeed, have left, precisely because of this, but Greenpeace vehemently denies that it has renounced its commitment to direct action where it thinks it advisable. FOE in the late eighties and early nineties appeared to be prioritising conventional tactics like participation in planning enquiries and producing expert reports, but it has become revitalised on the direct action front by way of the anti-roads protests precisely because its own supporters insisted upon getting involved. In short, the American argument that movements will probably become more conventional over time is true in so far as most British movements have included supporters who have argued for this to happen. As with the debate over the aims of movements, however, such changes have usually failed to come about because too many of those involved see unconventional tactics as a necessary and inherent part of their mission – their attitude on this is effectively non-negotiable, whatever the apparent advantages of toning down tactics might be.

Overall, then, most of the attitudes and actions of social movements in Britain 'fit' better with the prognosis offered by continental European commentators than with the American view. The American idea, that those attracted to social movements are outsiders seeking integration into the mainstream of politics, and who see movements as the best vehicle for achieving this, has its adherents in Britain, but they are outnumbered and outweighed by those who, as the Europeans suggest, are expressing something which they feel cannot be expressed within the confines of conventional politics.

SOCIAL MOVEMENTS AND PROTEST MOVEMENTS

I think the Europeans are right to argue that a 'pure' social movement is one which offers a fundamental challenge to the prevailing cultural, social and political or economic norms of a society. This will involve protest, to varying degrees, but the crucial point is that it also involves *identity*. With a new identity comes *autonomy*, in the sense that not only can such a movement dispense with formal organisation if it so wishes (because supporters are held together with emotive rather than formal ties), but also does not *have to* interact with the established political authorities. There will always be points at which such a movement will interact with the mainstream political system; radical feminists have views on the law relating to abortion rights, for example, or 'deep' greens on pollution or transport. A 'pure' social movement, however, has a life independent of such interaction, because it is primarily concerned with changing how people think and act in almost every aspect of their lives, not just the sphere of public policy. It is, literally, a 'way of life' – a way of seeing the world from a particular perspective, and acting in accordance with that. In contrast, there are organisations and more informal groupings which are often classified as 'social movements' when, in fact, they are better construed as 'protest' movements. Some of these address a particular issue which is part of a wider social movement's agenda – Earth First! and the environmental movement, for example – and draw their support from both those who are part of that wider movement and those whose only interest is the specific issue. Others are effectively stand-alone protests –

CND is an example of a protest movement which does not have an 'umbrella' social movement in the form of a 'peace' movement. It is for these protest movements that the American approach is particularly relevant. As protest movements, their prime concern is to affect public policy. They cannot enjoy the autonomy of 'pure' social movements, because they are more interested in political rather than cultural change. Therefore, they have to interact with mainstream political institutions – and this is an area in which the American approach has a lot to offer.

We drew a distinction earlier between protest campaigns and social movements. Now we need to construct another category, distinguishing between protest and social movements. This gives us the following three categories:

• Protest campaigns: centred upon a single issue, and of limited durability; an example would be the Anti-Poll Tax federation;
• Protest movements: organisations or groupings with a wider focus than protest campaigns; centred upon a single policy area, but incorporating different issues; persist over time, sometimes helped by a formalised organisational structure; examples include CND, Greenpeace, liberal and socialist feminists;
• Social movements: groupings which espouse a wide-ranging, comprehensive and radical ideology which rejects prevailing political, economic and social norms and conventional ways of practising politics; examples include radical feminists and 'deep' greens – FOE and the Green Party.

Protest campaigns are not really our concern. We are interested here in political behaviour which persists over time. Protest movements, however, are very much part of our agenda – not just because many dub them social movements, but because they are often the 'public' face of wider and deeper 'pure' social movements.

Does this mean, then, that the social movement theory we outlined earlier is deficient or just downright wrong? Not necessarily, because the differences and nuances we are discovering here can be explained by reference to some of those theoretical insights, in particular to ideas concerning Resource Mobilisation and Political Opportunity Structure. These are ideas which remind us that we have to assess movements within their own particular contexts. Resource Mobilisation directs our attention not just towards 'personal' resources like an individual's expertise in a particular area, but also to organisational resources. It contends that emerging movements will be influenced by other organisations which already exist, and may benefit from hanging on to their coat-tails. Similarly, the whole point of the Political Opportunity Structure line of reasoning is that it insists that movements in different countries have to cope with different situations and interact with different political systems. In other words, we can use these theoretical ideas to argue that there are and have been circumstances *specific to Britain* over the last thirty years which explain why Britain's social movements do not map neatly on to general theoretical paradigms. Let us develop this a little further by looking in turn at protest movements and social movements.

PROTEST MOVEMENTS

Probably the most clear-cut example of what we mean by a *protest movement* is CND. In our matrix above, we classified CND's ideology as 'reformist' – a label guaranteed to raise the hackles of many of CND's adherents. This is because we have to draw a distinction between a *peace movement* and an organisation such as CND. The distinction rests primarily upon ideology, rather than on organisation or tactics. Using our definitions, we would expect any peace movement which was a social movement to use both conventional and unconventional tactics. CND certainly does this, as NVDA has always been part of its tactical repertoire. This is not just because direct action and demonstrations are perceived as effective ways of forcing the issue into the public eye. It is also because CND has a belief that NVDA is *morally* justified and, indeed, necessary. CND does not require or request any change in its supporters' social and economic practices in everyday life, but it would like to think that most of them were prepared to 'bear witness' at least by participating in demonstrations, if not in more direct action. Tactically, then, CND would fit our definition of a social movement. Organisationally, CND is unusual in having such a formalised, national organisation. There are historical and contextual factors behind this, of course. CND was formed before the rise of social movements in the late sixties; given that so much of its initial support came from habitual Labour Party members and supporters, it is hardly surprising that it adopted a similar federalist, bottom-up decision-making structure. The way in which local groups enjoy some autonomy in terms of campaigning objectives, and the loose association with groups such as Cruisewatch and the Greenham women, mean that the organisation is more flexible than that of Labour. Moreover, in its day-to-day operations, CND's organisational *style* – exhortative rather than directive – is reminiscent of a social movement. Its decision-making *structure*, however, is much more centralised and – in the final analysis – authoritative than we would expect from a 'typical' social movement.

It is, however, the aims of CND which really mark it out as something other than a 'pure' social movement. We have defined social movements as having radical, challenging ideologies, aims which run counter to a prevailing consensus. In the area of 'peace', we would expect a social movement to have wide-ranging aims – opposing not only nuclear and chemical or biological weapons, but also conventional weapons and arguably even armed forces altogether. In other words, we would expect them to be pacifists, with all the ramifications for their view of international relations that this would entail. Such a movement would indeed challenge the prevailing norms of society and culture, and be a truly radical ideology. As it is, in the case of CND we have an organisation which opposes only weapons of mass destruction and, with less conviction, Britain's membership of NATO. As we have seen, CND certainly numbers among its supporters those who do espouse radical pacifist views, and those who would like to see Britain move to an international position of formal neutrality. The fact remains, however, that such views have never been accepted by the Campaign as a whole.

It is interesting to note the effect of a formalised organisation in this context. CND's Annual Conference, in theory, is the authoritative voice on both the aims and tactics of the Campaign. Its authority over tactics, in reality, is limited by the relative autonomy of local groups; if they do not want to campaign on a certain issue or in a particular way, then they won't, and there is little National CND can do except exhort them to follow the national line. When it comes to aims, however, the Annual Conference is in a position to define these. Neither those who would like to radicalise CND's agenda, nor those who would like to moderate it, have been able to command a majority for their viewpoint at the Conference – but, being the good democrats they are, each feels bound to abide by the Conference line. If CND did not have this internally-democratic decision-making procedure or such a formalised structure, each of these factions may well have drifted off to do their own thing, as has been the case in the women's movement. They could still have defected, of course, but in the certain knowledge that any splinter group would be almost invisible next to CND, given the Campaign's high public profile. Were cultural change the only concern, this might not be problematic; but, given that issues of public policy were central, and desired changes could only be delivered via the political system, this would be fatal.

Organisation, then, can be said to have given stability to CND and contributed to its longevity. This is in line with the American viewpoint, which stresses such advantages flowing from formal organisation. According to the American view, however, CND would seem to have been a prime candidate for some ideological trimming along the way; after all, CND had the Labour Party converted for a while, and it would surely have made the relationship much easier if CND had dropped its opposition to NATO membership, or even concentrated its campaigning upon just Trident and Cruise, rather than the whole of Britain's nuclear deterrent. Such a softening of aims would also have contributed to a closer relationship with the Liberals/Liberal Democrats.

Why, then, has CND not compromised? The answer lies in principles which become non-negotiable because of the moral motivation of so many of its supporters. Converts to the CND cause are not seeking recognition of the validity of alternative lifestyles, as are radical feminists; they are not seeking equality before the law and in representative institutions, as are liberal/socialist feminists. They are protesting because they see weapons of mass destruction as being *evil*, and therefore morally unacceptable. They are more than happy to advance pragmatic arguments as well – that deterrence actually only increases the risk of nuclear conflagration, for example – but even if possession of nuclear weapons could be 'proved' to deter aggression, CND supporters would still argue that it was morally indefensible to threaten others with such weapons, and that alternative methods should be adopted.

Morality is a powerful motivator; it underpins justifications for breaking the law, because protesters believe that in so doing they are obeying a 'higher order' of morality than acquiescence with state laws. It does mean, however, that CND does not have the freedom of ideological manoeuvre that American commentators assume social movements to have. Supporters who are motivated by morality, rather than a desire to become 'insiders' in the political system, will not contemplate ideological trimming. CND's supporters could not be convinced to drop or downplay their opposition to existing weapons systems or to a nuclear-based alliance like NATO because of their fundamental belief that *all* nuclear weapons and alliances were morally indefensible. Equally, however, a majority have only taken this moral stance with regard to weapons of mass destruction; their moral objections have not extended as far as all weaponry or armed forces. CND, then, is too narrowly focused to fit the European conception of a social movement, but its supporters have too many non-negotiable principles for it to fit the American vision of an adaptable, integrative organisation.

The liberal and socialist wings of the women's movement come closer to fitting the American idea of a social movement. There is an obvious difference from CND, in that both these wings are part of a wider movement. From the early eighties onwards, though, these wings have not only effectively coalesced into one, they have also grown apart from their sisters in the radical feminist camp. They have come together as they have come to share the same aim, which is a representational strategy. Both believe that getting more women into public life and political institutions is the best way forward. Liberal feminists may prioritise Parliament, business and commerce, and all the parties, while socialist feminists prioritise local authorities, the unions and the Labour Party in particular; but the thinking is the same. By gaining greater representation, women will be better able to ensure *equality* for women with men. The inspiration for their efforts stems from convictions about their *rights* rather than any moral stance against evil. Protest, in the form of demonstrations and limited incidences of NVDA, are part of their repertoire, but much more important has been working within established political institutions. It is a reformist rather than a radical ideology, in that its aims could be secured without a complete restructuring of economic and social life. To be sure, in its early days, one could argue that even an ideology of equality verged on the revolutionary, in that it introduced the notion of 'the personal is political'. As cultural values have changed such that at least lip-service is now paid to the idea of greater equality between the sexes in domestic and working life, however, so the liberal and socialist feminists have concentrated upon the public sphere. Their organisation is that of a social movement – a loosely connected set of networks and groups – but their ideology is one of a protest group, focused on gaining equality within the mainstream political system. Of course, they do not just want to be admitted into the system to play the game by exactly the same rules. They would like to see some changes in those ground rules to make them more 'women-friendly' – changing the working hours of Parliament to recognise that MPs may have child-care responsibilities, for example. In overall terms, though, the aim is to participate in conventional politics in order to secure legislative guarantees for equality of opportunity, rather than rejecting the practice of conventional politics in its entirety.

Among the greens, Greenpeace is also better conceptualised as a protest movement rather than a social movement. Greenpeace certainly adopts the same causal analysis of environmental problems as other parts of the green movement, condemning the exploitation of third world countries by the advanced industrialised nations, and criticising the practices of largely uncontrolled multi-national companies, for example. It does not, however, spend much time or energy on producing in-depth analyses of the structural deficiencies of the political and economic systems of advanced industrial societies. Rather, it is a very *focused* organisation, targeting specific instances of environmental problems and abuses, and concentrating its campaigning energies upon them. To be sure, it has always covered a wide range of such issues, from marine ecology to global warming. The fact remains, however, that it does not make the specific connection between these issues and the need for a more participatory style of democracy that FOE or the Green Party do. The job of persuading people that, in the long run, they should adopt very different political and economic frames of reference is something which Greenpeace largely leaves to others; it is more concerned with bringing to public attention specific problems which are happening *now*. Greenpeace is unique among all the movements and organisations we have looked at, in that it pays little lip-service to the idea of internal democracy or consultation. It is perhaps not surprising that it tends to have something of a reputation for aloofness verging on autocracy among the wider social movement community; it is respected and admired, but not often loved because of this. It has to be said that this is of little concern to the core activists within Greenpeace. They are not primarily concerned with attracting adherents in the way that the Green Party is, but more with exposing to the glare of national and international publicity the environmental abuses that preoccupy them. Supporters are encouraged to lead green lifestyles, but that is very much secondary to their role of providing the (primarily financial) support which is necessary for the core activists to undertake their campaigning. This 'distance' between supporters and activists is accentuated by the international nature of much of Greenpeace's campaigning. Although most British protest and social movements maintain international linkages, it is really only Greenpeace which fully integrates international with domestic campaigns – Mururoa and Brent Spar being recent examples of the way in which national Greenpeace organisations bring pressure to bear domestically, as Greenpeace International simultaneously coordinates the direct action. We have already noted that, in organisational terms, Greenpeace is analogous to a business corporation. In terms of its place within the green movement, Greenpeace's core activists are analogous to frontline troops – others can get on with the job of pondering the intricacies of Basic Income Schemes or interlocking, economically self-sufficient, communities, while Greenpeace gets out there and physically confronts the polluters on their own ground.

There are clear parallels here with newer groups such as Earth First! and Reclaim the Streets, which also prioritise physical confrontation and resistance. In their present incarnation, these are also protest movements, in that they have sprung into being in the UK primarily in response to one particular area of public policy – transport and the road-building programme. Having said that, Earth First! in particular may well evolve into a 'pure' social movement. It certainly has a holistic analysis of the environmental problem, questioning the pursuit of economic growth. Having mobilised support around the roads issue, it is now mounting workshops and training camps in techniques of NVDA and the underlying causes of environmental problems. It is only a subjective impression at the time of writing, as little research has yet been undertaken, but the anti-roads campaigning of Earth First! and related groups does seem to be attracting a lot of interest among young people in Britain. To the extent that mid-nineties Britain has an 'alternative' youth subculture analogous to the student movement of the late sixties, centred upon festivals, travellers and 'recreational' drugs, it is Earth First! that is attracting its interest and support rather than the longer-established environmental groups. Whether this will develop into an integrated movement with a coherent challenge to prevailing social and economic norms remains to be seen, but the potential is certainly there.

In all these cases, then, we are arguing that their activities are better conceptualised as evidence of protest rather than as social movements – which, of course, raises the question of why we should bother to make the distinction. In fact I believe we make the distinction because protest movements have to be assessed differently from social movements. Protest movements are seeking *political* changes, alterations to specific areas of public policy, while social movements devote at least as much attention to cultural as to political change. Motivations may differ – CND objecting to the immorality of weapons of mass destruction, Greenpeace to the immorality of bequeathing to future generations a poisoned planet, liberal and socialist feminists insisting on their right to equal treatment and representation. In each case, like social movements, protest movements want changes in values and attitudes; the primary aim, though, is to secure changes in public policy. Engaging with political authorities, either directly, as in the case of liberal/socialist feminists, or indirectly via protest, as in the case of CND and Greenpeace, is more important than persuading people to change their everyday behaviour. Protest movements' record of achievement is mixed. Liberal and socialist feminists have the most to show for their efforts, even if most of the promises that have been made to them by Britain's political parties have yet to be delivered. CND has the least; Cruise may have gone, but Britain still has a highly expensive and sophisticated nuclear deterrent, and both main political parties are firmly committed to retaining it. The impact of Greenpeace *et al.* is much harder to assess; the British government is committed to various environmental targets, and has scaled down specific initiatives like the road-building programme, but it is arguable that this has had more to do with other political pressures (particularly pressures stemming from the UK's membership of the EU, and localised pressures in marginal constituencies) than as a direct result of environmental protest. Direct action by Greenpeace, Earth First!, etc., certainly has an effect upon the political authorities – like guerrilla forces, they are a constant thorn in the side of the authorities, troublesome and expensive to counteract, but ultimately an irritation rather than a serious threat – but the main impact of such action is to ensure that the issues remain in the public eye, thus creating a general climate conducive to change, rather than forcing specific policy reversals.

As protest movements, each has had to operate with the particular Political Opportunity Structure that obtains in Britain. When CND revived in the late seventies, it was already well known from its previous incarnation of a generation earlier. The political and social rights of women have been on the British political agenda throughout this century. In both cases, many on the left of the political spectrum were already convinced of their basic arguments. This gave both of them an entrée to the Labour Party in particular. This was obviously an advantage, giving each a head-start in trying to convert at least one of the main political institutions. Against this, however, we should remember that each also had powerful opponents within Labour. For CND, it was those on the right of the Party and the more pragmatically-minded (usually found at the top levels of the Party) who either sincerely believed in the value of the nuclear deterrent, or were apprehensive of the electoral consequences of any fundamental change. For women seeking an extension to their political and economic rights, it was the trade unions who were fearful of the impact of such changes on their predominantly male membership. Opportunities and obstacles were finely balanced.

This has been most problematic for CND, addressing an issue which has been particularly 'closed'. Not only has there usually been a cross-party consensus in favour of the nuclear deterrent for most of the time over the last three decades, there has also been a strong convention that decision-making in such an area is the preserve of the Executive, rather than a matter for Parliamentary, let alone public, debate. The environmental groups have not found the door quite so firmly closed in their faces, but they also have been operating in a climate where parties and politicians committed to the pursuit of economic growth are happy to pay lip-service to the idea of preserving the planet, but reluctant to take any steps which may impact adversely upon such growth. In both cases, however, they have been bolstered and aided in their efforts by another feature of the Political Opportunity System (or, as I would prefer to think of it, the political culture), which is a special regard for *morally-inspired protest*.

We have to bear in mind that the British system is unlike those of America or continental Europe. All may be liberal democracies, but Britain is unusual in tolerating an electoral system which distorts voting preferences to produce single-party governments, with an executive branch of the government that is subject to few legal restraints, but instead is 'controlled' by a sovereign Parliament. Hand-in-hand with this goes a different approach to the question of rights in civil society. Most other countries spell these out, in the form of codified constitutions and/or Bills of Rights. In Britain, we have a *residual* system – that is, it is assumed citizens have the right to do anything which is not forbidden by law. This gives a special resonance to moral protest. Deprived of the opportunities which exist in other liberal democracies to challenge the actions of the government of the day, British citizens assume they have the 'right' to protest, particularly if the source of their grievance is of a 'higher order' than selfish pursuit of self-interest. Unlike Americans, who find it hard to understand why grievances cannot be pursued within conventional, mainstream politics, or continental Europeans, who tend to assume any protest must derive from a structural contradiction in society, the British are accustomed to protest, and see it as yet another of the informal safeguards against dictatorial government which abound in the British system. For protest movements like CND or Greenpeace, this means that the mainstream institutions they are trying to influence are more closed-off than, for example, their American counterparts – thus forcing the movements into protest rather than more integrative strategies – but at least the culture in which they are operating sees such protest as legitimate, and is usually prepared to ascribe positive motives to those who engage in it.

SOCIAL MOVEMENTS

All of our protest movements above are primarily interested in the *content* rather than the *style* of contemporary British politics. Although both CND and the liberal/socialist feminists have a preference for a relatively informal, participatory style of conducting politics, each has been forced by the nature of its objectives to work with and within the more formal and hierarchical mainstream institutions, and has not found this problematic – and Greenpeace, as we have seen, campaigns regardless of the nature of the institutions it is addressing. Social movements, however, have firm views upon the *way* in which politics is conducted, as well as *what* is done. They are much more 'outsiders' than are the protest movements, advocating a 'new politics' – wanting not just widespread change in policy terms, but also a different way of going about the whole process of politics itself. The elements we are identifying as social movements – 'deep' greens and radical feminists – want an end to hierarchical, elitist politics. Deep greens favour a dramatic decentralisation of decision-making in society; radical feminists want society to give them the freedom to realise a different and autonomous lifestyle. Although virtually all their support comes from those on the left of the political spectrum, they cannot engage with established left-wing members of the polity in the way that protest movements can attempt to do, because they are using a different *discourse* – they don't even use the same language as their more established counterparts. 'Democracy' for the mainstream means representative democracy; for the social movements, it means direct democracy. 'Economics' for the mainstream is about profits and growth; for the social movements, it is about sustainability. The 'state' for the mainstream is a mechanism for regulating individuals in society; for the social movements, personal autonomy is the goal.

Radical feminism is the best example in a British context of such a social movement. Radical feminists are not interested in redistribution of resources in society in the way that liberal and socialist feminists are. They are not seeking to participate in the existing system, so much as to turn their backs on it. In their eyes, conventional society is hopelessly imbued with patriarchal attitudes and values. Certainly they argue that society should rid itself of patriarchy, but, rather than expend their efforts seeking to convince others of this, they have turned instead to creating their own non-patriarchal subculture within society. Hence the emphasis upon 'self-help' initiatives like Rape Crisis Centres and women's refuges. It is not these visible products of their mobilisation which really mark them out from protest movements, however, but their emphasis upon changing people's values and behaviour in *all* aspects of their lives, not just the conventionally political. If radical feminism is about anything, it is about women's identity as women.

As we have seen, this stress upon a new consciousness about a different identity from that of men has, in its turn, led to the development of different identities between women. This has led to internal conflict, particularly between those who equate identity with sexual preference and those who believe a consciousness of being different from men can be combined with heterosexuality. Such fission has been criticised as limiting the political impact of the women's movement, but the central point about social movements is that we do not just look for political impact, but also for *cultural* impact. This is extremely hard to assess, as there are so many ways in which attitudes and values are revealed; it is made even harder by the fact that much of the radical feminists' agenda has been concerned with 'private' life, the ways in which women interact not just with men but also with other women. We cannot, then, look just at the political arena for evidence of change, we need also to examine the social arena – which in itself raises all sorts of awkward questions about how such evidence is filtered through the media. Despite this, we can see some clear signs of cultural change, leading, if only in some instances, to political change. The issue of male violence towards women, whether in the context of rape or of domestic violence (or the two combined, as in the concept of 'marital rape'), is now firmly on the media agenda, even if it has not produced much in the way of concrete political change. Lesbianism, once ignored or castigated by the media, is now portrayed as much less shocking and deviant, at least outside the tabloid press – although, once again, those on the right of the political spectrum are sufficiently powerful to block legislative changes like allowing lesbian couples to marry or to adopt children. Such changes have come about, not as a result of lobbying within established parties and groups, but because of women coming together in informal networks and using their collective energy and bravery to challenge society to take account of their ideas and attitudes. There is no process of mediation going on here. Radical feminists are not negotiating with established parties and institutions with a view to seeking power over others, but asserting their right to the autonomy they need to lead their lives as they wish.

'Deep' greens are in a rather different category. They are closer to conventional politics, in that they are primarily interested in the 'public' rather than the 'private' sphere. Granted, there is a clear expectation that individual lifestyles and practices will conform with ecological thinking. Members of FOE or the Green Party are under considerable peer pressure to recycle, minimise energy consumption, eschew pesticide use and so on in their everyday lives. Such changes in personal values and behaviour are not their *raison d'être*, however, as they are with the radical feminists. 'Deep' greens come into our category of social movements because of the scope of their radical agenda, and the way in which they put their commitment to direct participatory democracy before more pragmatic considerations like presenting a united front to the electorate. FOE may be a borderline case for inclusion as a social movement, just as Greenpeace is arguably at the borderline of our protest movement category, but I think a distinction between the two has to be drawn because of FOE's unshakeable commitment to autonomy at the local level, the stress it places upon activism by its supporters, and the explicit way in which it argues that true ecological change will not come about until there is real involvement by individuals in political decision-making. Like protest movements (and, indeed, conventional interest groups), FOE will engage in conventional lobbying where that is appropriate to the situation or issue being addressed. It does so, however, within the context of a movement which, as a whole, believes fundamental change will only come about if and when British society adopts a new form of politics. The same applies to the Green Party. Although the only one of our movements actually to engage in conventional electoral politics, we have seen in its development over the years that the Green Party's grasp upon mainstream politics is tenuous. Indicative of this is that, at the time of writing (August 1996), there are even calls from some members for the Party not to contest the next General Election (due in the spring of 1997), but to concentrate instead on the 1999 European Parliament elections. It has lost – some might say driven out – its charismatic leading figures; it refuses to countenance arguments that it must behave like a 'normal' political party; and – even more so than FOE – it clings persistently to an ideology which is so widespread and radical that it can really only be comprehended in terms of 'new' politics rather than the mainstream. It may call itself a political party, but it thinks and acts like a social movement.

END OF AN ERA?

We have seen that over the last thirty years in Britain there has been a wave of protests, often overlapping, some of which have coalesced into social movements. We know that this kind of approach to politics has been particularly attractive to the so-called 'new' middle class – but we are not sure why this has been so, and we know little about the many thousands who do not belong to this class who have also become involved. We know that protests and other types of activism have taken a wide variety of forms, such that we have argued that it is best to distinguish between protest campaigns, protest movements and social movements. We know that certain changes in the law and public policy have come about, although it would be a brave person who asserted that this could be proved to be the direct result of the 'new' politics (has Cruise gone because of CND, or because of quite separate changes in the international political climate? Is the British Government taking the threat of global warming seriously because it has been persuaded by the greens, or because the major insurance companies have now become worried about the impact of future claims resulting from much more volatile weather conditions?). We know that values and attitudes have changed, but, again, to prove causality would be immensely difficult. How are we to assess this, and what does the future hold?

It is part of our argument that protest movements have to be assessed differently from social movements. Protest movements engage directly with the political authorities. It has to be said that their concrete achievements seem few. Liberal and socialist feminists have made considerable headway in getting the mainstream parties and institutions to commit themselves to a greater role for women, but we are still waiting for most of them to deliver. Green protests have led to a few policy reversals and much rhetoric from the established parties about the desirability of a greener approach, but, again, Britain is a very long way indeed from being the kind of ecologically-sound society the greens would like to see. CND has the least to show for its activities; in the mid-nineties, the idea of unilateral disarmament is as far away from the mainstream political agenda as it was during the sixties – though it may, of course, revive if and when we have another Labour Government whose backbenchers no longer have to follow the tight guidelines of a party desperate to win the middle ground of the electorate.

Social movements are more problematic to assess, as it is much harder to identify changes in values and culture generally than specific policy changes. Subjectively, there does seem to have been a change in attitudes, but it is questionable how far attitudes have been translated into practice. Feminists and greens can take encouragement from the fact that they have made at least some of their aims not just acceptable, but actually desirable in the eyes of most. It is rare to find any public figure or major media outlet not at least paying lip-service to the idea of equality for women or the need to address ecological problems. It may be 'political correctness', but arguably we would not even have a concept of 'correctness' were it not for the efforts of the social movements. At the same time, it has to be acknowledged that there is little evidence of their more fundamental aims becoming part of the prevailing consensus. Neither the radical feminists' conception of accepting 'difference' in society, nor the 'deep' greens' questioning of economic growth and decentralised direct democracy, can be said to have gained much hold among the population at large.

Even if we are prepared to accept that the protest and social movements have made an appreciable impact, are we in any case witnessing their demise in the nineties? CND may have held on to a sizeable membership, but in terms of 'newsworthy' action it is clearly but a shadow of what it was in the eighties. The women's movement has forced its way into most of our political institutions, but its more radical, autonomous wing seems to be suffering from a degree of 'burn-out'. Environmental campaigners like Greenpeace and the Green Party have seen their support decrease significantly. Has the wave of protest and social movements subsided, not to return for another fifty years?

I think protest and social movements have made an impact, and I think they are here to stay. They have done two things – they have put issues on the political agenda, and they have changed the way in which we think about politics. Whatever one may think about their impact or lack of it, there can be no dispute that they have managed to alter the terms of political debate over the last thirty years. Disarmament may be out of vogue at the moment, but CND has shown that – providing it can keep a nucleus of support – interest can revive dramatically. Granted, such revivals are dependent upon external events – but who is to say that, for example, an accident involving nuclear weapons would not have the same effect as the introduction of new weapons did at the end of the seventies? Feminism (if only of the 'equality' school, rather than the 'difference' viewpoint) is clearly on the political and social agenda, and is not likely to go away. Green protest will stay with us, if only because ecological problems will get steadily worse if things continue as they are.

More importantly, protest and social movements have provided a model for political behaviour. There is nothing new about protest *per se*, of course; but the movements and groups we have examined have demonstrated that a mix of conventional and unconventional tactics, and informally-based network organisations, can give protest a permanence and a presence that one-off campaigns rarely achieve. What evidence we have suggests that young people in Britain today are not greatly enamoured of the 'classic' movements of the seventies and eighties – but when they come together to protest for animal rights or civil liberties, or against road-building or marine pollution, they are drawing on thirty years' experience of such protest, whether they realise it or not. In tangible terms, our protest and social movements have seen many of their aims and desires frustrated, but in less tangible terms – in people's attitudes, and the way in which they assess what is 'acceptable' and 'unacceptable' in politics – protest and social movements have much more to celebrate. We have not moved from 'old' politics to 'new' politics – but, thanks to protest and social movements, we have a *different* politics in Britain today.

Notes

1 INTRODUCTION

1 I Crewe *et al.*, 'Partisan Dealignment in Great Britain', *British Journal of Political Science*, 1977; G Parry, G Moyser and N Day, *Political Participation and Democracy in Britain*, Cambridge University Press, 1992, ch. 9.
2 G Almond and S Verba, *The Civic Culture*, Little, Brown, 1965.
3 A Marsh, *Protest and Political Consciousness*, Sage, 1977.
4 S Barnes *et al.*, *Political Action: Mass Participation in Five Western Democracies*, Sage, 1979.
5 S Beer, *Britain Against Itself: The Political Contradictions of Collectivism*, Faber, 1982.
6 Parry, Moyser and Day, *op. cit.*, ch. 2.
7 *Ibid.*, p. 41; published in 1992, the book is based upon surveys conducted in the mid-eighties.
8 *Ibid.*, p. 44.
9 *Ibid.*, p. 423.
10 *Ibid.*, p. 228.
11 The changes were brought about by individual MPs, as Private Member's Bills; neither Government nor Opposition was willing to risk the electoral consequences of adopting formal positions for or against, allowing their members a free vote.

2 DEFINING SOCIAL MOVEMENTS

1 See J Lovenduski and V Randall, *Contemporary Feminist Politics*, Oxford University Press, 1993, ch. 1.
2 See D Rucht (ed.), *Research on Social Movements; the state of the art in Western Europe and the USA*, Westview Press, 1991.
3 A Melucci, *Nomads of the Present*, Hutchinson Radius, 1989.
4 M Diani, 'The Concept of Social Movement', *The Sociological Review*, 1992, p. 14.
5 L Gerlach and V Hine, *People, Power and Change*, Bobbs-Merrill, 1970.
6 S Tarrow, *Democracy and Disorder*, Oxford University Press, 1989.

7 H Kitschelt, 'Political Opportunity Structures and Political Protest', *British Journal of Political Science*, 1986.
8 Melucci, *op. cit.*, pp. 28–30.
9 J Pakulski, *Social Movements: the Politics of Moral Protest*, Longman, 1991, p. 42.
10 One of the biggest demonstrations, in London at the end of March 1990, resulted in over 130 injuries, some 340 arrests and hundreds of thousands of pounds worth of damage.

3 THE RESURGENCE OF SOCIAL MOVEMENTS

1 B Klandermans and S Tarrow, 'Mobilisation into Social Movements', in B Klandermans, H Kriesi and S Tarrow (eds), *From Structure to Action*, JAI Press, 1988, p. 18.
2 CND itself developed from two groupings established in 1957: the National Committee for the Abolition of Nuclear Weapon Tests and the Emergency Committee for Direct Action against Nuclear War, the latter having the explicit aim of encouraging non-violent direct action; see P Byrne, *The Campaign for Nuclear Disarmament*, Croom Helm, 1988, ch. 3.
3 See R Taylor and C Pritchard, *The Protest Makers*, Pergamon, 1980.
4 See F Parkin, *Middle Class Radicalism*, Manchester University Press, 1968.
5 This did not include the French Communist Party (PCF), which viewed the events of May 1968 as a combination of adventurism, dangerous anarchism and political immaturity.
6 See G Hill, 'How trendy protests hardened into waves of mob violence', *The Times*, 2 April 1990.
7 An experience not confined to Britain; one of the leading American feminists, Gloria Steinem, recalls her experiences at the time in the US civil rights and anti-war movements: 'There was this idea – "Women say Yes to men who say No" – women were not only meant to do the mimeography but supply the sex besides. At least in the Republican Party you only had to do the mimeographing. And that helped us to realise there needed to be an autonomous women's movement – that even in these idealistic groups women were still being told our role was prone' (*The Observer*, 15 May 1994, p. 12).

4 THEORETICAL IDEAS

1 See D McAdam, J McCarthy and M Zald, *Comparative Perspectives on Social Movements*, Cambridge University Press, 1996, for a good overview.
2 R Turner and L Killian, *Collective Behaviour*, Prentice Hall, 1957.
3 W Kornhauser, *The Politics of Mass Society*, Free Press, 1959.
4 T Gurr, *Why Men Rebel*, Princeton University Press, 1970.
5 M Mayer, 'Social Movement Research in the United States', in S Lyman, *Social Movements: Critiques, Concepts, Case-Studies*, Macmillan, 1995.
6 M Olson, *The Logic of Collective Action*, Harvard University Press, 1965.

7 A Hirschman, *Shifting Involvements: Private Interests and Public Action*, Princeton University Press, 1982.

8 D Chong, *Collective Action and the Civil Rights Movement*, University of Chicago Press, 1991.

9 *Ibid.*, p. 233.

10 *Ibid.*, p. 79.

11 *Ibid.*, pp. 34–5; Chong makes the point that such social pressures can, of course, also be negative – social pressure dissuading you from participation in certain movements or causes.

12 *Ibid.*, p. 55.

13 A Oberschall, *Social Conflict and Social Movement*, Prentice Hall, 1973.

14 B Fireman and W Gamson, 'Utilitarian Logic in the Resource Mobilisation Perspective', in M Zald and J McCarthy, *The Dynamics of Social Movements*, Winthrop, 1979.

15 J McCarthy and M Zald, 'Resource Mobilisation and Social Movements', *American Journal of Sociology*, 1977.

16 J Lovenduski, *Women and European Politics*, Wheatsheaf, 1986, pp. 53–5.

17 L A Banaszak, *Why Movements Succeed or Fail*, Princeton University Press, 1996.

18 *Ibid.*, p. 221.

19 *Ibid.*, p. 220.

20 McCarthy and Zald, *op. cit.*; W Gamson, *The Strategy of Social Protest*, Dorsey, 1975.

21 R Dalton, M Kuechler and W Burklin, 'The Challenge of New Movements', in R Dalton and M Kuechler, *Challenging the Political Order*, Polity Press, 1990, p. 9.

22 L Gerlach and V Hine, *People, Power, Change*, Bobbs-Merrill, 1970.

23 R Eyerman and A Jamison, *Social Movements: A Cognitive Approach*, Polity Press, 1991.

24 *Ibid.*, p. 57.

25 A Melucci, *Nomads of the Present*, Hutchinson Radius, 1989.

26 A Melucci, 'Liberation or Meaning', in J Nederveen Pieterse, *Emancipations, Modern and Postmodern*, Sage, 1992, pp. 74–5.

27 C Tilly, *From Mobilisation to Revolution*, Addison-Wesley, 1978, and 'European Violence and Collective Action since 1700', *Social Research*, 1985, pp. 714–47.

28 S Tarrow, *Democracy and Disorder*, Oxford University Press, 1989.

29 S Tarrow, *Power in Movement*, Cambridge University Press, 1994.

30 K-W Brand, 'Cyclical Aspects of New Social Movements', in R Dalton and M Kuechler, *Challenging the Political Order*, Polity Press, 1990.

31 A Giddens, *The Class Structure of Advanced Societies*, Hutchinson, 1973, p. 35.

32 J Habermas, *Legitimation Crisis*, Heinemann, 1976.

33 A Touraine, *The Voice and the Eye*, Cambridge University Press, 1981; see also Touraine's 'An Introduction to the Study of Social Movements', *Social Research*, 1985, pp. 749–88. There is a good discussion of Touraine in A Scott, *Ideology and the New Social Movements*, Unwin Hyman, 1990, ch. 3.

34 Touraine, *The Voice and the Eye*, Cambridge University Press, 1981, p. 81.

35 W P Burklin, 'The German Greens', *International Political Science Review*, 1985, pp. 463–82.
36 B Frankel, *The Post-Industrial Utopians*, Polity Press, 1987.
37 C Offe, 'New Social Movements: challenging the boundaries of institutional politics', *Social Research*, 1985, pp. 817–68.
38 S Cotgrove and A Duff, 'Environmentalism, Middle Class Radicalism and Politics', *Sociological Review*, 1980, pp. 333–51; S Cotgrove, *Catastrophe or Cornucopia*, Wiley, 1982.
39 F Parkin, *Middle Class Radicalism*, Manchester University Press, 1968.
40 R Inglehart, *The Silent Revolution*, Princeton University Press, 1977; see also Inglehart's *Culture Shift*, Princeton University Press, 1989.
41 A Maslow, *Motivation and Personality*, Harper and Row, 1970.
42 Parkin, *op. cit.*, p. 29.
43 J Craig Jenkins and B Klandermans, *The Politics of Social Protest*, University College of London Press, 1995, ch. 1.
44 H Kitschelt, 'Political Opportunity Structures and Political Protest', *British Journal of Political Science*, 1986.
45 L A Banaszak, *op. cit.*
46 S Tarrow, 'National Politics and Collective Action', *Annual Review of Sociology*, 1988; see also Part One of McAdam *et al.*'s *Comparative Perspectives on Social Movements*.
47 H Kitschelt, 'Citizens, Protest and Democracy', in *Social Movements, Political Parties and Democratic Theory*, Annals of the American Academy of Political and Social Science, July 1993.
48 A Scott, *Ideology and the New Social Movements*, Unwin Hyman, 1990.
49 *Ibid.*, pp. 135–6.
50 *Ibid.*, p. 150.

5 WHO ARE THEY?

1 J K Galbraith, *The Affluent Society*, Hamish Hamilton, 1958.
2 D Bell, *The End of Ideology*, Free Press, 1960.
3 A Gouldner, *The Future of Intellectuals and the Rise of the New Class*, Seabury, 1979.
4 B Bruce-Biggs (ed.), *The New Class?*, Transaction Books, 1979, pp. 169–89.
5 F Parkin, *Middle Class Radicalism*, Manchester University Press, 1968.
6 P Nias, *National Membership Survey*, CND, 1982.
7 P Byrne, *The Campaign for Nuclear Disarmament*, Routledge, 1988.
8 M L Harrison, *CND – the Challenge of the Post Cold War Era*, unpublished PhD thesis, Loughborough University, 1994.
9 H Kriesi, 'New Social Movements and the New Class in the Netherlands', *American Journal of Sociology*, 1989, pp. 1078–116.
10 S Cotgrove, *Catastrophe or Cornucopia*, Wiley, 1982.
11 A postal survey of Green Party members in the East Midlands, conducted by Paul Byrne and Claire Page in 1991; 340 responses were received.
12 K Van Liere and R Dunlap, 'The Social Bases of Environmental Concern', *Public Opinion Quarterly*, 1980, pp. 181–97.

13 D Morrison and R Dunlap, 'Environmentalism and Elitism', *Environmental Management*, 1986, pp. 581–9.

14 C Offe, 'New Social Movements: Challenging the Boundaries of Institutional Politics', *Social Research*, 1985, p. 833.

15 G Parry, G Moyser and N Day, *Political Participation and Democracy in Britain*, Cambridge University Press, 1992.

16 *Ibid.*, p. 69.

17 *Ibid.*, p. 74.

18 *Ibid.*, p. 84.

19 *Ibid.*, p. 215.

20 *Ibid.*

21 R Rohrschneider, 'The Roots of Public Opinion toward New Social Movements', *American Journal of Political Science*, 1990, pp. 1–30.

22 *Ibid.*, p. 25.

23 Parkin, *op. cit.*, ch. 2.

24 D Fuchs and D Rucht, *Support for NSMs in 5 West European Countries*, ESF/ESRC Conference, Manchester, 1990.

25 van Liere and Dunlap, *op. cit.*, p. 191.

26 Kriesi, *op. cit.*, p. 1106.

27 Parry *et al.*, *op. cit.*, p. 144.

28 *Ibid.*, p. 145.

29 J Lovenduski and V Randall, *Contemporary Feminist Politics*, Oxford University Press, p. 117.

30 Harrison, *op. cit.*, pp. 162–3.

31 van Liere and Dunlap, *op. cit.*

32 Kriesi, *op. cit.*

33 W Rüdig, M Franklin and L Bennie, *Green Blues: the rise and decline of the British Green Party*, No. 95, Strathclyde Papers on Government and Politics, Department of Government, Strathclyde University, 1993.

34 S Barnes and M Kaase, *Political Action: Mass Participation in Five Western Democracies*, Sage, 1979.

35 Parry *et al.*, *op. cit.*, p. 160.

36 *Ibid.*, p. 214.

37 G Sianne and H Wilkinson, *Gender, Feminism and the Future*, Demos, 1995.

38 A Maslow, *Motivation and Personality*, Harper and Row, 1954.

39 R Inglehart, *The Silent Revolution: Changing Values and Political Styles among Western Publics*, Princeton University Press, 1977.

40 See also R Inglehart, *Culture Shift in Advanced Industrial Society*, Princeton University Press, 1990.

41 R Inglehart, 'Post-Materialism in an Environment of Insecurity', *American Political Science Review*, 1981.

42 S Flanagan, 'Value Change in Industrial Societies', *American Political Science Review*, 1987.

43 P Lowe and W Rüdig, 'Political Ecology and the Social Sciences – the State of the Art', *British Journal of Political Science*, 1986, p. 516.

44 Inglehart, *op. cit.*

45 W Rüdig and P Lowe, 'The Withered Greening of British Politics', *Political Studies*, 1986, pp. 264–5.

46 *Ibid.*

47 J Savage, 'Post Materialism of the Left and Right', *Comparative Political Studies*, 1985.
48 R Eckersley, 'Green Politics and the New Class', *Political Studies*, 1989, pp. 205–23.
49 *Ibid.*, p. 221.
50 C Offe, 'New Social Movements: Challenging the Boundaries of Institutional Politics', *Social Research*, 1985, p. 851.
51 O Knutsen, 'Materialist and Post-materialist Values and Social Structure in the Nordic Countries', *Comparative Politics*, 1990.
52 H-G Betz, 'Value Change and Post-materialist Politics: the case of West Germany', *Comparative Political Studies*, 1990.
53 N de Graaf and G Evans, 'Why are the Young more Post-materialistic?', *Comparative Political Studies*, 1996.
54 *Ibid.*, p. 834.
55 *Ibid.*
56 W Burklin, 'The German Greens: the post-industrial non-established party system', *International Political Science Review*, 1985.
57 B Frankel, *The Post Industrial Utopians*, Polity Press, 1987, p. 239.
58 F Parkin, *op. cit.*, p. 185.
59 S Cotgrove, *op. cit.*, p. 95: see also S Cotgrove and A Duff, 'Environmentalism, Middle Class Radicalism and Politics', *Sociological Review*, 1980, and 'Environmentalism, Values and Social Change', *British Journal of Sociology*, 1981.

6 CND AND THE PEACE MOVEMENT

1 Figures supplied by National CND, October 1995.
2 P Byrne, 'Pressure Groups and Popular Campaigns', in P Johnson (ed.), *20th Century Britain: Economic, Social and Cultural Change*, Longman, 1994, p. 455.
3 Put at five billion pounds in 1980 – and over ten billion by the time the first submarine was launched in 1992.
4 These are all CND's own estimates of turn-out; in each case, the police estimate was considerably lower. Even if CND's figures are exaggerated, there is no doubt that these were genuinely mass demonstrations.
5 It was known at the time that Heseltine was being backed by the efforts of a small team of civil servants within the Ministry of Defence known as DS19. Their official function was to assist in the drafting of speeches for Heseltine, prepare publicity material on the Government's defence policies, and deal with media enquiries; in practice, they appear to have spent their time advising ministers. The team was disbanded after the 1983 election. Two years after the election, it was alleged by an ex-employee of the Security Services that MI5 had been monitoring CND during the early eighties (tapping the phones of known members of the Communist Party among the Campaign's leadership, for example, and even allegedly introducing an agent into CND's headquarters), and passing information on to Heseltine's team. The charges were made by Cathy Massiter, who worked for MI5 between 1970 and 1985, when she resigned in protest at what she saw as improper conduct with regard to the Security Service's surveillance of CND. See *The Observer*, 24

February 1985, and *The Guardian*, 1 March 1985, for a full account of
her allegations; the aftermath, including an official enquiry which
effectively cleared the Government and the subsequent High Court
hearing, are discussed in P Byrne, *The Campaign for Nuclear
Disarmament*, pp. 186–91.
6 I Crewe, 'Britain: Two and a half cheers for the Atlantic Alliance', in G
Flynn and H Rattinger, *The Public and Atlantic Defense*, 1985.
7 Kinnock joined CND in 1961, when he was 19 years old.
8 J Ruddock, 'Post-War Plans', *New Statesman and Society*, 18 August
1989, p. 22.
9 M L Harrison, interview with Bruce Kent, 28 May 1991, in M L
Harrison, *CND – the Challenge of the Post Cold War Era*, unpublished
PhD thesis, Loughborough University, 1994.
10 For a fuller account, see P Byrne, *op. cit.*, pp. 111–13.

7 THE WOMEN'S MOVEMENT

1 This chapter is a revised and amended version of P Byrne, 'The Politics
of the Women's Movement', *Parliamentary Affairs*, January, 1996 – a
special issue also published as J Lovenduski and P Norris (eds), *Women
in Politics*, Oxford University Press, 1996.
2 D Dahlerup, *The New Women's Movement: Feminism and Political Power
in Europe and the USA*, Sage, 1986, p. 6.
3 J Lovenduski and V Randall, *Contemporary Feminist Politics*, Oxford
University Press, 1993, p. 3.
4 Two further aims were added in 1974 – financial and legal independence
for women, and no discrimination against lesbians – and a seventh aim in
1978 – freedom from intimidation by threat or use of violence or sexual
coercion.
5 Lovenduski and Randall, *op. cit.*, p. 305.
6 David Steel's Private Member's Bill on abortion reform which, when
passed by Parliament, provided for abortion in the first 28 weeks of
pregnancy, subject to the agreement of two doctors that the mother's
health was at risk or the baby was likely to be handicapped; the National
Health Services Family Planning Act gave local authorities the power to
provide free contraceptive aids and advice.
7 Lovenduski and Randall, *op. cit.*, p. 222.
8 Proposed by James White, a Labour MP.
9 D Marsh and J Chambers, *Abortion Politics*, Junction Books, 1981, p. 47;
see also J Lovenduski and J Outshoorn (eds), *The New Politics of
Abortion*, Sage, 1986.
10 Private Member's Bill proposed by James Corrie, a Conservative MP.
11 D Bouchier, *The Feminist Challenge*, Macmillan, 1983, p. 177.
12 E Wilson, *Hidden Agendas*, Tavistock, 1986, p. 99.
13 H Bradley, *Fractured Identities*, Polity Press, 1996, p. 86.
14 *Ibid.*, p. 87.
15 *Ibid.*, p. 88.
16 Lovenduski and Randall, *op. cit.*, p. 67.
17 Bradley, *op. cit.*, p. 97.
18 *Ibid.*, pp. 100–13.

19　See the chapter by L Loach, in H Benyon (ed.), *Digging Deeper: Issues in the Miners' Strike*, Verso, 1985.

20　Lovenduski and Randall, *op. cit.*, p. 124.

21　*Ibid.*, p. 340.

22　*Ibid.*, pp. 225–6.

23　*Ibid.*, p. 228.

24　*Ibid.*, p. 247.

25　The bill was 'talked out' by MPs. Alton announced in 1992 that he would not stand for the Liberal Democrat Party at the next election in protest at a decision to make abortion a policy issue rather than a matter of conscience.

26　Introduced as an amendment to the Human Fertilization and Embryology Act.

27　Lovenduski and Randall, *op. cit.*, pp. 251–6.

28　R Jowell, S Witherspoon and L Brook (eds), *British Social Attitudes: the Fifth Report*, Gower/SCPR, 1988, p. 193.

29　Lovenduski and Randall, *op. cit.*, p. 151.

30　The National Conference of Labour Women and the National Labour Women's Advisory Committee, as well as women's sections at a regional and constituency level.

31　H Margetts, 'Public Management Change and Sex Equality within the State', and I Forbes, 'The Privatisation of Sex Equality Policy', in Lovenduski and Norris, *op. cit.*, pp. 132–62.

32　G Parry, G Moyser and N Day, *Political Participation and Democracy in Britain*, Cambridge University Press, 1992.

33　L Brook, S Hedges, P Jowell, J Lewis, G Prior, G Sebastian, B Taylor and S Witherspoon, *British Social Attitudes Cumulative Source Book*, Gower/SCPR, 1992.

34　*The Guardian*, 15 February 1995, p. 21.

35　Lovenduski and Randall, *op. cit.*, p. 95.

36　G Sianne and H Wilkinson, *Gender, Feminism and the Future*, Demos, 1995; quotation taken from *The Guardian*, 6 March 1995.

37　B Ryan, *Feminism and the Women's Movement*, Routledge, 1992.

38　*Ibid.*, p. 62.

39　J Gelb, 'Feminism and Political Action', in R Dalton and M Kuechler, *Challenging the Political Order: New Social and Political Movements in Western Democracies*, Polity Press, 1990, p. 144; see also Gelb's 'Feminism in Britain: politics without power?', in D Dahlerup (ed.), *The New Women's Movement*, Sage, 1986.

40　A Melucci, *Nomads of the Present*, Hutchinson Radius, 1989, p. 44.

41　R Eyerman and A Jamison, *Social Movements: a Cognitive Approach*, Polity, 1991.

42　Lesbian groups may well be kept at a distance by political parties and institutions, but they are increasingly recognised by the market – as in, for example, the significant growth in the mid-nineties in films and books which celebrate lesbian culture.

8 THE GREEN MOVEMENT

1 This is a common distinction in the literature on environmentalism, although the terms sometimes vary; 'conservation' is sometimes termed 'nature conservation', 'light' or 'grey' green, or even 'environmentalism'; 'ecological' is also known as 'new environmentalism', 'dark', or 'deep' green.

2 D Richardson, 'The Green Challenge', in D Richardson and C Rootes (eds), *The Green Challenge: the Development of Green Parties in Europe*, Routledge, 1995, p. 7.

3 S Young, *The Politics of the Environment*, Baseline Books, 1993, p. 17.

4 R J Dalton, *The Green Rainbow: Environmental Groups in Western Europe*, Yale University Press, 1994, p. 32.

5 *Ibid.*, p. 35.

6 A conservation group founded in America in 1892, the Sierra Club stresses the importance of protecting biodiversity, has a particular interest in preserving America's national parks and forests; and uses conventional lobbying tactics, directing much of its argument towards Congress. As with most environmental groups, a brief summary of the group's aims can be found on the World Wide Web, the URL being *http://www.sierraclub.org/*

7 Figures from S Cotgrove, *Catastrophe or Cornucopia*, Wiley, 1982; G Frankland, 'Does Green Politics have a Future in Britain', in W Rüdig (ed.), *Green Politics One*, University of Edinburgh Press, 1990; Dalton, *op. cit.*; and *The Economist*, 3 March 1990.

8 See FOE's 'home page' on the World Wide Web; the URL is *http://www.foe.co.uk/*

9 F Pearce, *Green Warriors*, Bodley Head, 1991, pp. 49–51.

10 P Lowe and J Goyder, *Environmental Groups in Politics*, Allen and Unwin, 1983, p. 134.

11 Greenpeace Annual Report 1992–93; for a useful summary of current policies, see the Greenpeace 'home page' on the World Wide Web; the URL is *http://www.greenpeace.org*

12 The growth is worth recording (in round figures drawn from *Greenpeace Facts and Figures 1991*): 1976 10,000; 1977 15,000; 1978 20,000; 1979 30,000; 1980 90,000; 1981 200,000; 1982 300,000; 1983 500,000; 1984 750,000; 1985 1,000,000; 1986 1,250,000; 1987 1,800,000; 1988 2,800,000; 1989 4,000,000; 1990 4,800,000.

13 *Ibid.*

14 Richard Sambrook, in a debate at the Edinburgh National Television Festival, 1995 – *The Guardian*, 28 August 1995.

15 David Lloyd, senior commissioning editor of news and current affairs, Channel 4 – *Ibid.*

16 Thermal Oxide Re-Processing Plant.

17 *The Guardian*, 27 August 1996.

18 True to its organisational principles, there is no central site on the WWW for the UK arm of Earth First!; a useful summary can be found at the Manchester Earth First! web-site – the URL is *http://www.u-net.com/manchester/organisations/earthfirst!*

19 Reclaim the Streets has a national WWW site: *http://www.hrc.wmin.ac.uk/campaigns/RTS.html*

20   *The Guardian*, 27 August 1996.
21   R Garner, 'Political Animals', *Parliamentary Affairs*, 1993, pp. 333–52.
22   T Quirke, 'They shoot Scientists, don't they?', *The Times*, 7 November 1992.
23   S Parkin, letter to *The Times*, 14 June 1990.
24   C Rootes, 'Britain – Greens in a Cold Climate', in Richardson and Rootes, *op. cit.*, pp. 66–90.
25   Richardson, *op. cit.*
26   See H Ward, 'Green Arguments for Local Democracy', in D King and G Stoker, *Rethinking Local Democracy*, Macmillan, 1996.
27   Originating in the thirties, there were only a handful of such local exchange and trading schemes in 1990; by 1994, there were at least 200 in the UK, with perhaps as many as 20,000 people involved.
28   W Rüdig, L Bennie and M Franklin, *Green Party Members: a Profile*, Delta, 1991.
29   *The Sunday Times*, 30 August 1992.
30   *The Guardian*, 24 August 1994.

Bibliography

Almond G and Verba S, *The Civic Culture*, Little, Brown, 1965.

Bagguley P, 'Social Change, the Middle Class and the Emergence of New Social Movements; a critical analysis', *Sociological Review*, 1992.

Banaszak L A, *Why Movements Succeed or Fail*, Princeton University Press, 1996.

Barnes S and Kaase M, *Political Action: Mass Participation in Five Western Democracies*, Sage, 1979.

Beckford J, *New Religious Movements and Rapid Social Change*, Sage, 1986.

Beckwith K, 'Feminism and Leftist Politics in Italy', *West European Politics*, 1985.

Beer S, *Britain Against Itself: The Political Contradictions of Collectivism*, Faber, 1982.

Bell D, *The End of Ideology*, Free Press, 1960.

Benyon H, *Digging Deeper: Issues in the Miners' Strike*, Verso, 1985.

Betz H-G, 'Value Change and Post-materialist Politics: the case of West Germany', *Comparative Political Studies*, 1990.

Blanchard D, *The Anti-Abortion Movement*, Macmillan, 1994.

Bouchier D, *The Feminist Challenge,* Macmillan, 1983.

Bradley H, *Fractured Identities*, Polity Press, 1996.

Brand K-W, 'Cyclical Aspects of New Social Movements', in R Dalton and M Kuechler, *Challenging the Political Order*, Polity Press, 1990.

Brook L, Hedges S, Jowell P, Lewis J, Prior G, Sebastian G, Taylor B and Witherspoon S, *British Social Attitudes Cumulative Source Book*, Gower/SCPR, 1992.

Brown M and May J, *The Greenpeace Story*, Dorling Kindersley, 1991.

Bruce-Biggs B, *The New Class?*, Transaction Books, 1979.

Burklin W, 'The German Greens: the post-industrial non-established party system', *International Political Science Review*, 1985.

Burns R, *Protest and Democracy in West Germany*, Macmillan, 1988.

Byrne P, *The Campaign for Nuclear Disarmament*, Croom Helm/Routledge, 1988.

—— 'Pressure Groups and Popular Campaigns', in P Johnson (ed.), *20th Century Britain: Economic, Social and Cultural Change*, Longman, 1994.

—— 'The Politics of the Women's Movement', in J Lovenduski and P Norris, *Women in Politics*, Oxford University Press, 1996.

Carter A, *Direct Action and Liberal Democracy*, Harper, 1974.

—— *Peace Movements, International Protest and World Politics Since 1945*, Longman, 1992.

Chong D, *Collective Action and the Civil Rights Movement*, University of Chicago Press, 1991.

Clarke A, 'Moral Reform and the Anti-Abortion Movement', *Sociological Review*, 1987.

Cohen J, 'Between Crisis Management and Social Movements', *Telos*, 1982.

—— 'Strategy or Identity: new theoretical paradigms and contemporary social movements', *Social Research*, 1985.

Cotgrove S, *Catastrophe or Cornucopia*, Wiley, 1982.

Cotgrove S and Duff A, 'Environmentalism, Middle Class Radicalism and Politics', *Sociological Review*, 1980.

—— 'Environmentalism, Values and Social Change', *British Journal of Sociology*, 1981.

Crewe I, Sarlvik B and Alt J, 'Partisan Dealignment in Great Britain', *British Journal of Political Science*, 1977.

Dahlerup D, *The New Women's Movement: Feminism and Political Power in Europe and the USA*, Sage, 1986.

Dalton R, *The Green Rainbow: Environmental Groups in Western Europe*, Yale University Press, 1994.

Dalton R and Kuechler M, *Challenging the Political Order*, Polity Press, 1990.

Dalton R, Kuechler M and Burklin W, 'The Challenge of New Movements', in R Dalton and M Kuechler, *Challenging the Political Order*, Polity Press, 1990.

della Porta D and Tarrow S, 'Unwanted Children: Political Violence and Cycles of Protest in Italy', *European Journal of Political Research*, 1986.

Diani M, 'The Concept of Social Movement', *The Sociological Review*, 1992.

—— *Green Networks: a Structural Analysis of the Italian Environmental Movement*, Edinburgh University Press, 1995.

Diani M and Eyerman R, *Studying Collective Action*, Sage, 1992.

Dunleavy P, 'Group Identities and Individual Influence; Reconstructing the Theory of Interest Groups', *British Journal of Political Science*, 1988.

—— 'Mass Political Behaviour; is there more to learn?', *Political Studies*, 1990.

Eckersley R, 'Green Politics and the New Class', *Political Studies*, 1989.

Eder K, 'A New Social Movement?', *Telos*, 1982.

—— 'The "new social movements" – moral crusades, political pressure groups or social movements?', *Social Research*, 1985.

—— *The New Politics of Class*, Sage, 1993.

Eyerman R and Jamison A, *Social Movements: A Cognitive Approach*, Polity Press, 1991.

Fireman B and Gamson W, 'Utilitarian Logic in the Resource Mobilisation Perspective', in M Zald and J McCarthy, *The Dynamics of Social Movements*, Winthrop, 1979.

Flanagan S, 'Value Change in Industrial Societies', *American Political Science Review*, 1987.

Flynn G and Rattinger H, *The Public and Atlantic Defense*, Croom Helm, 1985.

Forbes I, 'The Privatisation of Sex Equality Policy', in J Lovenduski and P Norris, *Women in Politics*, Oxford University Press, 1996.

Foss D and Larkin R, *Beyond Revolution; a New Theory of Social Movements*, Bergin and Garvey, 1986.

Frankel B, *The Post Industrial Utopians*, Polity Press, 1987.

Frankland G, 'Does Green Politics have a Future in Britain', in W Rüdig (ed.), *Green Politics One*, University of Edinburgh Press, 1990.

Freeman J, *Social Movements of the Sixties and Seventies*, Longman, 1983.

Fuentes M and Frank A, 'Ten Theses on Social Movements', *World Development*, 1981, p.179–191.

Galbraith J K, *The Affluent Society*, Hamish Hamilton, 1958.

Gamson W, *The Strategy of Social Protest*, Dorsey, 1975.

—— 'Understanding the Careers of Challenging Groups', *American Journal of Sociology*, 1980.

Garner R, *Animals, Politics and Morality*, Manchester University Press, 1993.

—— 'Political Animals', *Parliamentary Affairs*, 1993.

Gelb J, 'Feminism in Britain: Politics without Power?', in D Dahlerup (ed.), *The New Women's Movement*, Sage, 1986.

—— *Feminism and Politics*, University of California Press, 1989.

—— 'Feminism and Political Action', in R Dalton and M Kuechler, *Challenging the Political Order: New Social and Political Movements in Western Democracies*, Polity Press, 1990.

Gerlach L and Hine V, *People, Power and Change*, Bobbs-Merrill, 1970.

Giddens A, *The Class Structure of Advanced Societies*, Hutchinson, 1973.

Goldstone J, 'The Weakness of Organisation: A New Look at Gamson's "The Strategy of Social Protest" ', *American Journal of Sociology*, 1980.

Gouldner A, *The Future of Intellectuals and the Rise of the New Class*, Seabury, 1979.

de Graaf N and Evans G, 'Why are the Young more Post-materialistic?', *Comparative Political Studies*, 1996.

Gurr T, *Why Men Rebel*, Princeton University Press, 1970.

Habermas J, *Legitimation Crisis*, Heinemann, 1976.

Harrison M, *CND – the Challenge of the Post Cold War Era*, unpublished PhD thesis, Loughborough University, 1994.

Hinton J, *Protests and Visions: Peace Politics in Twentieth-Century Britain*, Hutchinson Radius, 1989.

Hirschman A, *Shifting Involvements: Private Interests and Public Action*, Princeton University Press, 1982.

Hulsberg W, *The German Greens: a Social and Political Profile*, Verso, 1988.

Hunter R, *Warriors of the Rainbow; The Chronicle of the Greenpeace Movement*, Holt, Rinehart and Winston, 1979.

Inglehart R, *The Silent Revolution: Changing Values and Political Styles among Western Publics*, Princeton University Press, 1977.

—— 'The Impact of Values, Cognitive Level, and Social Background', in S Barnes and M Kaase, *Political Action: Mass Participation in Five Western Democracies*, Sage, 1979.

—— 'Post-Materialism in an Environment of Insecurity', *American Political Science Review*, 1981.

—— *Culture Shift in Advanced Industrial Society*, Princeton University Press, 1990.

Jamison A, Eyerman R and Cramer J, *The Making of the New Environmental Consciousness*, Edinburgh University Press, 1990.

Jenkins J Craig, 'Resource Mobilisation Theory and the Study of Social Movements', *Annual Review of Sociology*, 1983.

Jenkins J Craig and Klandermans B, *The Politics of Social Protest*, University College of London Press, 1995.

Johnson P, *20th Century Britain: Economic, Social and Cultural Change*, Longman, 1994.

Jowell R, Witherspoon S and Brook L, *British Social Attitudes: the Fifth Report*, Gower/SCPR, 1988.

Kerbo H, 'Movements of "Crisis" and Movements of "Affluence" ', *Journal of Conflict Resolution*, 1982.

King D and Stoker G, *Rethinking Local Democracy*, Macmillan, 1996.

King R and Nugent N, *Respectable Rebels*, Hodder and Stoughton, 1979.

Kitschelt H, 'Political Opportunity Structures and Political Protest', *British Journal of Political Science*, 1986.

—— 'The Internal Politics of Parties; the Law of Curvilinear Disparity Revisited', *Political Studies*, 1989.

—— 'New Social Movements and the Decline of Party Organisation', in R Dalton and M Kuechler, *Challenging the Political Order: New Social and Political Movements in Western Democracies*, Polity Press, 1990.

—— 'Citizens, Protest and Democracy', in *Social Movements, Political Parties and Democratic Theory*, Annals of the American Academy of Political and Social Science, July 1993.

Klandermans B, *Organising for Change: Social Movement Organisations in Europe and the United States*, JAI Press, 1989.

—— *Peace Movements in Western Europe and the United States*, JAI Press, 1991.

Klandermans B, Kriesi H and Tarrow S, *From Structure to Action*, JAI Press, 1988.

Klandermans B and Oemega D, 'Potentials, Networks, Motivations and Barriers: Steps Towards Participation in Social Movements', *American Sociological Review*, 1987.

Klandermans B and Tarrow S, 'Mobilisation into Social Movements', in B Klandermans, H Kriesi and S Tarrow, *From Structure to Action*, JAI Press, 1988.

Knutsen O, 'Materialist and Post-materialist Values and Social Structure in the Nordic countries', *Comparative Politics*, 1990.

Kolinsky E, *The Greens in West Germany*, Berg, 1989.

Kornhauser W, *The Politics of Mass Society*, Free Press, 1959.

Kriesberg L, *Research in Social Movements: Conflict and Change*, vol. 3, JAI Press, 1980.

Kriesi H, 'New Social Movements and the New Class in the Netherlands', *American Journal of Sociology*, 1989.

—— 'The Political Opportunity Structure of the Dutch Peace Movement', *West European Politics*, 1989.

Kriesi H and van Praag P, 'Old and New Politics: The Dutch Peace Movement and the Traditional Peace Organisations', *European Journal of Political Science*, 1987.

Liddington J, *The Long Road to Greenham: Feminism and Anti-militarism in Britain since 1820*, Virago, 1989.

Lofland J, *Protest: Studies of Collective Behaviour and Social Movements*, Transaction Books, 1985.

Lovenduski J, *Women and European Politics*, Wheatsheaf, 1986.

Lovenduski J and Norris P, *Gender and Party Politics*, Sage, 1993.

—— *Women in Politics*, Oxford University Press, 1996.

Lovenduski J and Outshoorn J, *The New Politics of Abortion*, Sage, 1986.

Lovenduski J and Randall V, *Contemporary Feminist Politics*, Oxford University Press, 1993.

Lowe P and Goyder J, *Environmental Groups in Politics*, Allen and Unwin, 1983.

Lowe P and Rüdig W, 'Political Ecology and the Social Sciences – the State of the Art', *British Journal of Political Science*, 1986.

Lyman S, *Social Movements: Critiques, Concepts, Case-Studies*, Macmillan, 1995.

Margetts H, 'Public Management Change and Sex Equality within the State', in J Lovenduski and P Norris, *Women in Politics*, Oxford University Press, 1996.

Marsh A, *Protest and Political Consciousness*, Sage, 1977.

Marsh D and Chambers J, *Abortion Politics*, Junction Books, 1981.

Maslow A, *Motivation and Personality*, Harper and Row, 1970.

Mattausch J, *A Commitment to Campaign: a Sociological Study of CND*, Manchester University Press, 1989.

Mayer M, 'Social Movement Research in the United States', in S Lyman, *Social Movements: Critiques, Concepts, Case-Studies*, Macmillan, 1995.

McAdam D, McCarthy J and Zald M, *Comparative Perspectives on Social Movements*, Cambridge University Press, 1996.

McCarthy J and Zald M, 'Resource Mobilisation and Social Movements', *American Journal of Sociology*, 1977.

Melucci A, 'The Symbolic Challenge of Contemporary Movements', *Social Research*, 1985.

—— *Nomads of the Present*, Hutchinson Radius, 1989.

—— 'Liberation or Meaning', in J Nederveen Pieterse, *Emancipations, Modern and Postmodern*, Sage, 1992.

Messina A, 'Postwar Protest Movements in Britain', *Review of Politics*, 1987.

Morrison D and Dunlap R, 'Environmentalism and Elitism', *Environmental Management*, 1986.

Muller-Rommel F, 'New Social Movements and Smaller Parties', *West European Politics*, 1985.

—— *New Politics in Western Europe*, Westview Press, 1989.

—— 'The German Greens in the 1980s', *Political Studies*, 1989.

Nederveen Pieterse J, *Emancipations, Modern and Postmodern*, Sage, 1992.

Nias P, *National Membership Survey*, Campaign for Nuclear Disarmament, 1982.

Norris P and Lovenduski J, *Political Recruitment: Gender, Race and Class in the British Parliament*, Cambridge University Press, 1995.

Oberschall A, *Social Conflict and Social Movement*, Prentice Hall, 1973.

—— 'Theories of Social Conflict', *Annual Review of Sociology*, 1978.

Offe C, 'New Social Movements: Challenging the Boundaries of Institutional Politics', *Social Research*, 1985.

Olofsson G, 'After the Working Class Movement: what's new and what's social in New Social Movements', *Acta Sociologica*, 1988.

Olson M, *The Logic of Collective Action*, Harvard University Press, 1965.

Olzak S, 'Analysis of Events in the Study of Collective Action', *Annual Review of Sociology*, 1989.

Opp K-D, 'Grievances and Participation in Social Movements', *American Sociological Review*, 1988.

Pakulski J, *Social Movements: the Politics of Moral Protest*, Longman, 1991.

Parkin F, *Middle Class Radicalism*, Manchester University Press, 1968.

Parry G, Moyser G and Day N, *Political Participation and Democracy in Britain*, Cambridge University Press, 1992.

Pearce F, *Green Warriors*, The Bodley Head, 1991.

Piven F and Cloward R, *Poor People's Movements: How They Succeed, Why They Fail*, Vintage Press, 1977.

Poguntke T, 'New Politics and Party Systems', *West European Politics*, 1987.

—— 'Unconventional Participation in Party Politics', *Political Studies*, 1992.

—— *Alternative Politics: The German Green Party*, Edinburgh University Press, 1993.

Porritt J, *Seeing Green*, Blackwell, 1984.

Price J, *The Antinuclear Movement*, Macmillan, 1990.

Richardson D and Rootes C, *The Green Challenge: the Development of Green Parties in Europe*, Routledge, 1995.

Rochon T, *Mobilising for Peace: the Anti-nuclear Movements in Western Europe*, Adamantine, 1988.

Rohrschneider R, 'The Roots of Public Opinion toward New Social Movements', *American Journal of Political Science*, 1990.

Rucht D (ed.), *Research on Social Movements; the State of the Art in Western Europe and the USA*, Westview Press, 1991.

Rüdig W, *Green Politics One*, Edinburgh University Press, 1990.

—— *Green Politics Two*, Edinburgh University Press, 1992.

—— *Green Politics Three*, Edinburgh University Press, 1995.

Rüdig W, Bennie L and Franklin M, *Green Partymembers: a Profile*, Delta, 1991.

Rüdig W, Franklin M and Bennie L, *Green Blues: the Rise and Decline of the British Green Party*, No 95, Strathclyde Papers on Government and Politics, Department of Government, Strathclyde University, 1993.

Rüdig W and Lowe P, 'The Withered Greening of British Politics', *Political Studies*, 1986.

Ryan B, *Feminism and the Women's Movement*, Routledge, 1992.

Salomon K, 'The Peace Movement – an Anti-Establishment Movement', *Journal of Peace Research*, 1986.

Savage J, 'Post Materialism of the Left and Right', *Comparative Political Studies*, 1985.

Scott A, *Ideology and the New Social Movements*, Unwin Hyman, 1990.

Sianne G and Wilkinson H, *Gender, Feminism and the Future*, Demos, 1995.

Staggenborg S, 'Coalition Work in the Pro-Choice Movement', *Social Problems*, 1986.

Sussman G and Steel S, 'Support for Protest Methods and Political Strategies among Peace Movement Activists', *Western Political Quarterly*, 1991.

Tarrow S, 'National Politics and Collective Action', *Annual Review of Sociology*, 1988.

—— *Democracy and Disorder*, Oxford University Press, 1989.

—— *Power in Movement*, Cambridge University Press, 1994.

Taylor R, *Against the Bomb: The British Peace Movement 1958–1965*, Clarendon Press, 1988.

Taylor R and Pritchard C, *The Protest Makers*, Pergamon, 1980.

Taylor R and Young N, *Campaigns for Peace: British Peace Movements in the 20th Century*, Manchester University Press, 1989.

Tilly C, *From Mobilisation to Revolution*, Addison-Wesley, 1978.

—— 'European Violence and Collective Action since 1700', *Social Research*, 1985.

Touraine A, *The Voice and the Eye*, Cambridge University Press, 1981.

—— 'An Introduction to the Study of Social Movements', *Social Research*, 1985.

Tucker K, 'Ideology and Social Movements; the Contributions of Habermas', *Sociological Inquiry*, 1989.

Turner R and Killian L, *Collective Behaviour*, Prentice Hall, 1957.

Van Liere K and Dunlap R, 'The Social Bases of Environmental Concern', *Public Opinion Quarterly*, 1980.

Veldman M, *Fantasy, the Bomb and the Greening of Britain*, Cambridge University Press, 1994.

Ward H, 'Green Arguments for Local Democracy', in D King and G Stoker, *Rethinking Local Democracy*, Macmillan, 1996.

Wilson B, *The Social Dimensions of Sectarianism: Sects and New Religious Movements in Contemporary Society*, Clarendon Press, 1990.

Wilson E, *Hidden Agendas*, Tavistock, 1986.

Yearly S, *The Green Case: a Sociology of Environmental Issues, Arguments and Politics*, Unwin Hyman, 1991.

Young S, *The Politics of the Environment*, Baseline Books, 1993.

Zald M and McCarthy J, *The Dynamics of Social Movements*, Winthrop, 1979.

Index